She-Smoke

A Backyard Barbecue Book

Julie
Reinhardt
Co-owner of Smokin' Pete's
BBQ, a Seattle joint

SEAL PRESS

She-Smoke
A Backyard Barbecue Book

Copyright © 2009 by Julie Reinhardt

Published by
Seal Press
A Member of the Perseus Books Group
1700 Fourth Street
Berkeley, California 94710

Library of Congress Cataloging-in-Publication Data

Reinhardt, Julie.
 She-smoke : a backyard barbecue book / Julie Reinhardt.
     p. cm.
 Includes bibliographical references and index.
 ISBN-13: 978-1-58005-284-9
 ISBN-10: 1-58005-284-3
 1. Barbecue cookery. I. Title.
 TX840.B3R453 2009
 641.7'6--dc22

                          2008051944

Cover design by Tim McGrath
Interior design by Tabitha Lahr
Illustrations by Tim McGrath
Printed in the United States of America
Distributed by Publishers Group West

As with any creative foray, the author can take no responsibility for your successes, nor for the fact that no two meals you prepare will be exactly alike. Practice may not make anything perfect, but you're guaranteed to have more fun. Author not responsible for sauce that's too spicy or meat that's too tough, smoky, well done, rare, fat, lean, or delicious. All recipes in this book were tested and then tested again. Barbecuing, grilling, smoking, and mopping can be dangerous and addictive. Consider yourself warned.

Dedication

To my sweet daughter, Eloise, who kicked me (literally)
out of bed each morning to write, and tested each
of the recipes in this book in vitro.

Contents

Preface

I will never forget my first taste of barbecue. I was at a hole-in-the-wall joint just outside of Trussville, Alabama; it offered classic two meat/three side combos, a huge selection of smoked meats, and sides like warm peaches drenched in syrup and creamed corn. When I first bit into those tender, smoky ribs, I had to take a moment of silence.

My journey into barbecue curved, stopped, looped, and stooped. It began in Alabama where my dad grew up. We spent summers there with my huge, glorious southern family. I worked in restaurants and catering companies for over twenty years; and though I tried, I never completely left the lure of the food business. I met a barbecue-loving chef, and twelve short years later we opened a barbecue restaurant, Smokin' Pete's BBQ.

Even so, I was past thirty before I learned how to properly cut a chicken. I destroyed carcasses for years, used dull knives, and gingerly held up meat between my fingers like something the cat dragged in. The fact that I now own a barbecue restaurant, grill like a she-Hulk, and cater for thousands means that you, too, can sidle up to the smoker. I made many mistakes along the way, and I share them gladly in hopes you will laugh with me, or at me if need be.

She-Smoke is a basic guide to get you started. I've also included a look at the greats for you to study, including a smokin' trail of female barbecue blazers out there. If you've thought that your grill could blow up at any moment or felt iffy with big hunks of raw meat, or if you've wondered

"Why?" when told the back-yard grill was the man's domain, then sister, this book is for you.

Together we will break down the barbecue barriers that exist in the "smokesphere" and that say you have to "be" from barbecue country, i.e., Kansas City, Memphis, the Carolinas, Texas, or regions in between; that barbecue is the stuff of secrets; and that barbecue is a man's world.

I may be "half southern" (I like my sweet tea cut with unsweet), but I'm also a Pacific Northwest left-coast girl. In honor of that I include a chapter on the traditional Northwest Salmon Bake. Also included is a whole mess of information about sources for buying local, natural meats and making sustainable choices, something everyone ought to be concerned about.

Though people the world over smoke and grill their food, the Church of Barbecue, that holy worship of smoke, resides right here in the United States. It's time that women stood up for their barbecue rights. So grab your tongs—it's time to journey into the smoke.

Introduction

"If you take barbecue away from men, Julie, what will we have left?" asked my friend Victor.

He didn't expect me to give him a history lesson. "Actually," I replied, "there is mounting evidence that it wasn't yours in the first place. Hunting, I'll give you, Victor, but fire tending, tool making, and food preparation were most likely the realm of women."

Because it was fire and food preservation that bumped us from Neanderthal and Homo erectus man into the Homo sapiens we are today, *weeeelll,* one can pretty much deduce that though you guys slew the beasts, without women, y'all might still be "a little behind" in the classroom. **Barbecue may well be what helped make early humans jump to modern humans, and back then, women were in charge of the barbecue**. My friend slumped away, poor guy, shaking his head and wiping the barbecue sauce from his chin.

Now, I'm not here to discredit men. In our postmodern world, where cooking so often involves picking up pre-packaged units from the freezer, it is the guys, for the most part, who have kept our slow, outdoor cooking tradition alive. If we are going to combat our fast-food, quick-'n-easy relationship to meal making, then we *all* need to learn to tend a slow fire.

Sister, *don't be afraid of the fire*. It won't bite. And if early woman *was* the keeper of the fire, then somewhere, deep inside, you know just what to do.

Have you always let someone else "man" the barbecue? We need to understand *why*. Why is barbecue such a man's sport in this country? Why are *you* and most of your girlfriends *not* out there with smoky tendrils dancing in your hair?

Most people say it's because women don't have time to stand around for twelve hours, drinking PBR and scratching themselves. We're doing *everything else*. This is true, but I think it goes deeper. I'm talking about the 1950s: the Renaissance of Backyard Cooking. Weber came out with its Kettle grill, and the patio daddy-O's started swinging out burgers and kebabs in a frenzy of martini-infused flames. This is where women at home got booted from all things fire, and separated from the smoke.

I bring you Exhibit A: my mother.

My mom married a wonderful, albeit at the time, traditional man. Without question, she assumed her role as housewife. Cooking was a forty-year chore for her, and it showed. "Quick-'n-easy" became her mantra. She loved that seventies Crock-Pot. While the kids chomped on cereal, she'd throw in a can of pineapple, a packet of sweet-and-sour mix, and chunked chicken, turn that baby on, and *voilà*! When hubby and the kids showed up frothing hungry at six, she had Hawaiian Chicken ready to roll.

In all those years of toil, fire never entered the picture. She never grilled, smoked, or turned the rotisserie outside. Why? Firephobia. Not the kind that requires therapy, but something pumped, pummeled, and propagandized into ladies' heads in the 1950s. She is still convinced that anything involving charcoal, propane, or wood chips might explode at any moment.

"It's that word 'propane,'" she said recently. "It sounds so ominous."

Now on to Exhibit B: Just read the cookbooks of the time. My good friend Christine collects old cookbooks and booklets like "Fun with Aspic!" and "Velveeta: Recipes for People Who Eat Food." (Clearly the goal of this book was to convince the reader that Velveeta is in fact food.) In the 1958 edition of *The Better Homes and Gardens Barbecue Book,* they practice not a speck of subtlety. The meat chapter's opening line? "This is Dad's domain. Sit back, Mom; admire Chef. He has the fascinating how-to on big steaks, and other juicy meats that take to charcoal." We laugh, but looking at them, you read the language pounded in through words, pictures, and titles: Dad is chef, Mom the salad gal. Illustrations place Dad at the barbecue, while Mom holds the fixin's platter. It is time, gals. Time to take back our place by the fire.

So what did I mean when I told Victor that women cooked the first barbecue? One anthropologist, Dr. Sonia Ragir, posits that because the larger males had first pick of the ripe fruit and other easy pickin's, it was the females who, out of necessity, invented tools for breaking down less desirable foods. Tough foodstuffs such as tubers, roots, and bulbs required mashing, fermenting, or drying to break down the "digestion inhibitors" and make them edible.[1]

Males adopted those same tools while hunting and began snagging larger prey. Once hunting became more efficient, there was more meat to go around. This, paired with the discovery of fire, changed everything. The new food abundance required a separation of labor to process and protect it. The family unit formed out of necessity, and it was most likely the females who stayed behind at "camp" to tend to the food and offspring.[2]

"The tendency of . . . females to forage close to the main group or camp put . . . [them] in a position to control the use of fire. Thus, it is likely that women were responsible for cooking and the innovations in human culture that followed from it," asserts Dr. Ragir.[3] More protein and nutrients meant higher birth weights, and the subsequent larger brains "catapulted" early man to the Homo sapiens we are today.

Whether it was woman or man who was the first to smoke up some woolly mammoth ribs may be argued, but what you have to remember is that barbecue is the simplest cooking there is. Early man *and* woman had little else than fire and wood. At its basic element, you can literally barbecue with sticks. Dig pit, rub sticks together, light fire. Whether that fire should be direct or indirect, whether the wood should be hickory, apple, or cherry, and how to make the best smoke are where it gets interesting.

Along with teaching you the basics of how to barbecue, this book will get you started on being a kickass 'cue girl. You are going to discover that barbecue is not the stuff of secrets. It is not impossible with a busy schedule. It is not one bit scary. Barbecue, sister, is *fun*.

The Difference between 'Cueing & Grilling

The first thing—the *very first thing*—is to understand the difference between true barbecue and grilling. Barbecue is about cooking with wood, slow and low, with indirect heat. As a method of cooking, it is at opposite ends with the grill. The word "barbecue" in America, however, also means the event and the whole realm of outdoor cooking. We'll cover grilling, too, because often you can do both on the same equipment, and getting comfortable with one technique lends itself to the other.

SMOKING

Even if you have some grill or barbecue experience, read through these first few chapters to familiarize yourself with the terms I use throughout the book. "Slow and low," the mantra of barbecue, means you will cook foods on a very low temperature (usually between 180°F and 225°F), for long periods of time (usually from 4 to 14+ hours). We make barbecue by cooking with indirect heat, meaning the food does not sit above the fire. We can do this with a variety of equipment, which you will learn about in chapter 1. The first two chapters cover equipment basics, fuel, fire starting, and fire tending.

GRILLING

Grilling sears food by direct heat fire, locking in the flavor. In the Grilling chapter we'll talk about the different levels of heat and grilling with a combination of direct heat and indirect heat.

How to read this book: While you might skip around when reading a cookbook depending on the recipe you want to try, it is best to read *She-Smoke* in order, at least for the first chapters. We start with the basics and build from there.

Chapter One

Tools of the Trade

EQUIPMENT

You can make great barbecue with an old refrigerator, an oil drum, or a pieced-together metal box—many have—but thankfully there are plenty of options for grills and smokers at your local fireplace dealer, hardware shop, or home improvement store. Once you get to competition- or commercial-level equipment, the scope (and cost) of equipment expands, but I'll focus on home-model equipment.

PIT BARBECUE—You hear "pit-cooked barbecue" advertised at restaurants, but what does that mean? Pit barbecue is the traditional way of barbecue—cooking with wood fire. Wood is burned down to coals, to keep temperatures consistently low, and meat is cooked indirectly, apart from the fire. This can mean the meat is placed on one side of the grill, the heat generated on the other, or that the heat and smoke are generated in a separate chamber and fed into the indirect oven where the meat cooks. Though a pit can just be a hole in the ground, regularly used pits were historically stationary structures, often in a building separate from the main kitchen. Today a "pit" means any smoker that burns wood or a combination of wood and charcoal, ranging in size from a small home unit, which can start at about $200, to a rig that "travels" via trailer, which can cost in the thousands or tens of thousands of dollars. What any of the equipment below is trying to do is create that same flavor of pit barbecue with a smaller, home-size unit, some using alternative fuels like gas, electric, or pellets, which we will discuss below. Many are set up for direct-heat grilling too but can be used for barbecue by adjusting how much fuel you use, using your grill vents to regulate the temperature, and keeping your food indirect from the heat source.

DEDICATED SMOKER—I call grills that are made specifically for barbecue "dedicated smokers." By design, these cook food indirectly from the fire, have the capability to maintain low temperatures, and often cannot cook at the higher temperatures for direct-heat grilling. Some examples of dedicated smokers below are the bullet "water" smokers, the box-style electric smokers, and grills with an offset fire box.

KETTLE GRILL, a.k.a **THE WEBER**—There are other brands of the kettle grill—so named because of its shape and dome lid—but the Weber is the original king of the kettle grill. Fifty percent of Americans own a charcoal grill, and chances are you are among them.[1] The invention of the Weber kettle grill in the 1950s began the back-yard grilling revolution. Its domed lid and vents gave flexibility to the cook in terms of even, all-around heat that the open braziers of the time couldn't achieve.

For barbecue, slow cooking on a kettle grill is just a matter of keeping a low charcoal fire indirect from the food. It takes more work to cook at low temperatures on a kettle grill, so you might consider one of the smokers listed below—but I love my Weber and list it first because you can do everything in this book on a kettle.

WHAT TO LOOK FOR IN A GRILL AND/OR SMOKER

When shopping for a grill and/or smoker, here are some points to consider that will help you make great barbecue, with greater ease.

1. Separate fire box or separate entry to the fire. One key element to maintaining the consistent low temperatures needed for slow and low cooking is keeping the grill lid down. You will need to "feed the fire" incrementally, and having access to the fire without opening the lid is important. You don't have this option with a Weber kettle drum, but you do with the bullet smokers and offset smokers listed below.

2. Vents. Opening or closing vents helps manage the fire temperatures by regulating how much oxygen feeds the fire. Choose a smoker with at least a bottom and a top vent for greater control. Some units have more elaborate venting systems.

3. Ash removal. Excess ash in the bottom of your grill or smoker can clog your vents, smother your fire, and, with a gust of wind, coat your food. Some grills make removing ashes easier than others.

4. Capacity and distance from fire. Size matters when you want to cook for a larger party. Look for smokers that have multiple racks or a chamber large enough to accommodate a whole brisket. The greater distance from the fire and the food in larger units also makes maintaining low temperatures easier.

5. Durability and thickness. Sturdier units with thicker walls will better insulate your fire, keeping temperatures more consistent (and that means less work for you!). They will also last longer and save money in the long run.

6. Built-in water pan. We will discuss water pans in greater detail in this chapter, but often in barbecue we place a pan of water or other liquids next to or in between the coals to create humidity in the cooking chamber. Water pans combat the drying effect of smoking foods and help regulate temperature. While you can easily place your own water pan in your grill, units that have a built-in pan, like the bullet smokers listed below, are handy.

7. Remote (external-read) thermometer. Knowing how hot the inside temperature of your smoker is takes the mystery and guesswork out of the equation. Some units have temperature gauges on the outside so you know the temperature inside without opening the unit. Others can be easily retrofitted with one, like the Weber Smokey Mountain smoker listed below. If your unit does not, have no fear—there are remote thermometers you can purchase that serve this function. I discuss this in the Favorite Tools section in this chapter and list a few options in the Resources chapter.

As you travel deeper into the 'cue, you will start to seek out the endless equipment possibilities in barbecue chat rooms, blogs, and web rings. Beware of future obsession.

BULLET SMOKER—The bullet-shaped smoker, often called a "water smoker" because of its built-in water pan, is a favorite in the barbecue world both for its features and its compact design. With two to three racks for food, bullet smokers are big enough to smoke a turkey, yet at only 17 inches in diameter, their footprint is minimal. A separate door to the fire and built-in water pan are key features, and while most do not come with a built-in thermometer, some units, like the favored model in the barbecue competition world, the Weber Smokey Mountain, are easily modified to include one. Called WSM's by those in the know, these shiny "bullets" stand like sentry guards, smoking through the night, at competitions (read more about the competitive world of barbecue in the Pork chapter).

While charcoal is a competition must-have (only wood or charcoal can be used as fuel), water smokers come in gas and electric, too. Lower-end bullet smokers, like the Brinkmann, run in the $50–$80 range, and the WSM runs about $250. Keep in mind that you get what you pay for. The Brinkmann does not have vents to monitor your heat and is made of a thinner metal, meaning less heat insulation. The electric Brinkmann, which is a convenient and inexpensive unit, keeps a consistent temperature of 225°F–250°F. But that is it. The only way to lower the temperature is to unplug the unit.

KAMADO GRILL AND THE BIG GREEN EGG—The Kamado grill and Kamado-style grills like the Big Green Egg are real lookers on a patio, but their true beauty is on the inside. Their shape and durable ceramic material create an insulated barbecue womb. Though they can reach kiln-level heat, their ability to maintain low temperatures with allover heat makes for great barbecue. You will use about one-fifth less charcoal than in a regular grill, and they are a snap to light.

The original Kamado-brand grills are mosaic works of art. People swear by these beautiful ceramic-tile grills. The only thing is you need to be committed to replacing the tiles when they pop off, which they do from time to time.

BOX-STYLE ELECTRIC SMOKER—Like little smoke shacks, some of the best smokers come in this style. Both the Cookshack AmeriQue and Bradley electric smokers are excellent for slow and low barbecue and can maintain temps low enough for cold smoking. With their three to five racks inside, you can smoke larger quantities in these

compact units. Both have external thermometers for monitoring temps. The Bradley unit has a separate smoke box—nice for adding chips without opening the oven section. Keep in mind, however, that more parts equals more maintenance.

THE HASTY-BAKE OVEN—This well-designed grill-smoker-oven includes features made for the regular outdoor cook such as a full-width fire door to access your fire without opening your grill lid. I particularly like the adjustable fire box. With multiple vents, it gives you one more way to control your heat.

GRILL SMOKER WITH OFFSET FIRE BOX—Plenty of companies make these, ranging from home models up to competition and commercial rigs and available in charcoal or gas. The separate-side fire box in this style of smoker is convenient because you can feed your wood and fuel to the fire without opening the main compartment. Smoke travels up to the main cooking chamber and out through a chimney that draws smoke across the meat. Lower-end models can be rickety. Choose one that is solid enough to withstand many seasons. A few well-known brands that make home-size models are Brinkmann, Char-Griller, and Bar-B-Chef. For an excellent higher-end brand, try Pitt's & Spitt's of Austin.

PELLET GRILL—Pellet fuel is just compressed-wood sawdust. The Traeger-brand pellet grills have a great reputation because of Traeger's understanding of barbecue. An electric rod lights pellets in a separate "hopper." An auger

She's Smokin': Buying Used Equipment

Lynnae Oxley, of Sugar's BBQ & Catering in Portland, Oregon, bought her first Weber at a garage sale for $5. "I learned everything on that thing—grilling, barbecue. . . . I like that the *story* of a grill gets soaked into it," she says. As she became more interested in barbecue, she upgraded her equipment, selling that same Weber for $5 at a garage sale to another woman. Though a chef for twenty-four years, Lynnae has been competing on the barbecue circuit for just one and a half years. She admits that being a chef doesn't necessarily translate to being ready for competition barbecue: "What makes barbecue an interesting endeavor is it comes out a little different each time, and you won't know what that is until ten hours later. There is no right or wrong way to barbecue—it's about how *you* feel about it . . . and obsess about it."

feeds the pellets to the fire so all you have to do is flip the switch to ON and indicate high, medium, or low, designated as "smoke," and make sure you have enough pellets for the length of your cooking. Some say the pellets give a different flavor than wood or charcoal. Units start at a little under $500 and quickly go up from there.

STOVETOP SMOKER—The Barbecue Queens* tip their crowns to the indoor smoker for those wet or freezing days when even the most hardcore barbecue fanatic just needs a night inside. The little smokers sit right on the stovetop burner, using either wood chips or wood sawdust to create smoke. A rack separates the

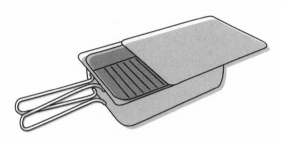

food from the wood, and the cover keeps the smoke inside. While they're fine for getting a "smooch" of smoke on foods, you won't be cooking a brisket on one of these. To me, a huge part of the enjoyment of barbecue and grilling is that it is outdoors, so I smoke it up postal-style: through wind, rain, sleet, and snow.

See Resources for info on these big-time barbecue gals' many cookbooks.

OTHER GRILLS

HIBACHI—You won't make barbecue on these little overlooked wonders, but when we get to the Grilling chapter, the hibachi is our friend. With their adjustable racks, they are versatile, space-saving, and fuel-efficient little hummers that are great as everyday grills or as second grills when your big-girl grill is overfull.

GAS GRILL—The choices are almost endless. Pick one that fits your space, needs, and budget. Do you like to rotisserie chicken? Then that bell or whistle might warrant the extra bucks. Choose a gas grill with a lid and one that has a minimum of two but preferably three burners for indirect-heat cooking. If the grill features many rack levels, make sure they are adjustable to accommodate large cuts of meat like a brisket or whole turkey. If a smoke box is an option, I'd get it. I find the usual method of creating smoke on a gas grill—putting wood chips wrapped in a foil pouch with holes, then placing them on the burner—an inadequate smoke producer.

Buying Equipment: A Cautionary Tale

When I started this chapter, I wanted to pump up my personal equipment arsenal for recipe testing. I had my trusty Weber, a gas grill with an offset smoker box, and a few other well-worn charcoal grills junking up the back yard, but owning a barbecue restaurant with commercial smokers at your fingertips means you neglect your home equipment.

I walked into my local fireplace and outdoor cooking store to basically decide between the Big Green Egg, which I'd been lusting after for years, and the Cookshack AmeriQue, a box-style electric smoker. Neither is cheap—they range from $900 to $1,550—so I was ready to spend some bucks.

"May I help you?" asked the salesman as he sidled up to me.

"Yeah, I like both these models and am just trying to decide which one to get." I went on a bit about both, so he'd know I was serious. His next utterance confused me.

"These are for smoking with wood," he said, pointing. "Here is where you put wood chips to create the smoke."

"Um . . . yeah, I know both these models," I said, cutting him off. Then I saw my favorite charcoal smoker, the Weber Smokey Mountain. Its sleek black bullet shape and great rep among barbecue competitors had it at the top of my list. I wanted to do some side-by-side comparisons with the WSM and a low-end Brinkmann smoker because the Brinkmann can be found just about anywhere.

He immediately saw his commission shrink with the $250 Weber Smokey Mountain, so he tried his best to sell me on the Cookshack electric model. "The great thing about this one is you can turn it on and go shopping!"

"Shopping?" I coughed. I didn't have a single pair of pants without a rip, stain, or missing button because there just wasn't time. I was too busy running a restaurant and catering company, raising a two-year-old, and writing a book. I didn't say all that. I told him I loved the flavor of charcoal-smoked foods, and of course the Weber bullet is a classic.

Then, of course, there are the BTU's (British thermal units), the measurement for heat output on a gas grill in relation to the size of the grill. Grill manufacturers will boast their BTU's like guys boast RPM's at a car show, but over a certain amount just becomes a waste of fuel. Usually all you need is 35,000–50,000 BTU's unless your grill is very large. Choose a grill that is sturdy. My guess is that the lower-end grills priced at $100–$300 are not going to satisfy you once you start grilling and smoking on a regular basis. You can find many good gas grills in the $500–$1,500 range, and if you have a spare $10K, you can buy the tip top of the line.

"Ah, but charcoal is so *messy*," he said. "The Cookshack takes all of the brain work out of the equation."

Hmm . . . so according to this guy, if you are a girl, a.k.a. a brainless bubble head who wants to go shopping, you should buy an electric smoker. I said thanks but no thanks, stewed out on the sidewalk, then walked back in.

"I want you to know I was ready to lay out some cash today, and you lost a sale. Shopping? Are you serious? I own a barbecue restaurant, and I'm testing recipes for my book."

He fumbled a lame excuse while his two buddies giggled in the back. Maybe at me, maybe at him.

The truth is, though, when you are choosing equipment, you do need to find a unit that fits *your* needs. Barbecue purists may admonish any equipment that isn't wood- or charcoal-fueled, but you may need an electric smoker so you can . . . take care of the kids, make that business deal with China, or finish your PhD. You might need to shop for some groceries too.

Get the equipment that will make you want to get outside and cook rather than what you think you should get. I love the simplicity of a Weber kettle grill. I know how much charcoal it needs; I can grill with direct heat, indirect, smoke slow and low; and I can do all three at once if I time it right. That said, it takes a lot of time to make and tend the coals for a brisket on a Weber. Once I had a child, I needed different equipment, at least for the early years. It is challenging to maintain a charcoal fire while chasing around a toddler! Sometimes you just need to turn on the gas grill and bang out your premarinated meats and veggies for a quick grilled meal. I also like my electric bullet smoker for the fact that I can turn it on and walk away. Though some call electric smokers "Lazy Q," I like to think of them as "Busy Q" smokers, for when you need to be less into process and more into end result.

TIP: You don't have to be limited to one piece of equipment. You may find that as you get more comfortable in your outdoor kitchen, you'll want to add a few things to *your* arsenal.

A note about gas grills and barbecue: As we will discuss below, true slow and low barbecue can often take 10 to 18 hours. Not all of it does; however, the biggies— pulled pork and brisket—need time. Gas grills, though wonderful for direct-heat cooking and for the indirect-medium cooking we will discuss, really aren't the right equipment for slow and low barbecue. If that is what you have, don't fret. You can do most of what you will learn in this book and take "shortcuts" that accommodate the gas grill.

TYPES OF FUEL

CHARCOAL BRIQUETTES—Made of charcoal dust and some sort of binder to keep in pressed form. Look for those that are bound with cornstarch or other vegetable binder only. More on charcoal, below.

ELECTRIC—Electric smokers operate much like their charcoal and gas counterparts. Wood chips or chunks are added near the heat element below, so they smoke up through the chamber. Most smokers of this style have a water pan, adding moisture to the drying process of smoking foods. Electric heat is good for slow and low cooking but can't get hot enough for direct-heat grilling.

GAS—Gas grills use propane gas or may be hard-wired for natural gas. Heat output in relation to the size of the grill is measured in BTU's.

LUMP CHARCOAL—Charcoal left in its natural state. Irregular chunks and flakes from the kiln process. Lump charcoal burns hotter and cleaner than briquettes. Cleaner because there's less ash to remove.

PELLETS—Compressed wood sawdust. Popular smokers that burn pellets are Traeger brand and Cookshack's Fast Eddy's smoker. The downside is that most require electricity to get started. The upside (though whether it's an upside is a source of debate) is that your fuel and smoke are one in the same.

SMOKING WOOD FORMS—Depending on your equipment, you will use wood chips, wood chunks, pellets, wood sawdust, or logs to generate your smoke. You can soak the chips and chunks but not the pellets or sawdust. See page 15 for wood varieties and their qualities for smoking.

WOOD—In most charcoal grills, you can use straight wood as your fuel. Dedicated smokers are made for both wood and charcoal. Most folks use a combination of the two because food can get oversmoked with straight wood. Many commercial operations are increasingly moving to gas- or electric-fired "pits" that burn wood for smoke only because wood is expensive, needs constant supervision, and makes it difficult to get insurance. At home you don't have to worry about the skyrocketing costs of fire insurance.

FIRE STARTERS

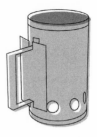

PREFERRED **CHIMNEY FIRE STARTERS**—The best $10–15 you will spend for lighting a charcoal grill. Makes lighting without fuels easy and nicely contained. See chapter 2 for details.

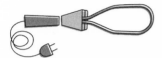

ELECTRIC FIRE STARTERS—Great if you have an outdoor outlet. Just place the mini electric element under your charcoal and plug in. Takes about 7 minutes to ignite.

Lighter Fluid—Don't Do It!

Would you pour petroleum over your cereal? Use it as a perfume? Then why cook with it? Even though they say petroleum "cooks off" before you begin, residue remains and permeates your food. You are going to learn how to light a fire without it. The same applies to using charcoal with fuel additives. That is even worse, because as you add coals to your fire, you are adding that petroleum directly to your cooking flames. Ick. Not to mention totally wimpy. You are an ancient fire starter, girlfriend—you don't need the stuff.

U.K. Consumer Affairs reports that 30% of all barbecue accidents are from improper use of lighter fluid.[2]

SAWDUST FIRE STARTERS—Usually a mix of sawdust and paraffin. While I don't love these because the paraffin scent remains for some time, they are handy in inclement weather, when you just have to get that charcoal lit. You light the fire starter, then place charcoal around it. Once charcoal is lit, you can remove any parts of the fire starter not yet burned.

FINDING SUSTAINABLE WOOD CHIPS AND CHARCOAL

Most of the charcoal briquettes offered in stores like the "self-lighting" stuff out there contain petroleum products and other fillers. These harm the flavor of your food and your health. Petroleum, though the claim is that it "burns off" before you begin cooking, tends to leave a residual flavor on the food. I spoke with Tom Mahowald of Nature's Grilling Products about the charcoal and barbecue wood industry and what sets NGP apart.

"Since 80% of the charcoal industry is dominated by one vendor," said Mahowald, "we started Nature's Grilling Products to fill an underserved niche." As there are no labeling laws for the charcoal industry, the first thing they did at Nature's Grilling Products was take mainstream charcoal to the lab for a burn test. What they found was the briquettes contained 20%–35% coal, plus other fillers like Borax and sodium nitrate. They wanted to produce an all-natural charcoal while keeping their company carbon footprint as low as possible.

How Is Charcoal Made?

There are different methods, but most charcoal is made in huge kiln vats, often dug in the ground, with air chimneys to control the oxygen. The kilns are covered to create a low-oxygen environment, extracting moisture and gases. Once the carbonization (burning of organic material down to carbon) occurs (often determined by sight—the smoke turns white and smells "different"), the remaining oxygen sources are smothered and the charcoal is left to cool slowly. Depending on the batch size, this can take a day to a week.

"Most of the charcoal sold in the U.S. is made in Paraguay and Argentina," says Mahowald. "Though we began getting our natural lump from Paraguay, the carbon footprint of shipping from a landlocked South American country was too great. Besides, Paraguay has almost no concept of forest management." Nature's Grilling Products built a plant closer to home in Monterrey, Mexico, and harvests wood sustainably by using pruned wood and trees from managing land the company owns or leases from the Mexican government. Their briquettes contain only 1% cornstarch to bind.

There are other companies following similar guidelines for their products. One of the easiest ways to barbecue sustainably is to use woods from your region (or from your back yard!). That said, I would hate to be without my hickory or mesquite, woods not native to my region. See the Resources chapter for companies I've found to have decent records.

TYPES OF WOOD

Whether your smoker or grill uses wood chips, chunks, logs, wood sawdust, or pellets, playing with the flavors of different woods enhances your barbecue. First try wood native to your region; then experiment with other woods. Most barbecue, hardware, or fireplace stores carry better barbecue equipment and a wider selection of woods than the megastores out there. You can shop online or ask your local store to special-order some of the more hard-to-get woods. Look for companies that advertise sustainable woods. If you are using cuttings from your own trees, season wood for at least six months.

ALDER—Being from the Northwest, this is one of the most readily available woods for me. I tend to suggest it too often in my recipes because I always have a stack of alder handy. Its mild flavor is a favorite for salmon and other seafood, or blended with other woods.

APPLE—Most fruit woods are great for smoking, and apple is one of my favorites. Save your pruning on your own trees and season for six months. You will have the most sustainably harvested barbecue wood on the block!

CEDAR—A popular wood for "plank cooking." I think that as a longer-smoking wood, it is too harsh, but you may disagree.

CHERRY—Sweet and aromatic, one of my favorite woods for smoking big cuts of meat. Try mixing it with hickory for a nice balance.

GRAPEVINES—Californians swear by the fruit smoke of their vines. I'm lucky to have a scraggedy vine that clings to our alley chain-link fence and that I clip and season year-round. With their mild to medium flavor, grapevines pair nicely with chicken, duck, pork, and lamb.

HICKORY—A true staple wood for barbecue. We smoke with hickory at Smokin' Pete's BBQ. I also like to blend it with a fruit wood like cherry or apple.

MAPLE—Canadian and eastern U.S. sources bring us this sweet, medium smoke.

MESQUITE—To bring out the Texas and Southwest flavors in your barbecue. Though I love the deep, musky flavor, I think this wood gets too bitter for the long time needed to smoke brisket or pork butt. Try it on shorter smokes, or only for a part of your smoking time.

TIP: Most hardwoods are smokable! Use what is available locally. Resinous soft woods like pine and other evergreens, however, can be toxic to humans. If you really aren't sure, just ask your local barbecue or hardware store.

OAK, WHITE OAK—Strong flavor. Often used in Texas barbecue.

PEACH—A mild, sweet wood. Use to smoke seafood, poultry, and cheeses.

PECAN—Milder than hickory, a favorite for smoked turkey and other poultry.

FAVORITE TOOLS

While you can practically barbecue with two sticks, a few key tools can make it easier.

- Long-handled chef tongs. Please don't use those ridiculous 2-foot "barbecue" clawed tongs they sell at stores. I swear they can give you carpal tunnel after one use. Simple chef tongs are the best.

- Long-handled spatula

- Heavy-duty hot pad or oven mitts. I don't like the restriction of the oven mitt, but you may like the coverage. Just be sure your hot pad is heavy-duty commercial, not one your aunt crocheted.

- Instant read thermometer. There are digital units and stay-in units, but I like the simplicity of the instant read. No batteries are required, and they fit nicely in an apron pocket. Just like the bathroom scale gets "off" and you have to subtract 5 pounds, instant read thermometers need to be calibrated from time to time.

- Remote-probe digital thermometer. Even if your grill or smoker has a temperature gauge, a remote thermometer can track the internal temperature far more precisely. I would say this is one of the most important

tools for your barbecue journey. The probe can be inserted into the meat or inside the grill so you can test your real cooking temperature. A long wire extends to the exterior of the grill so you can check the temperature without opening the lid. Most have a magnet that can stick on the outside of the grill.

You may also find there are hot or cold spots in your grill and can adjust where you place your meats. There are plenty out there—make sure yours has a range low and high enough (150°F–550°F). Prices start at about $30.

TIP: Calibrating your instant read thermometer is easy to do, using an ice-water bath. Fill a glass with ice and a little water. Place your thermometer in the bath for about 4 minutes. If it is calibrated correctly, it should read 32°F (freezing point). If not, use needle-nose pliers to turn the bolt until it reads 32°F (keeping it in the bath while you do it). You can do the same test with boiling water. Use 212°F (boiling point) as the base line.

- Small, portable cutting board

- A good, sharp knife; see section on knife sharpening, below

- Separate pans/platters for raw vs. cooked food

- Resealable bags for marinating

- Disposable foil pan, or an old pan to use as a drip pan. Use the 10 x 10 size (called a "half pan") or smaller.

- Heavy-duty foil if smoking/grilling fish or other "delicate" items

- Disposable latex gloves, for when you are adding unlit charcoal or handling raw meat

- Copper wire brush for cleaning grill before and after. Long handle preferred. Copper will last longer and not rust if you accidentally leave it out in the rain. I rarely clean my charcoal grill with soap and water. Clean and sterilize with oil and heat, as you would any cast-iron pan. If you do wash with soap and water, use a mild detergent and don't scrub off the black coating—this seasoning protects your food!

- Pastry brush for "mopping" or basting

- Long-handled lighter or fireplace matches

- Spray bottle for "mopping" with thin liquids like fruit juice.

SPECIALTY ITEMS

Once you get the bug, it can be difficult to stay out of cooking stores. A few things I cherish:

- Cedar "wraps": thin slices of cedar to wrap around your food, imparting the wood flavor. See chapter 5 for a recipe using wraps.

- Banana leaves for making seafood pouches and wrapping food for pit cooking. See chapter 6 for a Jamaican Buried Jerk Pork recipe using banana leaves (pg. 139).

- Beer-can chicken stand. See chapter 8 for a Smoked Beer-Can Chicken recipe (pg. 176).

- Grill basket for smaller veggies and delicate items like fish.

HOW TO SHARPEN KNIVES

Keeping your knives sharp not only makes your life easier, it is safer. Dull knives need so much pressure to work, they can slip and, though dull, can still cut you badly. I met with Donna Gerhart of Kitchen Song in Seattle. This knife-wielding babe has owned her knife-sharpening business for sixteen years. Here are her tips on choosing a knife and keeping kitchen knives optimal:

1. **Pick a knife that is right for you. You don't have to spend big bucks.** One of Donna's favorite knives costs only $10. She loves it because it is easy to sharpen and feels good in her hand. When shopping for a knife, try many of them in your hand. Mock chop on the store's cutting board. Does the knife have a nice, even rock to it from front to back? Does it feel heavy or too light? As for price, each knife brand has its own metal composite, and the better brands tend to have higher-quality steel and composition.

2. **Choose the right knife for the job. A big, burly chef knife might** look bad-ass in your hand, but the angle might be too wide for the bulk of your cooking needs, like vegetable chopping, boning, and paring. Neither do you need twenty different specialty knives on hand. I recall my recent annoyance when a friend kept insisting I use the cheese knife to cut cheese. I felt the utility knife already in my hand was just fine for the job, even without the special-cut cheese squeeze holes.

3. **Don't try to hone a dull knife. Sharpening and honing are two** different things. Sharpening cuts or *revises* the angle of your knife; honing sharpens the blade within that angle. Steels and most other home-sharpening systems are for *honing*. If you try to take a steel to a dull knife that has been lying around a drawer, you will be frustrated because it won't sharpen. Donna suggests getting your knives professionally sharpened, say, once a year or more depending on use, then honing them yourself after reading some material on how to do it properly. You will spend about $2–$5 per knife. If you want to learn how to sharpen on your own with a stone, read up about it or take a class.

4. **Remember that consistency is key. Keep the same angle when** honing a knife. It's often best if one person in the household does the honing to maintain consistency. Using a steel takes some practice, but it can

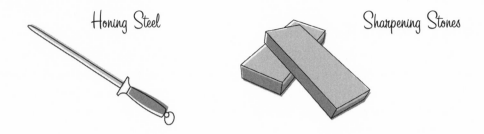

Honing Steel   *Sharpening Stones*

be fun to learn. Keep in mind that it is more about finesse than speed and power. Those guys who flurry their knives in the air on a hand-held steel may not be doing much good for their knives. Donna suggests holding the steel vertically, keeping it stable on the table, then consistently running the blade at the same angle a few times. I asked her about the pre-set sharpeners out there where you just run the knife through the middle. "I've tried them all and the only one I like is the Fiskars Roll-Sharp," she says. "It costs about $15." She likes it because it is set at a good angle for most utility knives, and it is ceramic and takes the guesswork out of honing.

5. Take care of your knives. Here are her tips:

- Donna finds the biggest problem out there is storing knives poorly (ie., the thrown-in-the-drawer method). Store them with a protective cover like a knife caddy or an edge guard.

- Don't put knives away with any moisture on them. Corrosion can occur.

- Though it is better to wash and dry good knives by hand because high heat can dull knives, most home dishwashers don't get as hot as commercial dishwashers and are safe for knives.

- Don't scrape the cutting edge of the knife across the cutting board; instead, flip the knife and use the back edge to clear.

- Remember: A knife is not a screwdriver, hammer, or can opener.

HOW TO TAKE CARE OF YOUR GRILL

Maintaining a grill or smoker is simple, but it's easy to neglect. After cooking all day with the flames, hosting the party, and cleaning up, it's easy to forget the grill until next time. Don't.

Before you get your unit hot, spray nonstick cooking oil on the inside of your lid and cooking grates. This will make cleanup easier later. Be sure to spray both away from the grill so you do not spray oil into the fire chamber.

Before you start to cook, remove enough ash from your charcoal grill to make sure the bottom vents are clear. One gust of wind will coat your food. I like to put the ash in the compost. I can do this since I only use natural charcoal and wood, so no chemicals are going into the garden—another argument for cooking clean and green.

Before you place your meat on the grill, clean the rack with heat. Preheat your grill and put the lid down for 10–15 minutes to get it hot. Brush the grate with a wire brush.

After you have cooked and removed all your food, close the lid with the fire going for about 10 minutes. Then take a wire brush and give the grill a quick scrub to remove any food bits. Wipe down the inside and outside with a dry rag. *For charcoal:* Close all vents and let cool with the lid on. *For gas:* Turn the gas off at the tank, close the lid, and cover when cool. For electric smokers, unplug. When cool, wash water pan and racks with hot, soapy water.

GETTING TO KNOW YOUR GAS GRILL

As someone who would rather chew Styrofoam than read the owner's manual, I must say, "Do as I say, not as I do." Read the manual, gals. But go one step further: Read it in front of your unit, and examine each section of it. Touch it; fiddle with the knobs. You know how to do this.

TIP: Just as you need to add a protective coat of oil to your cast-iron pans and grilling surfaces before cooking, you need to season your gas grill before you cook for the first time. Gas grills don't need oil. You can season simply by preheating your grill with grill grates in place, leaving it on medium for 1–1½ hours with the lid on, then turning it off and letting it cool down with the lid down.

HOW TO FILL UP A PROPANE TANK

This is one of those truly simple things that can scare away a propane-phobe like my mom. Think of it as getting a refill on your coffee. Make sure your propane tank under your grill is off (as it should be after each use). Unscrew the tank from the hose. Take it to a gas station or other store that offers propane, transporting it in a milk crate or other container that will keep it stationary. Guess what? They fill it for you. In fact, you aren't even allowed to do it yourself—it requires certification.

GAS GRILL MAINTENANCE

Keeping your gas grill maintained will extend its life. First, find your owner's manual. Look at the diagram of your grill and get familiar with the anatomy of your grill. In case it is lost, refer to this basic illustration of a gas grill.

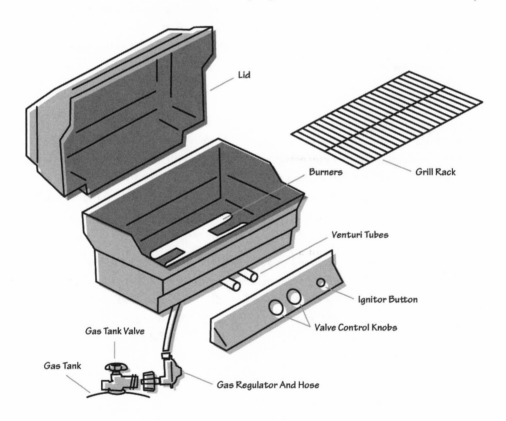

Lid

Burners

Grill Rack

Venturi Tubes

Ignitor Button

Valve Control Knobs

Gas Tank Valve

Gas Tank

Gas Regulator And Hose

TROUBLESHOOTING PROBLEMS WITH A GAS GRILL

Gas grills, by virtue of the fact they are more complicated than charcoal grills, get flanked by some common problems: Heat output is uneven, they won't light, they won't get hot enough, and others. First ask yourself, how old is my gas grill, has it been left out in the rain for season after season, do I clean it regularly, and was it the cheapest model in the store? If your grill is old and you answered yes to most of these, you might just need a new grill. However, some basic maintenance can extend its life.

My dad has a long history of buying lemons. Whether he buys cars, land, stocks, or gas grills, he'll land the one that gets recalled, won't perk, takes a sudden nose dive, or, in the case of his fancy new grill, wouldn't get hot enough. He is the quintessential helper to those in need, and somehow this carries over to inanimate objects as well. Dad's fancy new grill never reached past 300°F. (My brother's grill, too, was plagued with problems. I knew just by looking at *his* that it was from lack of maintenance.)

As part of my research for this book, I made it my goal to fix these two sickly grills. I'm not particularly handy, mind you; I can put a towel bar in the bathroom, I know how to calk a shower, and *sometimes* my shelves are straight. Troubleshooting a gas grill was definitely out of my comfort zone. If I can do it, *you* can.

Some common problems with gas grills *do* have solutions. Here are a few problems you can diagnose. Always follow your owner's manual and refer to the manufacturer's instructions.

PROBLEM: Does not get hot enough.
SOLUTION: There is a thingy on your gas hose connecting your gas tank to the grill called a "regulator." This little guy gets clogged or wears out. To check and correct a clog, first turn off the gas at the tank and disconnect the gas line. With the grill lid open, turn all control valves on high and light. Keep them open for a minute or so; then turn all the controls to OFF. Reconnect the gas at the line; then *slowly* turn on the gas from the tank. Relight your grill and turn valves to high. If they get hot, then it was a clog. If not, call your manufacturer and ask about a replacement regulator. They are easy to install: All I had to do on my dad's grill was unscrew the old hose and regulator attachment from the tank, and screw on the new one.

PROBLEM: Gas output is uneven.
SOLUTION: Most likely the burner holes are blocked from food dripping on them. Do the following:

1. Make sure the gas is turned off at the tank.

2. If you can, remove the burners and clean with a stiff metal brush, using hot, soapy water. On some grills, burners aren't removable. Get in there with your stiff brush and scrub them, wiping with a clean, damp rag.

3. If holes are "glued shut" with drippings, use a skewer to poke through the holes.

PROBLEM: You are constantly filling up the fuel tank, yet heat output is low.
SOLUTION: There may be a small leak in your gas line, or the hose is clogged. To see if you have a leak, first make sure you are in a well-ventilated area, away from any open flame or heat sources. Next, check for leaks using the "bubble method" (as always, consult your owner's manual and follow *those* instructions if different from mine):

1. Mix 1 cup of water with 1 cup liquid dish soap.

2. Make sure all control knobs are off. Turn the valve at the gas tank one click only. Do not light the burners.

3. With a rag or pastry brush, wipe the following areas with the soap and water solution: around the top and bottom rings of the hose that connects from the tank to your grill, on the bottom ring of the tank, and any welding spots on the tank. All hose connection points. All valve connections.

4. If any bubbles "grow" in an area, you have a leak. If you do have a leak, do *not* use the grill. Shut off gas at the source, remove the gas tank, and for repair call an appliance repair store or the store where you purchased your grill.

PROBLEM: Flame is yellow or orange, not blue.
SOLUTION: Gas flames should be blue at their core. If yours aren't, first try cleaning the burners, and then let them burn on high for 10–15 minutes. If that doesn't work, then your venturi tubes, the hoses that connect the burners to the control valves, may be clogged, out of alignment, or rusted. Spiders or other bugs consider these tubes their winter home. Often the venturi tubes are connected to the burners, so you can remove the entire unit, clean it, and position it back in easily. Refer to your owner's manual on how to clean, adjust, or replace them, as there are a number of different designs. Generally, though, a narrow pipe cleaner can clean them. In my brother's case, he'd left his grill out in the Seattle rain. His entire venturi tube and burner unit was corroded. We

easily found the replacement parts he needed for under $100, a far smaller amount than the cost of replacing his grill.

For all grills, no matter what the fuel, use a **grill cover** to keep rain out of the works. Rust is the number one maintenance enemy.

Chapter Two

Playing with Fire
Getting Started

GETTING STARTED

Okay, you have learned about your equipment or purchased something new. You have your fuel on hand and wood to start smoking great barbecue. Now what? Before you prepare your fire, read through Fire-Tending Basics, page 30. We will focus on three levels of heat from fire:

direct-heat grilling   **indirect medium-heat grilling**   **smoking slow and low**

Each recipe in the book is noted as one of these three or a combination. You may refer back to this section to review your fire-making techniques.

FIRE-STARTING BASICS FOR CHARCOAL
How To Light a Fire on a Charcoal Grill

Most books won't spend the time I'm about to on lighting the fire. You may be one of those people who light the match and—*poof!*—have a fire worthy of instant camp-song singing. For the rest of you, let me give you advice from one of the biggest failures at fire starting (me). Sometimes learning from the expert is not always the best. As a fire *failure* expert, I can talk you through just about any problem you may encounter in turning a non-fire into a fire.

#1 PYRAMID METHOD—Wad up about 5 or 6 sheets of newspaper. Stack 3 in the middle; then build a pyramid of charcoal around them, placing the remaining balls throughout. Lump charcoal works better than briquettes for the pyramid method because it doesn't roll off the paper. For briquettes, try #2, the Modified Pyramid Method.

#2 MODIFIED PYRAMID METHOD—If your briquettes continually tumble down from your newspaper balls, try this: Make a pile of newspaper balls underneath the bottom grill grate and stack twigs and small kindling sticks like a teepee around those. Place the bottom grate over that and stack your charcoal in a pyramid over your paper/stick pile. With a long fireplace match or a long-handled lighter, light the paper under the charcoal.

If #1 and #2 prove less than consistent for you, or you find they work only with nasty lighter fluid, by all means try my preferred charcoal-lighting method, #3, the Charcoal Chimney Starter.

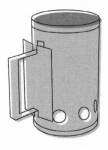

#3 CHARCOAL CHIMNEY STARTER—Many brands make chimney starters, and frankly, they are all about equal. It's a simple design, but I didn't have the instant success advertised on the label or in other barbecue cookbooks. It is partly because I grew up with so many men; I just couldn't break through their circle to ever make a fire. I am also a Pisces, and well, there is something to that. Try this:

1. Turn your chimney upside down. Ball up 3 pages of newspaper tightly and tuck them in the wire rack.

2. Fill or partially fill the chimney with charcoal. If you are using lump charcoal, sometimes the little bits fill the spaces too much and don't allow enough air flow. Or, if pieces are all large, they won't ignite. Be sure to have a good mix of large and small pieces.

3. Place the chimney either on the lower grill rack or on a level, non-flammable surface.

4. Using long fireplace matches or a long-handled lighter, light the paper.

It should start to smoke right away and within 5–7 minutes be showing licks of fire. If your chimney just smolders for a long time and then duds out, try these things first before starting completely over.

a. Light the match/lighter and hold the flame underneath the chimney. Your paper may not have fully lit.

b. Wad up a larger ball of newspaper, place it under the chimney (no need to tuck in), and light this. Be careful when you lift up the chimney—your coals, especially the bottom ones, might actually be lit and quite hot.

c. Poke through the bottom holes with a thin stick to make an air passage in case fire is smothered.

d. If you have to start over, take your coals out with long-handled chef tongs and place them in your grill. Most likely some coals are lit, but not enough to get the whole bunch lit. Then add new paper balls to the bottom ring again, keeping space in between for air flow. Put coals back using tongs and relight. Once the paper flame wanes, fan the flames.

FIRE STARTING BASICS FOR GAS
How To Light a Fire on a Gas Grill

Always light a gas grill with the lid fully open. Turn on a control valve while pushing the IGNITE button. Repeat until all burners are lit. Preheat burners on high for 10–15 minutes; then turn down to desired temperature.

If your igniter does not work, use a long-handled lighter to light each burner. Turn on the gas for only one burner at a time when doing this, and turn dials to a medium setting to avoid burns. Remember that propane "sinks," so if you have the gas on, but it is not lighting, gas can pool around the burner and suddenly *whoosh* when lit. Turn off the gas for a minute and try again. If your grill still won't light, see the Troubleshooting Problems with a Gas Grill section in chapter 1 (pg. 23).

FIRE-TENDING BASICS

Direct-Heat Grilling

Direct-heat fire sears your meat and rapidly cooks it over the flames. Direct-heat grilling works great for chicken breasts, kebabs, and steaks—though we'll get into some finer points on steak later. This is *not* barbecue. It *is* grilling and a tasty way to cook your meal. Often you will cook with a combination of direct-heat grilling, following by indirect-heat cooking. You may direct-heat grill on any charcoal or gas grill. Any of the electric smokers listed will not get hot enough for grilling. **The target temperature for direct-heat grilling is 400°F–500°F for high, 350°F–400°F for medium-high, and 300°F–350°F for medium.** Specific recipes will note which temperature you need.

MAKING YOUR FIRE

DIRECT-HEAT GRILLING ON A CHARCOAL GRILL.
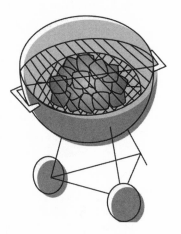
Use a full charcoal chimney to start your coals. If you are using the Pyramid Method, once the smaller pile of coals is lit, add fresh coals to the pile. When they are red hot, pour into your grill and spread them out in one layer, with little to no space in between the coals. (If a recipe calls for *really* high heat, you may be directed to have two to three layers of coals in a section of your grill. For most direct-heat grilling, one layer is fine.) Add more fresh coals around the edges.

   Important Note #1—Keep one quarter of your grill without any coals for an emergency cool spot in case you need to quickly move your food off the fire.

   Important Note #2—If you are going to be cooking with a combination of direct-heat grilling and indirect-heat cooking, cover only half of the space with coals. We will talk about combination grilling in chapter 5.

DIRECT-HEAT GRILLING ON GAS. The beauty of gas is how quickly it fires up. Preheat your gas grill for 15 minutes on high with the lid down. After it has preheated, turn the controls down to the desired temperature. Grill directly over your flame. If you are cooking with a combination of direct and indirect medium-heat grilling, turn one of the burners off after the preheating stage. You can regulate your heat with your control dials. If your grill has a top rack, use this to remove food during a flare-up or for indirect-heat cooking.

Indirect-Heat Grilling

Are you a one-sided gal or two-sided? Make your fire on one side of the grill, or on two sides, with enough space in between for your meat to cook without flames directly below it. Use indirect heat for larger cuts of meat like half or whole chickens, thick steaks (after searing on direct heat), pork loin, or anything else that takes more than 20–30 minutes to cook all the way through. *Target temperature for indirect medium heat is 300°F–350°F.*

Most of the barbecue recipes in this book can be prepared this way. They will cook a little faster than with a smoker at slow and low temperatures and have a more roasted texture and taste, rather than a slow-smoked quality. For brisket and pork butt, I prefer going slow and low, but I like poultry and less fatty cuts better at the slightly higher temperatures of indirect heat.

MAKING YOUR FIRE

INDIRECT MEDIUM HEAT ON A CHARCOAL GRILL. Pour coals from one *half* of a chimney starter on one side of the grill (about 30 briquettes or the equivalent in lump charcoal). When the coals have turned a light gray, spread most of them evenly in one half of the grill. Place a drip pan in the other half. You may also split up your coals on either side of the grill and place your drip pan in between. I'm a one-sided coal gal, because I think you can keep the temperatures lower. If you're using a kettle grill like a Weber, position the food grate so that the handle holes are over the coals.

Coals die out after about 45 minutes, and when you start with this few coals, you will need to feed the fire. **The best way to maintain an even temperature is to feed your coals with already hot coals.** Do this by lighting a new batch of about 10–15 coals in your charcoal chimney or a second grill. You will need to fire up your coals about 20–30 minutes after your initial fire, so that you are adding hot coals at the 45-minute mark. Transfer the hot coals to your pile with long-handled chef tongs. If you have a Weber, you can sneak in the hot coals through the handle holes. Offset fire boxes or grills with a separate door to the coals make transferring easy.

If you do not have a charcoal chimney starter, or a second grill to light fresh coals, feed your fire with fresh coals. The issue with adding fresh coals is that they generate flames and burn hotter at first, so they need to be away from the food. Add about 10 fresh coals on top and around your lit coals. Do this 30 minutes after you have initially dumped your coals and then every 30–45 minutes until your food is done.

HOW TO "GET YOUR SMOKE ON"—Once your coals are ready, put 1 or 2 wood chunks or ½ cup of wood chips (soaked or not; see later notes in this chapter) directly on your charcoal. Close the grill lid for 10 minutes to create a smoky chamber. Then place your items on the grill.

INDIRECT MEDIUM HEAT ON A GAS GRILL. Most gas grills have three burners. Preheat all three on high; then turn off the middle burner and turn the other burners down to medium. If your grill has only two burners, preheat both on high; then turn one off and the other to medium. Place meats over the unlit burner. If your gas grill has a mini top rack, as many do, you can place foods there after some time on indirect heat, to cook even slower. I often do this when I have multiple items to cook.

"Getting Your Smoke On" on a Gas Grill

If your gas grill does not have a smoke box, try one of these methods.

FOIL POUCH METHOD—Soak wood chips for 20–30 minutes. Cut off a piece of foil and fill it with 1 cup of soaked wood chips. Fold the foil into a pouch, seal, and poke a number of holes into it. Place the pouch directly on one of the high burners during the preheating stage. Make sure the pouch has begun to produce smoke before you turn down the burner to medium for indirect heat.

holes

WOOD CHUNK METHOD—I often have wood chunks on hand so I will take a medium to larger chunk and place it directly on the grill over the burner. Your food will be on the indirect side, and the lid will be down, so there's no need to fear the flames.

Slow and Low

The difference between slow and low cooking and indirect-heat cooking is temperature and time. Your target temperature range for slow and low is 200°F–250°F. Any charcoal grill, dedicated smoker like an offset smoker or bullet water smoker, Komado-style grill like the Big Green Egg, or electric smoker can maintain these low temperatures. Remember that when you are smoking over the course of 10–14 hours, temporary spikes or dips in temperature are no need for panic. It evens out over time.

MAKING YOUR FIRE

SLOW AND LOW HEAT ON A CHARCOAL GRILL. Your two best friends in keeping your fire low are managing the quantity of coals and managing your vents. First, start with a small number of coals to make a low fire—about 20 briquettes or the equivalent in lump charcoal. Get them hot and ash gray in a charcoal chimney lighter, or by the Pyramid Method as described above. *Keep the pile tightly stacked instead of spreading the coals out.* Then feed your fire with coals already started in a charcoal chimney starter or secondary grill, so that you are adding ash-gray coals to the fire rather than fresh coals. Fresh coals will burn hotter at first,

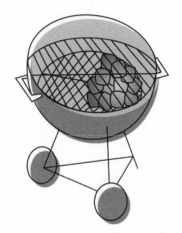

upsetting that delicate temperature balance you've achieved. Light a new batch of 15 coals 20–30 minutes after you have added hot coals to your fire, so that you replenish hot coals to the low fire every 45 minutes to an hour. I *highly* recommend using a **remote thermometer** so you know your internal grill temperature. If your fire is too low, add more coals; if it is too high, back them off and use your vents to slow down the fire. This is your second best friend: the vents.

FIRE MANAGEMENT WITH VENTS. The second way to manage your low fire is through your vents. Keep the bottom vents open or partially open, keeping airflow to the fire so it won't snuff out. Then adjust the top vents according to your need. Open vents allow more oxygen, creating a higher fire. Closed vents will damper the fire and heat.

A COUPLE OF OTHER METHODS IN YOUR POCKET: If your temperature is much higher than ideal, take off the lid for a minute to let heat escape. This is only a temporary fix, but it can get you back in "the zone." If your grill has the feature, you can also lower or raise the grill rack depending on your heat needs.

Water Pans

Water pans accomplish three things for you: They collect drips from your meat, minimizing flare-ups; they add back moisture via steam into your grill; and the water in them maintains a consistent temperature in the chamber. You may pour the same mop sauce or marinade you are using on the meat in your water pan, or a simple mix of water and apple juice as well. Leave at least 1 inch from the top to allow for the incoming drips. Disposable aluminum pans make great water pans, but if you have an old pan you don't mind getting sooty, use that. I have a dented round cake pan that serves me well. Add more water or marinade to your pan about every 3–4 hours as needed.

SLOW AND LOW ON A GAS GRILL. You can achieve delicious barbecue on a gas grill with indirect medium heat. For the recipes in this book that require *looooong* smoking times, like pork butt and brisket, I recommend gas shortcuts (discussed in the recipes). Cooking this long on a gas grill will be a waste of fuel for the result. For gas grills, I prefer smoking for 2 hours on indirect medium heat and then finishing off in the oven.

SLOW AND LOW ON AN ELECTRIC BULLET SMOKER. As with all of these, follow the manufacturer's instructions. Place wood chunks or pellets near the element but not touching. Fill the water pan with water or marinade up to 1 inch from the top. Be careful not to spill it on the element, as doing so can damage it. After preheating the smoker for 15 minutes, place the food on the racks and close the lid. Leave it alone for at least an hour. To lower the temperature, unplug the smoker for 20–30 minutes, leaving the lid on. Plug the unit back in when you've reached the desired temperature.

SLOW AND LOW ON A BIG GREEN EGG. Follow the lighting instructions in the owner's manual. Put down the lid and leave both the top and bottom vents wide open. Once the coals are ash gray, open the lid to release some heat; then close it and turn the vents nearly closed to get the temperature down. Once the temperature hits about 300°F (it will take about 25 minutes), put your meats in. By the time you've placed them, the temperature will be down to about 250°F, and temperature in these units can be easily maintained with the vents. To maintain 200°F–250°F, keep the top vents open a bit, and bottom vents open a few inches. The Big Green Egg does have a ceramic form that you can buy to place between your meats and the grill for true indirect heat. I don't think it is necessary—the ceramic insulation keeps the fire low enough that the effect is the same. For larger or fattier cuts like pork butt, brisket, and duck, you will need a V-shaped roasting rack placed in a drip pan.

HOW MUCH CHARCOAL?

A charcoal chimney fits about 70 briquettes. In most cases, you won't need a full chimney to start. If you are direct-heat grilling smaller cuts like chicken thighs, smaller pork chops, or a piece of fish, a half chimney full of coals should be enough. For indirect-medium or slow and low fires, you always want to start with fewer coals: 15–20 briquettes for slow and low or no more than a half chimney for indirect medium.

If you want to grill veggies in the hot part of the grill while smoking a larger cut of meat, feed more coals to the hot side at the *end* of your cooking when you are going to grill.

TIP: A common mistake with charcoal is starting to cook before the coals are ready. Let your coals turn completely ash gray. Put your hand over the coals—if you can leave it there for 10–12 seconds, your fire is right for slow and low barbecue. If you can't, it's still too hot. It took me a long time to get this through my watery head, but once I had that "aha moment," I haven't looked back at a temperature reading of 398°F since.

Hand-Test Method: How Hot Is Your Fire?

You can gauge a fire's heat by holding your hand 3 inches above the grill grate and counting.

2–3 seconds = high heat
4–5 seconds = medium-high heat
6–8 seconds = medium heat
9–12 seconds = slow and low

HOW MUCH WOOD?

I prefer wood chunks to chips because they burn more slowly. For either, add 1–2 chunks of wood or ½ cup of wood chips directly to your fire every hour as needed. If your wood still smolders nicely, there is no need to add more. *One of the most common mistakes beginners make is that they oversmoke their meat.* This makes the meat taste bitter or, worse, like creosote. My advice is to go lighter on smoke at first. You can always add more the next time. You want a definable smoke flavor, yet you don't want to burp up smoke flavor for 3 hours after eating a pork sandwich.

The meat benefits most from the smoke in the first 3 hours of cooking, before the "bark" forms. For pork butt and brisket, you may not need to add wood after this, even though they will both cook for 8–14+ hours. You certainly won't need more if you are cooking with charcoal; however, I continue to add small chunks of wood for up to 5 hours if I'm cooking with an electric or gas smoker.

TO SOAK OR NOT TO SOAK

Whether or not to soak your wood chips is a source of debate. I don't soak my wood except when I'm using gas. The idea behind soaking is that it slows down the burn and creates more smoke. I think there is an acidic flavor to soaked wood chips. Wood chunks will burn more slowly, solving the problem altogether.

"GET YOUR SMOKE ON"—This is my term for adding wood chunks or chips to your fire before you start cooking. I've explained how to do this above, whether using charcoal, gas, or electric. For all three fire levels, you need to place your wood on the coals once they are ash gray or once the gas grill or electric smoker is preheated. Place the wood on the hot fire and give the grill about 10 minutes with the lid closed to generate a nice smoke. **If you see "Get your smoke on" in a recipe, this is what I mean.**

". . . I Turn, Turn, Turn to That Burnin' Ring of Smoke . . . "

The smoke ring in barbecue is a symbol of true 'cue. When you slow-smoke meats, a red or pink ring penetrates inside the meat because of a chemical reaction between the smoke and moisture in the meat. Though perhaps too much emphasis is placed on this ring (you can get a "smoke ring" on a slow-cooked oven roast too), be proud of your first smoke ring: You've crossed the line from a grill scab to a real barbecue chick.

AND FINALLY . . . NO FUSSING!

The biggest obstacle to your fire management is *you*. You want to check what's going in there, but every time you lift the lid you lose valuable smoke and heat. It takes at least 20 minutes for your grill to get back to temperature when you open it. Every time you open your lid, you add to your cooking time. Keeping your temperature consistent is one of the most important elements to great barbecue. ***Keep the lid on!***

Campfires and Pit Fires

Just because you're camping doesn't mean you only get to eat hot dogs and s'mores (not that there is anything *wrong* with that). Here are two campfire building methods that will allow you to (a) show off your fire-building skills to your camping buddies and (b) make your fire substantial enough to seriously cook with the coals once the fire burns down.

TEEPEE STYLE—At the base of your pile, put 3–6 paper balls, topped with small sticks you've gathered for kindling. Use dry sticks. If you have no paper, gather dried plant material, such as dry moss, leaves, or bark, or just shred small sticks for the initial sparks.

Stack your wood around the pile, leaning into each other. Light your fire. As it grows, add larger logs to the pyramid, always making sure that air can enter through the bottom (like the bottom vents on your grill) to keep oxygen feeding the flames. Sometimes it takes only a slight adjustment of the burning logs to change a fire from smoldering to blazing.

LOG CABIN STYLE—Follow the same initial kindling instructions. Stack your wood in rows: Place two parallel pieces on either side of your paper and kindling pile; then place two more on top of those logs, perpendicular. Keep stacking your wood up for about five rows. Light the bottom pile, adding sticks and other kindling until the log cabin catches fire.

Safety First Dept.

1. Never, ever pour lighter fluid on lit coals. Since you are never going to use the stuff, this point is moot.

2. Never grill with charcoal or gas indoors. Every year there is a story of someone who died doing this. It seems obvious, but there you are— Darwinism front and center. Charcoal fumes are poisonous. I like to make sure grills are also far enough away from the house that fumes won't waft in. If you are grilling on a deck near the kitchen, keep doors and windows closed.

3. If you store your charcoal grill in a garage, wait a full day after cooking before putting it inside to avoid residual carbon monoxide.

4. Wash your hands with hot, soapy water after handling raw meats. Wash for 20 seconds (about the time it takes to sing "Twinkle, Twinkle Little Star"). Most food-borne illnesses occur via cross-contamination caused by handling already prepared foods with raw meat juices on hands.

TIP: Using gloves: When it comes to using gloves, I prefer disposable gloves when handling raw meat. That way I can just discard the gloves and keep working, without having to run inside to wash my hands. *However,* gloves can cross-contaminate just as hands do. Remember to take them off after handling raw meat before you touch prepared foods or turn a door handle. As restaurant owners we must bend to the public fear of bare hands, even though washing hands properly is as safe as, or *safer* than, using gloves—safer because cooks get a false sense of security using gloves and forget to change them, whereas with bare hands we feel the goop that needs washing off.

5. Keep kids away from the grill. Little hands want to help so badly and do whatever Mom and Dad do. I let my son play on a mini (unlit) kettle away from the main grill area. He "grills" painted rocks and flips them with a stick. What the rocks are changes, but his favorite things to grill are pancakes or cereal. You'll have to ask him for the recipe because I just can't figure out how to grill those items.

6. Don't grill in your nice, butterfly-sleeve blouse that can catch on fire. Cooking outside gets grubby. Keep dangling accessories to a minimum, and wear a working apron, changing into your party clothes later on.

7. Don't baste meat with marinade used on raw meat. If you want to baste with the same marinade, set aside extra for that purpose, but throw out marinade used on raw meats. If you misjudged the quantity and don't have extra for basting, cook the raw-meat marinade on a high boil for 5 minutes or more. This will kill any bacteria.

8. Keep raw and cooked platters separate. Bring out your meats to be cooked on one platter, and take them off the grill for serving on another to avoid cross-contamination.

9. Keep your grilling area free of anything that can burn. This includes plastic-handled utensils, matches or lighters, or spare wood. I like to keep a small folding table or TV tray next to my grill for all my utensils and ingredients.

10. Remove ash before you grill, rather than after. It can take hours for coals to completely snuff out after a cookout, which is why I prefer to do this step before I begin the next time. Often ash will contain small, lit bits. If you must remove your ash after cooking, scoop it into a metal can, douse it with water, and discard it in a non-flammable container. Be careful—it may be hot and cause a steam and ash cloud.

The Danger Zone

"The Danger Zone" refers to the temperature range that encourages bacteria to grow. Keeping raw foods cold and cooked foods hot, in addition to cooling foods properly, will keep your foods safe from food-borne illness. Follow the rule of four: Keep cold foods under 40°F, hold hot foods over 140°F, and keep all foods out of the danger zone for 4 hours or less.

FLARE-UPS

Flare-ups happen when grease or oil drips into the fire or when excess liquid from basting drips onto the coals. You don't want fire to char your slow-smoked barbecue. Many well-known folks out there suggest you keep a spray bottle to damper down flare-ups on the grill. I don't like to spray the flames because it's too easy to cause coal dust flurries to coat your food. My favorite method is to immediately close the grill lid and close the vents. This will damper the flames. You can avoid flare-ups by keeping a drip pan under your meats and only adding finishing sauces in the last 20–30 minutes of cooking.

LETTING MEAT REST

Rather than put this recommendation at the end of every recipe, this holds true for all: It is important to let meat rest before slicing. Heat drives juices to the outside of the meat. Allow meat to sit at room temperature for about 10 minutes so juices can spread back evenly into the meat. Meat will continue to cook during the resting process, so factor that into your cooking times and internal temperatures. I prefer to pull meat off the grill or out of the smoker just before it reaches the correct internal temperature, so as not to overcook it.

HOLDING MEAT

Because of the variables in barbecue times, your meat may be ready before you are. You may wrap it in plastic wrap or foil while hot and either hold it in a low oven or in a pre-warmed cooler. To warm up the cooler, pour hot water in it, close the lid, and swish the water around. Pour out the water and place your wrapped meat. Meat will hold above the "danger zone" temperature of 140°F for 2 hours or more.

About the Recipes in This Book

Each recipe I've chosen reflects a learning technique in barbecue. There are plenty of great barbecue *cookbooks* out there, many of which are listed in the back of this book. Once you've tried the basics, try experimenting with different flavors from some of the greats out there.

The times and temperatures may vary slightly with your equipment, weather conditions, and the particular piece of meat. If you live in a hot climate, back off the times listed a bit. If you are smoking a pork butt in Minnesota in November (and kudos to you if you are!), your cooking time will be a little longer. As you get to know your equipment, you will be able to adjust any recipe from any book to work for you. As always, go with your gut.

Chapter Three

Barbecue Smoke & Mirrors

An Elusive History

Defining barbecue is like striving to reach Nirvana: The moment you think you've reached it, classified it, you've lost it. It is meant to be experienced in the present, with all your senses wholly activated, not analyzed in a book or dissected tendon by tendon. Perhaps because this food gets literally buried in pits, or cooks under closed lids, surrounded by smoke, it escapes a clear or linear history. Now, we all know the *early* history of barbecue in the world. Woman, the fire tender, smoked up some woolly mammoth, and it was *gooood*. But *American* barbecue, as we know it, "happened" haphazardly from the joining of people from many walks of life and cultures, much like *a* barbecue brings folks together. Here are just some of the waging historical theories in this deceptively simple cuisine.

Much speculation surrounds the origins of American barbecue. The most accepted of this elusive history is that the Caribbean Taino Indians cooked on *barbacoas*, high wooden racks above wood fires. Columbus took this knowledge back to Spain. The Spanish, in turn, brought pigs to Florida. Those pigs bred like bunnies and spread throughout the Southeast. Pigs became so abundant, early settlers had to hunt them in order to keep their crops safe from packs of feral pigs. Thus American barbecue was born.

....

From Rodrigo Rangel's journal about De Soto's path through South Carolina: ". . . and the Indians came forth in peace and gave them corn, although little, and many hens roasted on barbacoa." Circa 1540.[1]

....

41

Another well-known theory about the origin of the word "barbecue" is that it comes from the French **barbe à queue,** meaning "from beard to tail." This fits well into the whole hog barbecue definition; however, the Spanish had a larger influence on the region than the French, and they brought the first pigs. Most agree on the **barbacoa** etymology or influence of the word.

A number of southern states fight for the birthright of barbecue. Because barbecue has remained so regional, and differences in preparation so hotly debated, the claim of "first" is naturally followed by the claim of "true" barbecue. The title "first" gets muddled, however. Are we talking barbecue the food, the cooking method, the event, or the word itself?

Andrew Warnes, in his book *Savage Barbecue—Race, Culture, and the Invention of America's First Food*, explores the idea that American barbecue was invented as something "savage" and "barbaric" by Europeans, both craving that encounter with the uncivilized New World and at the same time banding together against this savagery.[2] He challenges the stock acceptance of the barbacoa connection, claiming that early on people accepted this etymology of the word without questioning its authority.

His notion is that barbecue is an entirely "invented" name, much like "America" came from names and places of the time. According to Warnes, references like *barbacoa, Barbados, barbarian*, the Island of *Babeque* that Columbus and crew sought out for its myth of unending gold, and another cooking frame, the *babracot*, used by the French, all helped shape the word "barbecue." The Europeans' need to define the unknown as barbaric and put barbecue cooking front and center as a *symbol* of that barbarism shaped our American barbecue tradition. "Barbecue, then, was America's first food, and it was so because it entered European consciousness at roughly the same time and from roughly the same rhetorical circumstances as those that gave America its name," writes Warnes.

The truth is that woman and man have been cooking with wood, outdoors, using the naturally occurring smoke, or purposefully enhancing that smoke on their food, since our ancestors discovered fire. Smoke as a way of curing meats was mighty handy before the advent of refrigeration, but smoke-curing is different from the smoke we seek in barbecue.

Early woman dug a hole, filled it with rocks, and then burned wood on top of the rocks. She did this in part because she had no cooking pots. People still cook this way, whether it's the whole hog buried in a pit or salmon and clams as the Pacific Northwest Native Americans do (see chapter 10 on The Salmon Bake) or one-pot meals like chili or hunter's stew in camp cooking with a Dutch oven. The barbacoa was just another pot-less, indirect cooking method.

Every culture creates some form of barbecue **the cooking method**. You've most likely sampled Chinese barbecue pork and Peking duck or Jamaican jerk, and perhaps you've swayed your hips at a pit barbecue luau in Hawaii. While barbecue **the food** refers to purists' strict definition of seasoned pork cooked slowly over an indirect wood fire, I think what stirs our star-spangled hearts is really barbecue **the event**: those family gatherings filled with laughter and recipes handed down through the generations,

or the broader religious or political gatherings where barbecue is the pork glue, so to speak, to a community of people coming together to break bread (or meat).

American barbecue in its broader sense, and in southern cuisine, evolved from the intersection of cultures of the time that made up this country: Native Americans, European settlers, and African slaves. Much of our southern comfort food developed largely out of slave plantation cooking. African slaves found the sweet potato a close substitute to the yam, and today we enjoy spicy whipped sweet-potato pie at picnics and maple-glazed sweet potatoes at Thanksgiving. Whole-hog smoking, no matter its origins, was typically done by the resident slave smoke master, often "hired out" to other plantations at a profit. Though English cooking dominated the early settlers' cooking, the Native, African, and regional foodstuffs crop up plenty in the early cookbooks.

Native American smoking techniques mixed with the recipes from Scottish settlers in the Carolinas who brought the vinegar sauces of Carolina barbecue; German settlers brought mustard sauces to South Carolina and Georgia and smoking techniques to Texas; Chinese rail workers put their spin on it all as they traveled with the tracks.

Later in our history, the spread of barbecue to Chicago, Kansas City, and beyond follows the path of African Americans' migration to the cities in the 1920s. Barbecue joints could be opened with little cost, and barbecue cooking in the African American community remained a strong part of their cultural identity and a source of income when options were limited.

Barbecue hardliners will admonish any use of the word "barbecue" that includes grilling, that direct-heat, open-flame cousin to barbecue. We're not going to exclude grilling (see chapter 5) or that softer-line mix of direct and indirect cooking. Grilling, as a *cooking method*, and an important part of barbecue *the event*, has a rightful place in the discussion of barbecue. That said, let's look at some of the regional differences and definitions of "true" barbecue in this country before we start firing up our grills.

A Lady's Barbecue Introduction

By the time Mrs. Hill wrote her *Southern Practical Cookery* in 1867 (originally called *Mrs. Hill's New Cook Book*), Georgia was limping along after a bloody civil war. Mrs. Hill was widowed; her nest of eleven children, seven of whom survived infancy, was empty; and her means diminished such that she took up work as a principal in an orphan school. Her cookbook, however, derives from her earlier times of having grown up on a large and wealthy plantation.

Her instructions for barbecue are about the most thorough I've found in early texts. She most surely did instruct her slaves just so. The likelihood of Mrs. Hill, a society lady with a plantation to manage, actually stoking the coals is pretty slim. Still, it was her domain, not her husband's.

"To Barbecue Any Kind of Fresh Meat—Gash the meat. Broil slowly over a solid fire. Baste constantly with a sauce composed of butter, mustard, red and black pepper, vinegar. Mix these in a pan, and set it where the sauce will keep warm, not hot. Have a swab made by tying a piece of clean, soft cloth upon a stick about a foot long; dip this in the sauce and baste with it. Where a large carcass is barbecued, it is usual to dig a pit in the ground outdoors, and lay narrow bars of wood across. Very early in the morning fill the pit with wood; set it burning, and in this way heat it very hot. When the wood has burned to coals, lay the meat over. Should the fire need replenishing, keep a fire outside burning, from which to draw coals, and scatter evenly in the pit under the meat. Should there be any sauce left over, pour it over the meat. For barbecuing a joint, a large gridiron (grill) answers well; it needs constant attention; should be cooked slowly and steadily."[3]

REGIONAL DIFFERENCES IN BARBECUE

Most of the differences derived from folks' using what they had on hand. Two states claim to be the birthplace of American barbecue—South Carolina and North Carolina. In both, pork was and still is the *only* meat of barbecue. It is the *definition* of barbecue. It is said that vinegar and pepper sauce—with no or little tomato—was used because settlers to the region thought tomatoes were poisonous. What started out as using what was in the larder, however, has become fodder for fierce battles on the definition of barbecue and every nuance about it.

As you travel west and south, the smoke gets heavier, as does the sauce. For most people, their general idea of barbecue is more in line with that of Kansas City or Memphis, with a sweet and hot tangy barbecue sauce on deeply smoked meats. Come take a tour on the barbecue map.

NORTH CAROLINA—EASTERN REGION. North Carolina claims to be the "Cradle of 'Cue." The eastern part of the state employs a lighter smoke than the rest of the country, and in my opinion it's truer to the *early* American barbecue as described by Mrs. Hill, above. Here, whole smoked hogs reign as the definition of barbecue. Pork is "pulled" off the pig, or chopped, then mixed with a vinegar-pepper sauce.

NORTH CAROLINA—PIEDMONT OR LEXINGTON. The basic methodology is the same, but in Lexington you'll find less whole hog, more pork shoulder, often called pork butt (from the Boston butt section of the shoulder). The sauce tends to have a smidgen of ketchup, but vinegar is still the key ingredient.

Taking Sides

North Carolinians are stubborn about their sides, too. You'll find hushpuppies in the west but cornbread "sticks" in the east. They also argue over slaw. In the east it's a tangy mayonnaise-dressed slaw, while in the Piedmont region you'll find "red slaw," which includes ketchup and hot sauce in the dressing. Both areas agree on Brunswick stew—though not on who invented it. In North Carolina, you can hardly host a political event or church social without Brunswick stew. It originally contained anything on hand, including squirrel or possum, but today's community events feature their stew with chicken, pork, and vegetables. The matter of which vegetables is of course yet another source of regional strife.

SOUTH CAROLINA—"South Carolina is the only state in the nation that has the four kinds of barbecue sauces," states Lake High, president of the South Carolina Barbecue Association. He refers to the vinegar-pepper sauces, tomato-based vinegar sauces, the thicker sweet and tangy tomato sauces, and the state's famous mustard sauces. Pork still reigns as the meat. You will find only one definition of barbecue here, and that's the noun.

GEORGIA—Georgians love their mustard sauce, too. Ribs, chicken, and occasionally beef grace the sauce-stained menus in this barbecue-loving state.

Barbecue Birthrights

Lake High champions South Carolina as claiming the barbecue birthright. He argues that if barbecue had started in Florida, it would have "stuck," as it has in South Carolina. As for the North Carolina claims as first in line, High notes that the Spanish never went past Cape Fear. "North Carolina may be the inventors of the first barbecue restaurant," says High, "and mind you, they have some great barbecue there, but the Spanish kept excellent records, and they didn't go there." Now you may not know it, but I may have just started a war between those two states.

ALABAMA—I have to give Bama its own line, since my family hails from there. The "Heart of Dixie" state serves it up like most of the Deep South: pork as the meat, dressed with sweet and tangy tomato-based sauce. You won't find brisket, except at competitions, but Kathy Swift of the Wild Bunch Butt Burner's competition barbecue team says their own Conecuh sausage (named after the county where it's made) is notable. "We use this sausage a lot in competition, and folks from all over ask us where to get  it," she notes. An unusual Alabama sauce is a white barbecue sauce with a mayonnaise base, made famous by Big Bob Gibson's restaurants. Bamaites serve up the white stuff with chicken.

FLORIDA—Florida Barbecue Association officer Ricky Ginsburg acknowledges that "Florida barbecue is really just an amalgamation of tastes from around the country. You get the sweet sauces in the South, due to the East Coast influence, and tangier varieties as you head north." As with sauce, you will find it all in Florida meat—beef, pork, chicken, and sausage. Ricky notes that the Hispanic influence brings  flavors of Cuba and South America to Florida, including spicy smoked pork, usually cut in chunks, and the use of many varieties of hot peppers in sauces.

MEMPHIS—Within the city of Memphis, named the "Barbecued Pork Capital of the World," there is a long-standing debate: whether to sauce or not to sauce. Ribs are  served up "dry," meaning dry-rubbed with spice and smoked with sauce served on the side, or "wet," meaning dry-rubbed and smoked but mopped in sauce while cooking.

Some of the most famous barbecue restaurants in Memphis are Corky's and Interstate Bar-B-Que, but to find those hole-in-the-wall joints that do it so right, without a marketing department, read guides to Memphis barbecue or some of my favorite barbecue travel books, like Lolis Eric Elie's *Smokestack Lightning: Adventures in the Heart of Barbecue Country*. I've listed others in the Resources chapter.

Memphis in May is the largest pork barbecue competition in the world, with over 250 competitors smoking through the night. It's a huge party, and the big competitors put on elaborate hospitality tents and even participate in piggy skits that toe the line between funny and squealingly bad puns.

KANSAS CITY—Home to the Kansas City Barbeque Society, which sanctions close to 300 events all over the country for the competition barbecue circuit, Kansas City is often called the crossroads of barbecue. Because of this, you will find it all: pork, ribs, beef, and everything else you can slow-smoke over coals. Sauce is sweeter and thicker than in most other places and closest to what the masses consider "regular" barbecue sauce, because it is home to the successful KC Masterpiece barbecue sauces.

TEXAS—Texas is beef country, and the Lone Star State's deeply smoked brisket is what it's all about. Hickory and mesquite add the wood smoke, and while sauce may be slathered on the brisket, more often it is served on the side or not at all.

KENTUCKY—Mutton takes the main stage in Kentucky, sheep country of past. It's served up with the state's own special stew, *burgoo*, made of mutton, chicken, and vegetables. Burgoo is really Kentucky's counterpart to Brunswick stew. Both started out using more humble meats like squirrel and possum, and both are featured at political rallies, church socials, and special events, which in Kentucky means the Derby. Sauce: While you will find tomato-based sauces here, Kentucky has a unique black sauce made of Worcestershire sauce, vinegar, lemon, and peppers. Though I've never traveled to Kentucky, I ordered barbecue mutton and Black Dip from the famous Moonlite Bar-B-Q Inn in Owensboro online. Voted best in Kentucky, the inn has been hickory-smoking traditional mutton since 1963.

PACIFIC NORTHWEST—In the Northwest, our alder-smoked salmon is traditionally served at salmon bakes. See chapter 10 to learn a little history about salmon bakes and to try it yourself. Though latecomers to the long tradition of barbecue, we are experiencing a barbecue renaissance right now. Places pop up (and *go* if they can't cut the mustard, vinegar, or tomato), and the Pacific Northwest Barbecue Association has grown from 20 members to over 400. Tom Wallin, president of the association, attributes the overall growing interest in barbecue in the country to "the Food Network, Steve Raichlen, and so many cooking shows featuring barbecue."

CALIFORNIA—This is also not native barbecue land, but California's introduction of grapevines and oak wine caskets for smoking has been a nice addition to the barbecue world. Their connection to southwestern and Mexican flavors also adds mesquite and a wide variety of chilies to the mix.

Chapter Four

Meat Mixology
Rubs, Marinades, Mops & Sauces

Barbecue may be about slow-cooking the meat, but what you do to prepare that meat gives it spin, personality, and zing. Whether you dry-rub your meat hours before you stoke the coals, mop it in the middle, or paint on a heavenly barbecue sauce at the end (or do all three), each application serves a purpose in terms of flavor, moisture, personal taste, and presentation. What does it all mean? Here are some basic definitions to help get you in the know.

BRINE—a combination of water or other liquids, with salt and usually sugar. The saline solution will cause your meat to swell and take on the additional moisture. Pastrami, hams, and often turkeys are brined. For the brine to be most effective, you must submerge meat in the brine for 8–24 hours.

DRY RUB—a dry spice mixture, applied to meat half an hour to a day ahead of cooking.

GLAZES, FINISHING SAUCES, AND TABLE SAUCES—This includes the whole gamut of barbecue and other sauces both to cook on the meat toward the end of the cooking time and to serve with the finished product.

MARINADE—usually a mix of oil, vinegar, and spices to tenderize and flavor the meat. Best for smaller, leaner cuts, especially for keeping grilled items moist. Larger cuts like pork butt and brisket won't absorb enough of the marinade to make a difference.

MOP—a thin sauce to baste your meat throughout the cooking process, often done with a small cotton mop. Though the actual mop gives this application its namesake, a common tool used for mops is a spray bottle. Sometimes you see the term *sop*. This is just a mop applied with a rag.

PASTE—a wet spice mixture applied like a rub before cooking.

SLATHER—a somewhat thin sauce, typically made with mustard, to help the rub "stick" to the meat.

Write It Down!

Keep a barbecue journal as you try new recipes. After you are happily sated in a meat coma, your creative innovations may end up lost from memory forever. I like to note ingredients I substituted from a cookbook recipe, cooking time, wood used, and techniques used if different from my usual, like "tried coals on both sides of drip pan vs. one sided." Note any problems or issues during the cooking, rate the end product, and write down what, if any, changes you want to try the next time.

RUB BASICS

Rubs are dry spice mixtures that you use to coat your meat 30 minutes to 1 day ahead. They store well and therefore can be made far in advance. While plenty of fine spice rubs grace the grocer's shelves, it's about the easiest thing you can make yourself. Many commercial blends also contain MSG and too much salt for my taste. Any spice I use regularly, I buy in bulk or larger quantities at restaurant supply stores or price clubs.

Follow the simple three-part premise to make your own house rub:

SEASONING—salt, pepper, sugar. Try kosher salt or sea salt for smoother flavor. Pepper is a preference; add a well-ground pepper or a nubby cracked pepper for a crust. I often don't use sugar in my rubs because I tend to like sweeter finishing sauces. If you are using only a rub, a little brown sugar adds a nice level to a rub.

FLAVOR—any spice that adds its own unique signature to a rub, like cumin, paprika, turmeric, Chinese five-spice, dried thyme, ground ginger, etc.

HEAT—How hot do you want your rub? In this category I put chili powder, dried pepper flakes, smoked habaneros, etc.

How To Apply a Rub

First, don't be shy, and second, this isn't a massage. In other words, generously coat the meat with the spice rub. I obliterate all view of actual flesh. Don't worry that it will be too spicy. In comparison to the quantity of meat that is there, it still is a thin layer. Pat the rub on the meat—don't actually rub it in because you can tear the meat fibers. When it soaks in, it will become moist and a little sticky. This means your meat is ready to put on the grill.

 TIP: If you purchased meat in a Cryovac pouch or plastic bag, always rinse the meat, and then pat it dry with a paper towel before applying the rub. Meat can get what I call "Cryofunk" on it. It isn't spoiled, but there is something not right about the smell.

RECIPES
Basic Barbecue Rub

Make this in equal ratios. Add cayenne pepper and black pepper for a little more kick. Make a big batch and use it year-round. The rub can be stored in a sealed jar or a plastic sealable bag for up to six months. It won't go bad after six months, but spices tend to lose their punch over time.

INGREDIENTS

½ cup kosher salt
½ cup cumin
½ cup chili powder

A NOTE ON SALT: I use kosher or sea salt in my recipes. If you're using table salt, cut the quantities in half at first, and then add more to taste. Table-salt granules are much finer, and therefore denser, than the larger kosher flakes or sea salt crystals.

Substitutions

Don't worry if you are missing an ingredient in your rub (except for salt and sugar). There is more than one way to rub your meat, so don't get too hung up on the spice rack. Feel free to substitute with another on hand. While some flavors may define a rub, others add depth and complexity. Also, stick to dry ingredients in a rub. Fresh herbs will clump with the other spices and flake off rather than adhere to the meat. Make a note in your barbecue journal in case you really liked it and want to duplicate it next time.

Pacific Rim Rub

INGREDIENTS

2 tablespoons dry mustard

¼ cup packed brown sugar

1 teaspoon Chinese five-spice

1 teaspoon red pepper flakes

2 teaspoons ginger powder

Hotter'n Heck Wing Rub

INGREDIENTS

3 tablespoons cayenne pepper

3–4 dried or smoked habaneros

½ cup kosher salt

1 tablespoon fresh ground pepper

2 tablespoons paprika

NOTE: You can buy dried habaneros and other dried hot peppers in the Thai or Mexican section of your grocery store. If your local grocery store doesn't carry these, try specialty markets. Or, see below to learn how to smoke-dry your own peppers. I run dried or smoked peppers in the food processor. You may also use a mortar and pestle to grind the peppers into fine flakes. Always use disposable gloves when handling hot peppers.

Feisty Girl Rub

INGREDIENTS

3 tablespoons brown sugar

2 tablespoons sea salt or kosher salt

1 tablespoon fresh ground pepper

2 teaspoons dried mustard

1 tablespoon paprika

1 tablespoon Cajun seasoning mix

A few dashes of cinnamon

1 teaspoon ground ginger

Cocoa Bliss Rub

I love this rub on pork loin or ribs. A sweet crust forms and accents the smoke. Try it on duck too.

INGREDIENTS

1½ cups packed brown sugar

2 teaspoons Dutch processed cocoa

2 tablespoons kosher salt

2 tablespoons paprika

1 tablespoon red pepper flakes

2 tablespoons chili powder

2 tablespoons dried oregano

SLATHER BASICS

Mustard slathers are made up of a condiment, something to thin them, and spices. I usually just make a slather with what I have in the fridge. Though classically made with mustard because its consistency helps dry rubs adhere to the meat, slathers may also contain mayonnaise, butter, yogurt, oil, and/or butter. Thinning ingredients can be vinegar, pickle juice, broth, and beer or wine. Spices are anything goes, but remember that you will also apply a rub to the slather, so you don't need to get too complicated.

WHEN TO USE A SLATHER: While some folks use them every time they smoke a large cut of meat like pork butt or brisket, I slather only lean cuts because I find the slather adds a layer of moisture. Some examples of when I use them are as follows: (1) on brisket when smoking the flat only. You will learn about the parts of a brisket in the Beef chapter. The flat is the thinner, less fatty section of the brisket; (2) on grass-fed meats. Grass-fed meats are wonderfully flavorful and very lean compared to grain-finished; (3) on lamb shanks and other lean cuts.

Here is one simple slather I like, in part because I always have these ingredients on hand. Feel free to experiment with your own—add a little brown sugar or honey to sweeten it up; add Worcestershire sauce, balsamic vinegar, lemon juice, or soy sauce to get some zing; add cayenne, hot sauce, or other peppers to feel some heat.

Mustard Mummy Slather

INGREDIENTS
½ cup yellow mustard
¼ cup dill pickle juice
1 tablespoon dry mustard
2 teaspoons chili powder
1 teaspoon kosher salt
1 teaspoon fresh ground pepper

Smoking Your Own Peppers

It's easy to smoke hot peppers to use in dry rubs or to make hot-pepper-infused oil. Hot pepper oil keeps for at least six months and can be used to heat up any sauce. Buy peppers in the late summer when they are in season and least expensive. Choose a variety of jalapeños, habaneros, poblanos, and other favorites. If you are mixing peppers, as I usually do, keep in mind that different sizes need more or less time.

1. Wash your hands and use disposable gloves when handling hot peppers.

2. Wash the peppers, and then dry on a paper towel.

3. Make a slow and low indirect fire and "get your smoke on."

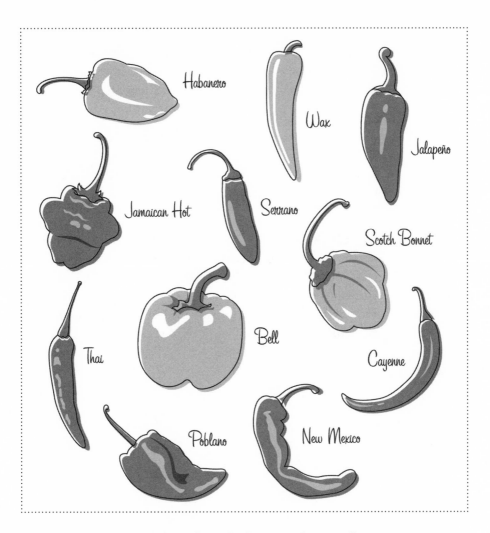

Habanero

Wax

Jalapeño

Jamaican Hot

Serrano

Scotch Bonnet

Thai

Bell

Cayenne

Poblano

New Mexico

4. Place peppers directly on the rack of your smoker or grill, at 185°F–200°F on indirect heat. *NOTE: Smaller peppers like habaneros and jalapeños can shrink enough to fall through the slats on your grill. Place a cookie cooling rack or second grill rack, turning the bars perpendicular to your main rack, to create a "net." A vegetable grill basket also works great if you have one.*

5. Smoke for 6–8 hours. Add wood as needed—a chunk every hour for the first 3–4 hours, or ½ cup soaked wood chunks, depending on your equipment.

6. Once cool, dry in open air for 1–2 days on a baking rack. Using disposable gloves, transfer to jars or plastic sealable bags. **Caution: The**

oils that coat these peppers after smoking are extremely spicy. Take care to avoid rubbing your eyes or other sensitive areas when handling them. Disposable gloves are highly recommended, as are tongs.

 TIP: These make great gifts for friends, too! Decorate jars or put a nice label on bags with a sauce or rub recipe that uses the peppers. Or, bottle up the hot pepper oil, below, for gifts. Leave a few peppers whole in the oil to make it pretty.

HOW TO MAKE HOT PEPPER OIL: Remove stems from peppers. Don't remove the inner ribs and the seeds—this is where the heat of the pepper resides. Grind up peppers finely in a food processor, until flakes are the size of peppercorns. Heat 3 parts canola oil to 1 part ground peppers (for example, 6 cups of oil to 2 cups of ground peppers), on medium-low heat for 30 minutes. Watch that the mixture does not smoke, and be sure to lower the temperature if it does. Let the mixture cool. Use oil to add heat to barbecue sauces, stir-fries, the Hot Wing Tossin' Sauce (pg. 71) or the Smoked Romesco Sauce (pg. 210).

Jamaican Jerk Dry Rub

This Jamaican jerk spice blend isn't shy about the heat. Great on pork or chicken.

INGREDIENTS
2 tablespoons dried chives
4 teaspoons dried thyme
2 teaspoons allspice (Jamaican allspice if you can get it)
4 teaspoons kosher salt
2 teaspoons fresh ground pepper
2 teaspoons cayenne pepper
2 teaspoons chili powder
¼ teaspoon cinnamon
¼ teaspoon nutmeg
1 tablespoon dried onion flakes

Fiery Jerk Paste

Here's an example of a wet rub, or paste. For the recipe on page 139, I prefer this wet style. This paste is hot. See also restaurateur Donna Moodie's family jerk recipe on page 110.

INGREDIENTS
1 smoked or reconstituted dried poblano pepper
2 smoked or reconstituted dried hot peppers like habaneros or scotch bonnet (for a milder jerk, use jalapeños, guajillo, or other medium-hot peppers)
8 whole scallions
3 tablespoons apple cider vinegar
½ teaspoon lemon juice
1 teaspoon salt
2 teaspoons fresh ground pepper
1 teaspoon allspice (Jamaican allspice if you can get it)
1 tablespoon fresh thyme

TOOLS
Food processor

STEP BY STEP

1. If you're using dried peppers, reconstitute by pouring boiling water over them and soaking for 15 minutes. Trim off tops. Remove seeds.

2. Mix all ingredients very well in a food processor, stopping to scrape the lid and sides as you go. Use the whole scallion, including the greens.

3. Once the paste is fully blended, store it for up to a month in the refrigerator.

SMOKED SEA SALTS & SPICES

Smoked sea salts and spices are all the foodie rage and fairly easy to do at home. I've seen some exorbitant prices for nicely packaged "Smoked Sea Salt" in the gourmet spice section. Unless they say otherwise, most of these products are infused with liquid smoke rather than truly smoked. Let me give you some advice. Take two steps to the right, look down at the bottom shelf, pick up a low-cost canister of sea salt, and then smoke it yourself.

Another place to find bulk sea salts is at soap and cosmetic supply stores or online. You can smoke paprika and other spices too. Smoked spices are lovely in rubs and give non-smoked foods a hint of smoke.

Plenty of misinformation about smoked salts exists out in the blogosphere. Most blogs just offer recipes infusing salt with liquid smoke (yuck), and others will tell you to hot-smoke the salt for an hour on indirect heat. It's enticing, but the salt you smoke for an hour won't last much longer than that. Over time and if exposed to air, salt will lose the smokiness. For the best results, cold-smoke salts or smoke at temperatures under 100°F. I found a great blog on smoking salts on chilifire.com after many of my initial so-so attempts. I do some things differently, but the basics are the same: Smoke low and smoke long for best results.

Gourmet Smoked Salt

COOKING METHOD
Cold-Smoked or Slow and Low Heat under 100°F

INGREDIENTS
Large, coarse sea salt

TOOLS
Make a salt screen to place over your grill grate, so the smoke will pass through the salt. To do so, take a piece of metal window screen (non-galvanized) and cut it in a circle approximately 16 inches in diameter. (This will cover the entire grill grate of a bullet water smoker or be small enough to stay on the indirect side of a larger charcoal grill.) Hardware stores sell screening in bulk on rolls. Wrap a strong wire around the edge of the screen; then press the screen edges around it.

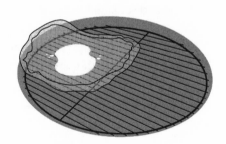

BEST EQUIPMENT
Charcoal bullet water smoker, any offset smoker, or a cold smoker. An electric water smoker won't go low enough, though you can get a milder smoke on your salt with one, turning it off and on to lower the temperature.

PREFERRED WOOD—This is an instance where the wood *is* the recipe. Do you want hickory salt? Alder salt? Apple salt? You decide.

STEP BY STEP

1. Make a very small fire in your smoker. Start with about 7 charcoal briquettes or lumps.

2. Once the fire is ready, add 2 small chunks of wood, or ½ cup soaked wood chips.

3. Fill a water pan and place it next to the fire, or, if using a bullet water smoker, place the water pan above the fire in its normal place. Keep the lid closed until chamber is fully smoky.

4. Pour a layer of sea salt on your salt screen, no more than ½ inch deep.

5. Place the screen on the grill rack, indirect from the fire. Aim for a temperature of 60°F–70°F, with a top temperature of 100°F. To maintain such a low temperature, follow these tips:

   a. Always feed your fire with ash-gray-ready charcoal, rather than unlit charcoal or red-hot charcoal.

   b. Keep the amount of fuel you use small.

   c. If using an electric bullet smoker, turn off the smoker once it reaches 70°F–80°F and turn it back on when it dips down to 50°F–60°F.

TIME

Smoke for at least 5 hours, but over 12 is best to achieve a deep brown color. If you have a cold smoker, or a higher-end model in which you can preset your temperature, smoke for up to 24 hours.

When your salt turns color, first gray-brown, then amber brown, it's ready. Turn off the smoker or let your fire die out completely to let the salt cool with the smoke. I did this accidentally at first and found my results were better! Store salt in an airtight container. Grind the salt in any pepper mill.

NOTE: You may notice I don't include flavored salts like garlic salt or onion salt in my rubs. This is just a personal preference. I feel that they overpower the other spices and that the flavor "sticks" to my tongue. Garlic salt and onion salt are common ingredients in rub mixes, so use them if you like the taste. I do like *smoked* salts in rubs, non-barbecue dishes, faux oven-baked "barbecue," on grilled meats, or as an ingredient in barbecue sauce.

Gift It!

As you might gather, I'm a big fan of homemade gifts. Smoked salt is an easy one. You will want to make a batch big enough for the effort anyway, so why not package it up in cool jars, make fancy labels, and mail it off to the relatives? See the Resources chapter for bulk online stores to buy larger quantities of sea salt.

MARINADE BASICS

Marinades infuse flavor in your food and tenderize at the same time. You don't need to buy store-bought marinades and can easily make any marinade from stock out of your refrigerator and cupboards. Combine marinade ingredients well; then pour over food so it is covered. I like to place meats and marinade in a plastic sealable bag. Less marinade is required to cover food, and you can shake up or turn over the bag for better coverage. Refrigerate marinated foods for at least 30 minutes, more depending on the recipe. Follow the simple premise below and create your own marinade.

2 PARTS ACID—This can be any vinegar like apple cider, balsamic, rice wine, or red wine vinegar, but it can also be citrus juice and combinations of these.

1 PART OIL—Olive oil is great for flavor and health, but a good canola or other vegetable oil works well, too. When using specialty oils like sesame oil or grape-seed oil, use a vegetable-oil base and add a small amount of the specialty oil.

TIP: Use a lower-grade olive oil for marinades, because extra virgin will coagulate when refrigerated. The oil will chunk up and may cause flare-ups once on the grill. If you have only extra virgin in the house, let the marinated meats sit out for about 20 minutes so the olive oil will disperse back in.

SPICE—This is where the fun comes in. Do you want a sweet marinade? Add brown sugar, jam, or marmalade. Do you want heat? Add pepper flakes, Tabasco, smoked chilies. Do you want an Asian-style or an Italian-flavored marinade? Use herbs and spices that complement the acids and oils of those regions. Don't forget about pepper and salt. *A note about salt*: Salt draws out the moisture of your meat to the surface, so use salt and soy sauce sparingly in marinades and rubs when you're applying them a day in advance. You may add in more salt or soy sauce 1 hour before cooking.

Burn, Sugar, Burn!

I'm a big fan of sweet marinades and sauces. I like how the sweet interacts with the smoke. But sugar marinades *can* cause flare-ups on the grill. This isn't so much of an issue with slow smoking or indirect grilling with a drip pan underneath, but when grilling with high heat, be sure to shake off the marinade before cooking to minimize the sugar burn. All glazes and finishing sauces should be added only in the last 20–30 minutes of cooking.

Simple Pleasures Marinade

Keep it simple! So often we try to reinvent the culinary wheel by pairing strange flavors just because we can or because nobody else has done it before. Relish in the simplicity of this one:

INGREDIENTS
1 part balsamic vinegar to 2 parts olive oil
Salt and fresh ground pepper, to taste

Kalbi Marinade

Marinate Kalbi Beef Short Ribs (pg. 103) with this Korean-inspired marinade. It's also great on chicken, pork tenderloin, and veggies.

INGREDIENTS
¼ cup sesame oil
½ cup soy sauce or tamari

½ cup rice wine vinegar
½ cup packed brown sugar
1 teaspoon dry ground ginger
2 tablespoons finely grated fresh ginger
2 tablespoons chili flakes

Thai Satay Marinade

Great on chicken or pork satay kebabs.

INGREDIENTS
6 garlic cloves, finely chopped
4 teaspoons grated or finely chopped fresh ginger
¼ cup packed brown sugar
½ cup soy sauce
¼ cup lime juice
6 tablespoons canola oil
½ teaspoon fresh ground pepper
4 teaspoons ground coriander
¼ cup fresh cilantro, finely chopped

Easy Steak Marinade

For the more economical steaks, like skirt or flank steaks, that need a little tenderizing. Marinate steaks for 4–8 hours.

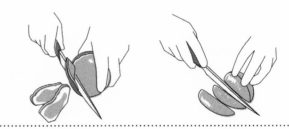

Cut outside peel off entire orange. Cut wedges from there to get membrane-free slices. Save the juice and put in the marinade.

INGREDIENTS
4 tablespoons Worcestershire sauce
3 tablespoons brown sugar
1 large orange, peeled, membrane removed from sections, plus juice

BRINING BASICS

Brines are an excellent way to add moisture and flavors to large cuts of meat. I especially like them for whole smoked turkey because they help fight that pesky problem of the breast drying out before the dark meat is done. A brine must be saltier than the meat is naturally for it to draw in the solution.

Other flavors can be added to the brine, and liquids like beer or vinegar may be substituted for all or part of the water. Below are some simple brines. See the Holiday Barbecue chapter for a Brined Smoked Turkey recipe (page. 222).

STEP BY STEP

1. Fully submerge meat into brine. A plastic bucket works well, or use a large food-grade plastic bag filled with the meat and brine, and set it in a large pan for stability. Tightly secure the top of the bag.

2. In the first 5 hours, dunk your meat and slosh the brine around to make sure the meat gets completely covered. Brines require 8–24 hours to fully penetrate the meat, depending on the weight, with a maximum time of 48 hours. Factor at least 1 hour per pound of meat.

3. After you remove meat from the brine, pat it dry with a paper towel before your next step, be that adding a rub or slather before you barbecue.

Basic Brine

INGREDIENTS
1 gallon water
½ cup kosher salt
½ cup sugar
½ cup apple cider vinegar

Citrus & Clove Brine

Try this on your Thanksgiving turkey (pg. 222).

INGREDIENTS
1½ gallons water
1 cup kosher salt
1 red onion, cut into wedges

1 cup lemon juice
1 orange, cut into wedges
1 tablespoon whole cloves
3 garlic cloves
1 tablespoon fresh ground pepper

Beer Brine for Beef
....

I like this brine for beef, but I think it is a little strong for poultry. This is enough to cover a large brisket.

INGREDIENTS
96 ounces beer (about 8 cans)
1½ cups kosher salt
1½ cups packed brown sugar
¾ cup apple cider vinegar
1 tablespoon fresh ground pepper
4 garlic cloves, minced

MOP BASICS

Mop sauces add moisture back into your food as it cooks. I like to keep it simple because this is where you can fuss too much, and if you are fussing with barbecue, ie. opening the lid, you are losing smoke and consistent heat. Generally my advice is to leave it alone. That said, mops, bone sauces, and bastings are often where the pros tinker to make their barbecue stand out.

You can mop your meats with the marinade you set aside (not the marinade you used on your raw meat). I like to mop meats with fruit juice like apple or pear when I'm adding coals or turning the meat. Here are two other simple mops to try.

Really Basic Cheap Beer Mop
....

I use this on beef dishes, especially brisket. Mix together, then mop on meat with a cotton mop, or use a spray bottle to apply.

INGREDIENTS

2 parts your favorite cheap beer, 24–40 ounces (2–3½ cans)
1 part apple juice or a blend of juices
A dash to a shot glass of Worcestershire sauce

Bone Sauce

A mop made with stock is often called a bone sauce. You can make your own stock for this recipe or use store-bought beef broth. I have added very little salt because commercial broths contain so much. If using your own stock, salt to taste. Mop the brisket, prime rib, or pork with these bones.

INGREDIENTS

½ onion, finely chopped
½ stick butter, melted
1 tablespoon dry mustard
1 tablespoon chili powder
1 tablespoon Worcestershire sauce
¼ cup apple cider vinegar
4 cups beef broth
1 whole bay leaf
¼ teaspoon kosher salt

STEP BY STEP

1. Sauté the onion in the butter until it starts to turn clear.

2. Stir in the dry mustard, chili powder, Worcestershire sauce, and vinegar.

3. Add the broth and bay leaf.

4. Simmer for 1 hour, or keep hot on the grill for mopping.

5. Add the salt in the last 20 minutes.

FINISHING SAUCE & GLAZE BASICS

Finishing sauces and glazes are brushed on in the last 20–30 minutes of cooking. Because of their higher sugar content, putting them on sooner will cause flare-ups. If you are of the Memphis "dry" mindset, one we espouse at Smokin' Pete's, you put your finishing sauce on the table, not on the meat. At home, however, I love playing with finishing sauces.

For any smoked meat recipe, go classic and finish with your favorite barbecue sauce. Try my No-Fail Barbecue Sauce below or one of the variations listed. Or, you can get uppity and try one of the "Fancy Pants" sauces that correspond to recipes in the book, like the Orange-Currant Glaze or the Drunken Port Sauce with Dried Fruit & Stilton (pg. 69). A glaze differs from a finishing sauce in that a glaze contains enough sugar and often margarine or butter to give the meat a shine.

RECIPES
No-Fail Barbecue Sauce

Use this sauce as a base and change it according to your taste, mood, and creativity. I've made it purposefully mild. Heat it up with the hot pepper oil you learned to make above, with commercial red pepper sauces or some cayenne. Use this sauce base also to make Kansas City– or Memphis-style sauces, with some adjustments noted below.

INGREDIENTS

½ cup vegetable oil or 4 tablespoons butter
3 garlic cloves, finely chopped
1 teaspoon cumin
½ teaspoon chili powder
1 teaspoon allspice
1½ tablespoons brown sugar
1 tablespoon molasses
2 cups ketchup
½ cup plus 1 tablespoon apple cider vinegar, divided
½ teaspoon salt (optional: substitute onion salt)
1 teaspoon fresh ground pepper

STEP BY STEP

    1. Heat oil or butter on medium-low heat. Once it's hot, add garlic, cumin, chili powder, and allspice. Caramelize together for 5 minutes.

    2. Add in brown sugar and molasses and cook for another 5 minutes.

    3. Add in ketchup, ½ cup of the cider vinegar, salt, and pepper, and simmer for 1 hour.

    4. Add another tablespoon of apple cider vinegar at the end before cooling the sauce. Set aside for 1 hour; then bottle and refrigerate with the lid off until completely cool.

Northwest Blackberry Boldness

INGREDIENTS

2 cups No-Fail Barbecue Sauce (facing pg.) or your favorite liquid smoke-free sauce
½ cup blackberry puree or blackberry jam
¼ cup red wine
3 tablespoons hot pepper oil (pg. 56) or 2 dried hot chilies, reconstituted and pureed

STEP BY STEP

    Combine all ingredients and simmer for an hour before serving.

Plum-Bourbon Barbecue Sauce

I make this velvety sauce at summer's end when my plum tree starts dropping its plums faster than I can harvest them. Great for pork or chicken.

INGREDIENTS

1 tablespoon butter
1 cup chopped plums
¼ cup water
2 cups No-Fail Barbecue Sauce (facing pg.) or your favorite liquid smoke-free sauce
2 tablespoons bourbon
1 teaspoon molasses
1 teaspoon honey

1. Heat a sauce pan on medium heat. Add butter. When the butter melts, add the plums and sauté for 2 minutes; then add water.

2. Stew the plums until they are soft enough to mash.

3. Add remaining ingredients: No-Fail Barbecue Sauce, bourbon, molasses, and honey. Boil down for 5 minutes; then simmer for at least 20 minutes.

TIP: Doctoring the sauce "in the fridge" adds your own spin to a store-bought sauce without reinventing the wheel. Most barbecue-sauce bases are the same—ketchup, vinegar, Worcestershire sauce, garlic, and spices. Adding fruit compotes, hot pepper oil, or sautéed sweet onions picked from your garden can zip up a generic sauce. Beware—many commercial brands contain liquid smoke, high-fructose corn syrup, and a host of other preservatives. Since you are making real barbecue, adding liquid smoke to smoked food will taint the 'cue and overkill the taste buds. You want your sauce to complement your meat, not compete with it. Pick a sauce off the shelf with minimal ingredients. If the ingredients list reads like novel, move on.

Fig & Mint Chutney

Use this as both a finishing sauce and a table condiment. Great on lamb and chicken.

INGREDIENTS
1 cup chopped dried figs, stems removed
½ cup chopped dried apricots
2 tablespoons finely chopped or grated fresh ginger
1 teaspoon coriander
½ teaspoon cumin
1 cup balsamic vinegar
¾ cup red wine
1 tablespoon fresh mint, chopped
Optional: 3 tablespoons toasted pine nuts, added at the end

STEP BY STEP

    1. Heat all ingredients except the fresh mint on low heat for 20 minutes.

    2. Take off heat and stir in mint and pine nuts. For a table condiment, chill in refrigerator and sprinkle some fresh mint as a garnish.

Orange-Currant Glaze

Great on duck, chicken, or pork chops.

INGREDIENTS

2 cups orange marmalade
4 tablespoons Worcestershire sauce
4 tablespoons rice wine vinegar
⅔ cup packed brown sugar
½ cup dried currants
2 teaspoons finely grated fresh ginger
½ cup orange juice for finishing sauce

STEP BY STEP

    1. Whisk all ingredients until sugar is dissolved.

    2. Split into two portions: one for basting, the other to make a finishing sauce.

    3. Brush on meat in the last 20–30 minutes of cooking.

Drunken Port Sauce with Dried Fruit & Stilton

Try this "Fancy Pants" sauce on pork tenderloin (pg. 133), as a variation on the Smoked Cornish Game Hen (pg. 227), or as a dessert sauce with poached pears. Be careful not to burn your finger when licking every last drop in the pan.

INGREDIENTS

2 cups port wine (cheaper variety)

1 cup heavy cream
¼ cup Craisins (or fresh figs when in season)
2 ounces Stilton or other blue cheese

STEP BY STEP

1. Using a heavy-gauge pan, heat port on medium high. Stir occasionally with a whisk. Reduce for about 20 minutes until it starts frothing.

2. Add heavy cream and stir constantly until it gets back up to a boil and reduces to one third less volume. One way to tell when you are "there" is that the bubbles, which start out quite large, start to get tighter. This means the sauce is getting denser, heavier, and is right where you want it.

3. Add the dried fruit; stir for another 5 minutes.

4. Take off heat and drizzle over your sliced pork.

5. Crumble the Stilton on top.

Apricot-Zing Glaze

This is a variation of Karen Putnam's Apricot-Maple Glaze in her book *Championship BBQ Secrets for Real Smoked Food.*[1]

INGREDIENTS

1 cup apricot preserves
¼ cup maple syrup
¼ cup packed brown sugar
4 tablespoons apple cider vinegar
2 tablespoons dried mustard
1 tablespoon grated ginger
1 teaspoon Worcestershire sauce

STEP BY STEP

Combine ingredients in saucepan on medium heat for 20 minutes. Whisk until all sugar and preserves are blended.

VARIATION

Try any fruit preserves you have in the fridge. Each will impart a different flavor, but the results of sheen, caramelization, and yummy crust are the same.

Hot Wing Tossin' Sauce

The original hot wings, first made in Buffalo, New York, were deep fried and then tossed in a sauce of butter and hot pepper sauce. Here is a hot wing sauce with plenty of punch, flavored with a tomato-based barbecue sauce. Try this on *smoked* wings (pg.181).

INGREDIENTS

½ cup hot pepper oil (pg. 56)
¼ cup vinegar
½ cup No-Fail Barbecue Sauce (pg. 66) or your favorite tomato-based barbecue sauce
3 tablespoons red pepper sauce (Like Frank's or Tabasco)

STEP BY STEP

Heat sauce on medium low. Toss smoked wings in bowl with the sauce until combined.

REGIONAL BARBECUE SAUCES

You've read about the historical differences—now here is some context for your mouth.

North Carolina Eastern Vinegar Sauce

An Eastern sauce is butt simple! Start with 2 cups of apple cider vinegar and add black pepper, red pepper flakes, and salt, to taste. I've never seen the sauce go bad in my refrigerator, but then again, it doesn't sit too long.

INGREDIENTS

2 cups apple cider vinegar
1 tablespoon fresh ground pepper
2 tablespoons red pepper flakes
1 tablespoon kosher salt

North Carolina Lexington Style

One of my favorite Lexington sauces is from Bob Garner's book *North Carolina Barbecue: Flavored by Time*.[2] Over time I've tweaked it here and there, mostly because I like it just a bit hotter. Here is my version, inspired by Garner.

INGREDIENTS

2 cups apple cider vinegar

1 cup white distilled vinegar

½ cup packed brown sugar

½ cup ketchup

3 tablespoons red pepper sauce (any decent vinegar-based hot sauce will do—I'm partial to Frank's)

1 teaspoon salt

1 teaspoon fresh ground pepper

1 teaspoon crushed red pepper flakes

1 teaspoon Worcestershire sauce

STEP BY STEP

Combine ingredients. Refrigerate for up to 4 months. Shake or stir well before each use.

Smokin' Pete's BBQ Carolina Sour Sauce

Use this sauce to baste pork; then add it to the chopped or pulled pork, and put it on the table. See the Pork chapter for further discussion. This is our version of a Carolina sauce—in line with an eastern sauce but with a few flavors added.

INGREDIENTS

1 cup lemon juice

1 cup white distilled vinegar

1 teaspoon ground red pepper

¼ cup paprika

2 tablespoons kosher salt

STEP BY STEP

Combine ingredients. Refrigerate for up to 4 months. Shake or stir well before each use.

South Carolina Mustard Sauce

This sauce is just my own mishmash of other mustard sauces on the market. Some recipes call for red wine vinegar, which gives the sauce more tang. I like the mellower apple cider vinegar, but both work. Georgians love their mustard sauces, too.

INGREDIENTS

⅔ cup yellow mustard
⅔ cup apple cider vinegar
¼ cup packed brown sugar
1½ teaspoons butter
2 teaspoons salt
1 teaspoon fresh ground pepper
1 teaspoon Worcestershire sauce
½ teaspoon red pepper sauce (more if you like it hot)

STEP BY STEP

1. Stir all ingredients in a sauce pan on medium-low heat until butter melts.

2. Simmer for 20 minutes before serving, or cool and store in refrigerator for up to 3 months.

Memphis Barbecue Sauce

A Memphis sauce, while a rich tomato-based sauce, is not as sweet as a Kansas City sauce. Here is how to turn the No-Fail Barbecue Sauce (pg. 66) into a Memphis-style variety. Use the directions for the No-Fail sauce, making the following adjustments:

1. Cook ¼ cup finely chopped onions with the garlic.

2. When adding the molasses and brown sugar, also add 3 tablespoons yellow mustard and 3 tablespoons Worcestershire sauce.

3. Add 3 tablespoons red pepper sauce to the ketchup, or more to taste.

Kansas City Barbecue Sauce

Host to the sweetest of regional barbecue sauces, Kansas City embodies what much of the country equates with barbecue. The success of KC Masterpiece barbecue sauce is a great contributor to this. To make a Kansas City–style sauce, take the base No-Fail Barbecue Sauce recipe on page 66 and make these changes:

1. Add 1½ teaspoons celery seed to the initial spices.

2. Increase the brown sugar to ½ cup.

3. Add 2 tablespoons yellow mustard.

4. Substitute white distilled vinegar for the apple cider vinegar.

Kentucky Black Dip

You will find "regular" tomato-based barbecue sauce in Kentucky, but the Kentucky Black Dip sauce is one that sets them apart. Made to go with a local meat of choice, mutton, this sauce is flavorful enough to hold up to old sheep. (I mean that in a good way!) Some recipes, like this one, call for a hint of nutmeg and cloves. The slight sweetness mellows the mutton. I like my dip heavier on the onions than is traditional. You can back it off if you find you prefer a thinner sauce.

INGREDIENTS

½ cup finely chopped onion
2 garlic cloves
¼ cup olive oil
½ cup Worcestershire sauce
3 tablespoons brown sugar
3 tablespoons lemon juice
⅓ cup distilled white vinegar
1 teaspoon salt
½ teaspoon fresh ground pepper
⅛ teaspoon ground nutmeg
⅛ teaspoon ground cloves
½ cup water

STEP BY STEP

1. Sauté onion and garlic in olive oil.

2. Add remaining ingredients and simmer for 30 minutes to 1 hour before serving.

Texas All-Nighter Sauce

Texans like their sauce a little thinner, tangier, and more pepper-centric than their Kansas City and Memphis pals. I added the coffee one late night sitting up with a brisket and liked it!

INGREDIENTS

½ cup finely chopped onion
2 garlic cloves, minced
1 teaspoon chili powder
1 teaspoon cumin
¼ teaspoon kosher salt
1 teaspoon fresh ground pepper
¼ cup canola oil
2 whole bay leaves
1 tablespoon brown sugar
¼ cup strong black coffee
1 cup ketchup
½ cup apple cider vinegar
¼ cup Worcestershire sauce
½ teaspoon molasses
1½ tablespoons finely chopped chipotle peppers or chipotle paste

STEP BY STEP

1. Lightly sauté onion on medium heat until it begins to turn clear.

2. Add garlic and stir in chili powder, cumin, salt, and pepper.

3. Add remaining ingredients and simmer for 1–2 hours before serving.

Northwest Blackberry Boldness

The Pacific Northwest is not normally on this list, but I have a personal goal of getting Northwest barbecue on the map. We are known for alder-smoked salmon. Try it with a little Northwest Blackberry Boldness (pg. 67) on the side.

Chapter Five

Grilling Basics

I decided to start with what *isn't* barbecue—grilling. I want you to get your feet wet working with live fire and enjoy the instant gratification of grilling. Then we will dive into the longer cooking times of slow and low barbecue.

The first time I had to grill by myself was for one of the biggest and most well known military officers of the world. The *first time*. The couple who hired me for the catering event (they told me nothing about it) thought I was a cook. I was strictly "front of the house" at this point, in my twenties, but the hosts seemed pretty stressed already and I didn't want them to freak out on me. So I winged it.

My first problem was I had no idea how to turn on the grill. I grew up with three brothers and was never let near the grill. Luckily, it was outside with no one looking, because I touched, turned, and poked every knob on the gas thing. Finally it lit with a *whoosh,* full throttle. My second problem was I couldn't get it to lower the flame without going out. So I cooked fires a-blazin'. I grilled mini-burgers until they were black on the outside and gray on the inside. The hosts were perfectly happy with the charred balls, stating, "Good, they are well done. They're kosher." Note to self, I thought then: Don't order kosher burgers in a restaurant. Excruciatingly long minutes of pushing, pulling, and turning knobs later, I got the thing to turn off.

After three fast-paced prep hours, chopping vegetables, making salads and canapés, and horrific grilling, I heard sirens. *Oh, god,* I thought, as I rushed out to the grill. Phew, it was still off. My next thought was, *Who got robbed?* No one, I soon discovered. It was the police escort for the guest of honor: then-General Ariel Sharon, who later became the president of Israel. Hopefully, as you begin grilling, you can do so in the privacy of your back yard and can make mistakes without any heads of state looking over your shoulder.

ELEVEN GRILLING TIPS

The beauty and the beast of grilling is that it is fast. You can marinate your meats before you head off to work or take the kids to school and at the end of the day bang out dinner in 30 minutes or less. You can get beaten by the speed of grilling, however, so before we begin, here are my top 11 grilling tips. That's right—these go to 11!

#1 GET YER SH-- TOGETHER! The French have a term that serves as a mantra to line cooks around the world—*mis en place*—meaning that everything is "put in place." No matter how you say it, it is the cornerstone of successful grilling. Have everything you need at your fingertips, prepared ahead of time, because once that meat, vegetable, fruit, or pizza hits the heat, you do not have time to run into the kitchen for forgotten items. When grilling, you often have only a few minutes between "done" and "dried-out tire."

#2 CLEAN OUT YOUR ASHES BEFORE YOU BEGIN. Never clean out ashes directly after you grill because some coals may be still live. I have an old hand brush to sweep my ashes out into a coffee can before I begin. Some grills are better than others in terms of ash removal. A gust of wind can send unwanted ash flurries to coat your food. For gas grills this won't be a problem, but cleaning and maintaining your fire vents are important. Review the gas maintenance tips in the Getting Started chapter.

#3 PREHEAT THE GRILL. For gas you need 15 minutes with burners on high and the lid down to preheat the grill fully. Once the grill is preheated, you may turn down the heat to the temperature desired. For charcoal, once you dump the coals and spread them out, place your grate and close the lid for 10 minutes. Food will stick less to a hot grill rack.

TIP: Don't forget to follow your grill-cleaning lessons: Clean the grill while it's hot, being sure to use some swipes with your grill brush before laying down fresh food.

#4 TURN ONCE. In general you want to turn your food over once. If you are continually turning your food, not only are you making multiple grill marks, but it means you aren't letting your meat or veggies cook enough on each side. There are some exceptions, like the Bistecca Fiorentina, which I will note.

#5 COOK ROOM-TEMPERATURE MEAT. This is different from my advice for barbecue. Because you are hitting the meat with quick, direct heat, your meat will cook more evenly if it begins at room temperature.

#6 KEEP LIKE WITH LIKE. It's important to always keep raw foods on separate platters and containers from cooked foods to avoid cross contamination. In the speed of the grill, you can forget this and suddenly get caught with no place to put your perfectly grilled steak. Include a clean platter when you set up so you have a place to put your finished product. Use disposable gloves when handling raw meats; then remember to take them off once you start cooking.

#7 KEEP IT SIMPLE. Grilling brings its own delicious flavor to the food— you don't need to drown it in sauces, overcomplicated rubs, and extra steps. Often the simple mix of olive oil, salt, and pepper is all you need.

#8 KEEP IN MIND THAT A SPATULA IS NOT AN APPLE PRESS. In other words, don't press down on foods on the grill. This just squeezes the juices out, juices you want in your food.

#9 CHOOSE THE RIGHT COOKING METHOD FOR THE FOOD. Smaller, lean cuts can be grilled right over the flames. Larger cuts might be seared over direct heat, then finished on indirect heat (combination), and still larger, on-the-bone pieces need indirect heat all the way. Generally if your food is thicker than 2 inches, it will need to be cooked with a combination or indirectly. Remember also that ***not everything you grill***

should be cooked on high heat. In fact, medium-high or medium flames are more the norm.

#10 GIVE YOURSELF SOME SPACE, SISTER. I always leave myself an "indirect space" on the grill, even if what I am grilling requires direct heat. My gas grill has an upper rack that suffices, but when I'm grilling with charcoal, I leave a quarter to a third of the grilling surface without fire underneath. This is so I have a place to move the food in the event there is a large flare-up, I didn't follow my own step #1, and I *have* to get something in the kitchen, or if one of the pieces I'm grilling is larger than the rest and needs a little more time to cook away from the flames.

#11 RELAX. It sounds fluffy, but grilling with a calm demeanor truly makes a difference in the success of your meal. We get behind in time and rush things out to the grill, throw them on the fire, and then forget the basting brush or hastily turn the kebabs before they've fully seared and they stick. . . . Take a deep breath, look to see that you have everything you need, and calmly place your food on the grill. Then stand back and watch while the heat and the meat do the work.

A Review of Fire Tending

Refer to the Getting Started chapter on fire-tending basics. In *this* chapter we'll focus on direct-heat grilling, and combination grilling, in which you first sear foods on direct heat, then move to indirect heat to finish. Combination grilling works great for larger cuts like bone-in chicken breasts, thicker steaks, half chickens, pork tenderloin, and chops.

Cooking with Live Fire

GRILLING WITH CHARCOAL—As we discussed in the Getting Started chapter, fill a charcoal chimney with charcoal and light it, dumping the charcoal when it is red hot.

For **high heat,** make a two-layer fire. Once you dump the first chimney of coals, add half of that amount in fresh coals to make a second layer to the hot and ready coals. Begin to grill when the second layer is red hot.

For **medium-high heat** (for most of your grilling needs), make a single layer with no space in between the coals, and leave yourself a quarter to a third of an area of indirect space "just in case."

For **medium heat,** spread out the coals and put a little space in between them. Don't add any fresh coals unless you didn't fire up enough in the first place. Medium heat is good for fish, chicken on the bone, and larger cuts that you will move to indirect cooking once you grill on direct heat.

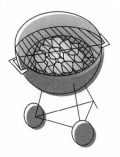 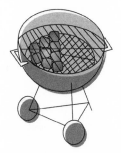 

 High Heat   Medium-High Heat   Medium Heat

Visual Method: How Hot Are Your Coals?

Take these visual clues to gauge the heat output of your coals:

Red glow = high heat (400°F–500°F)
Slight coating of ash over red glow = medium-high heat (350°F–400°F)
Ash coating = medium heat (300°F–350°F)
Thick coat of ash with coals significantly smaller = slow and low (200°F–250°F)

GRILLING WITH GAS—Preheat your burners on high for 15 minutes; then adjust according to what you are cooking. Remember to turn down your burners! Medium-high heat is your all-purpose heat for most foods. High heat works for thin marinated meats like skirt steak and Kalbi Beef Short Ribs (pg. 103), which will cook very quickly. Use medium heat for fish, chicken on the bone, and larger cuts that you will move to indirect cooking once you grill on direct heat.

For Charcoal and Gas
USE YOUR LID AND YOUR VENTS—Our dads may have grilled with flames licking the meat with the lid off, and subsequently we ate many charred lumps of meat. We know better than that. After you initially sear with high heat, the fat in your meat will begin to

Grilling Times and Temperatures

CUT	COOKING TEMPERATURE	COOKING METHOD
CHICKEN		
Whole Chicken *	Med-high	Combination
Half Chickens	Med-high	Combination
Thighs	Med-high	Combination
Breasts, skin on, bone in	Medium	Indirect-Medium
Breasts, boneless/skinless	Med-high	Direct
Legs	Medium	Direct
Chicken Skewers	Medium	Direct
BEEF AND PORK		
Burgers	High/Med-high	Direct
Steak, boneless		
Rib Eye, Spencer, Top Sirloin	Medium/Med-high	Combination
Steaks, bone in		
T-Bone, New York, Porterhouse**	Medium/Med-high	Combination
1½"-2" steaks	Medium	Combination
Beef Skewers	Med-high	Direct
Beef Short Ribs, cut Korean style	High	Direct
Pork Tenderloin	Medium	Combination
Pork Chop (½" thick)	Medium	Direct
Pork Chop, thick cut (1")	Medium	Direct

* butterflied or "spatchcocked" to lie flat   ** medium rare

WEIGHT	TIME	INTERNAL TEMPERATURE WHEN DONE
3-5 lbs.	1-1½ hr	165
1-2 lbs.	30 min-1 hr	165
4 oz.	5 min per side plus 10 min indirect	165
8 oz.	10-15 min per side	165
4-6 oz.	5-8 min per side	165
4 oz.	8-12 min per side	165
2 oz.	3-5 min per side	no pink
under 1"	4-6 min per side	160
		145
¾"–1"	5-6 min per side	145
		145
1"	5-7 min per side	145
2"	7-12 min per side	145
3 oz. each	4-5 min per side	145
3-5 oz. each	2-3 min per side	145
1-1½ lbs.	20-30 min per side	160
4-6 oz.	3-4 min per side	160
6-8 oz.	5-6 min per side	160

(continued on next page)

CUT	COOKING TEMPERATURE	COOKING METHOD
LAMB		
Ground Lamb Kebabs	Med-high	Direct
Rack of Lamb	Med-high	Direct
FISH		
Halibut Fillet	Medium	Combination
Salmon Fillet	Medium	Combination
Halibut Steaks	Med-high	Direct
Salmon Steaks	Med-high	Direct
Fish Grilled in Packets	Med-high	Direct
Shellfish, clams, mussels, and shrimp	Med-high	Direct
Shellfish, clams, mussels, and shrimp	Med-high	Indirect

WEIGHT	TIME	INTERNAL TEMPERATURE WHEN DONE
4 oz. each	5-7 min per side	160
3 oz. each	4-5 min per side	145
	4-5 min direct, 5 min indirect	160
	3-4 min direct, 5 min indirect	145
	2-3 min each side	145
	2-3 min each side	145
	approx. 10 min	145
	2-3 min	open
	5-10 min	open

IMPORTANT NOTE: Internal temperatures are based on USDA-recommended minimal temperatures. Cooking times are estimated and may vary according to equipment, weather conditions, and other factors.

These are the "end" target temperatures. Meat internal temperatures will rise 5-10 degrees in the resting period. I factor this in and pull from grill just before meats reach target.

melt and pour out. Putting down the lid will slow down the fire, cutting down on flare-ups from the fat hitting the fire, and create an oven in which to cook your meat so there is less loss of moisture. Vents allow air intake to fuel the fire. For direct-heat grilling, keep the top and bottom vents fairly open. For indirect cooking, keep the bottom vents open and the top about a quarter to half open. To smother a flare-up, close the lid and the vents.

Hand-Test Method: How Hot Is Your Fire?

You can gauge a fire's heat by holding your hand 3 inches above the grill grate and counting.

2–3 seconds = high heat
4–5 seconds = medium-high heat
6–9 seconds = medium heat
10–12 seconds = slow and low

SEARING—Food is hit with high heat to create an instant crust that seals in the flavor.

COMBINATION GRILLING—In combination grilling, you first cook over direct heat, then move food to an indirect-heat side of the grill to cook more slowly.

SLOW AND LOW—Slow-and-low smoked foods can be cooked in the reverse. Slow-cook your food and then grill at the end to get a nice grilled crust. I love doing this with chicken because often smoked chicken gets rubbery skin. A mop and quick grill at the end can crisp up the skin and give you the best of both worlds.

APPETIZERS
Grilled Eggplant Rolls with Goat Cheese & Roasted Red Peppers

COOKING METHOD: Combination, Medium-High Heat

This is one of my easy standards that can be banged out in no time, yet it is always a crowd pleaser. You can fire-roast your own peppers and roll goat cheese in fresh chopped herbs. You may also buy both at the grocery store and just grill the eggplant.

INGREDIENTS
5–10 Japanese eggplants: these longer, thinner eggplants make the rolls easier to manage both in the making and the eating. Choose the straightest eggplants in the bin.
Olive oil
Salt and fresh ground pepper
1 package herbed goat cheese (4 ounces)
Roasted red peppers (either fire-roast them yourself or buy canned). Once cooked, cut thin slices if whole; chopped is fine, too.

TOOLS: Long-handled chef tongs, spatula
MAKE AHEAD: Make this 2–4 hours before serving.

STEP BY STEP
1. Start your fire for medium-high direct heat (charcoal or gas), leaving about ⅓ of your grill without heat.

2. Cut eggplants lengthwise into long planks, approximately ¼ inch thick. You will get about 3–4 slices per eggplant, so buy as many as you need for your group (factor 1½–2 pieces per person).

3. Brush liberally with olive oil. Salt and pepper both sides. Grill for 3 minutes on each side. Move over to the indirect-heat side and close the lid. Cook for another 10 minutes, until eggplant is *just* soft. Remove eggplant from the grill with a spatula, taking care not to tear.

4. Once cool enough to touch, spoon ½ teaspoon herbed goat cheese and 2–3 slices of roasted peppers ¼ of the way down each eggplant slice.

5. Roll slices up and, with end of rolls on bottom, arrange on platter.

How To Fire-Roast Your Own Peppers

Give peppers a light coating of oil; then put peppers whole, directly on the grill. Leave until skin begins to blister and blacken; then turn, repeating this on four sides. Remove from the grill and cool slightly. Place peppers warm in a plastic sealable bag and let them steam for 10 minutes. The skin will loosen in the bag and remove easily by rubbing the bag. Peel parts that don't fall off in the bag with a paring knife. Cut open, remove seeds, and use immediately or store in the fridge for up to a week.

Grilled Saffron Shrimp

COOKING METHOD: Indirect Heat, Hot Heat

This is a quick appetizer to stave off the hunger before your grilled or smoked main course. You need only about 5 minutes for these shrimp on indirect heat if your grill is high and ready for direct-heat grilling.

INGREDIENTS
1 stick butter, divided
Saffron, about 20 threads
3 tablespoons lemon juice
2 pounds shrimp or prawns, size 16/20 or larger
½ teaspoon kosher salt
Optional: Chopped herb garnish like parsley or rosemary

TOOLS: Pastry brush, long-handled chef tongs

STEP BY STEP
1. Melt half the butter with the saffron in a microwave or stovetop. Heating saffron releases the color and flavor. Add lemon juice. Let stand for 10 minutes.

2. Cut the remaining cold butter into chunks and stir in until mixture is creamy.

3. Rinse, then butterfly shrimp by running knife down back to open up the shellfish without cutting all the way through. Remove legs, but keep the shell on. Press down shrimp to flatten.

4. Sprinkle salt on shrimp, then spoon 1 teaspoon of butter mixture inside each shrimp.

5. Place shrimp, shell side down (with butter mixture facing up), on indirect side or section of a hot grill and close the lid for 5 minutes. *Do not turn over.* Remove from grill. Sprinkle with an herb garnish of your choice, and serve immediately.

SIDES
Grilled Vegetables

COOKING METHOD: Direct-Heat Grilling, Medium Heat

Simple grilled vegetables are my favorite in the summertime. Serve them hot, or chill them for a cold salad.

INGREDIENTS
Olive oil
Balsamic vinegar
Salt and fresh ground pepper
Assorted veggies of your choice. Some that work best on the grill: eggplant, zucchini, yellow squash, red and yellow peppers, onions, asparagus
Optional ingredients to make a Mixed Grilled Vegetable Salad: pine nuts, goat cheese, balsamic vinegar, and cilantro

STEP BY STEP
1. Cut vegetables into thick "planks," or long slices, approximately ¼ inch wide. Drizzle with olive oil and balsamic vinegar, and lightly sprinkle on salt and pepper. Make sure both sides of vegetables are lightly coated but not drowning.

2. Place directly over coals and leave until clear grill marks are showing. Turn and grill on second side.

3. After grilling, lightly sprinkle with salt and pepper again and serve them as is, or cut them up in a warm Mixed Grilled Vegetable Salad with pine nuts, goat cheese, balsamic vinegar, and fresh chopped cilantro. Chill the salad for a cold side on a hot day.

Grilled Pineapple (& Other Fruit)

COOKING METHOD: Direct-Heat Grilling, Medium-High Heat

Grilled pineapple can send the winter blues packing, make a sizzling summer side dish, or provide a delicious low-fat dessert. Grill it with jicama to make the Island Slaw on page 235.

INGREDIENTS
1 ripe pineapple (reserve half for Island Slaw recipe)
1 jicama (reserve half for Island Slaw recipe)
3 tablespoons melted butter
Squeeze of lemon

TOOLS: Pastry brush, spatula

STEP BY STEP
1. *Pineapple:* Cut off ends, then cut off outer skin. Quarter pineapple and cut out the core. Cut long, into ½-inch wedges. *Jicama:* Cut outer peel, then cut into ¼-inch slices.

2. Place pineapple and jicama directly over heat. Leave for approximately 5 minutes on first side, then flip. *Lemon butter:* In a separate pan, melt butter on low heat and add lemon juice, stirring to combine. Brush pineapple with lemon butter and close lid.

3. Grill for another 5–7 minutes.

4. Serve plain or dice for Island Slaw.

Other fruits that grill well:

- Apples, cut across entire apple for whole circle slices. Serve with Smoked Pork Loin on page 135.

- Orange and lemon slices. Add these as a garnish with grilled fish.

- Mango. Top the Jamaican Black Beans on page 247, or use in a mango salsa.

- Any other fruit that isn't too juicy, watery, or delicate.

GRILLED FRUIT DESSERT—Drizzle honey butter over grilled fruit (1 part honey, melted with 1 part butter), and garnish with powdered sugar.

Grilled Balsamic Greens

COOKING METHOD: Direct-Heat Grilling, Medium Heat

Your kids might even eat these greens, and they take only a few minutes.

I like to mix escarole and radicchio when in season. The balsamic vinegar and grilling sweeten up the bitterness of these full-of-goodness greens. They also mix well with smoked meats. Add a glass of red wine and you just might live to one hundred.

INGREDIENTS
½ cup balsamic vinegar
½ cup olive oil
1 head escarole, quartered
1 head radicchio, quartered
Salt and fresh ground pepper

STEP BY STEP
1. Make your fire for direct medium heat.

2. Mix olive oil and balsamic vinegar and pour over cut greens. Shake out excess marinade before placing on grill.

3. Grill on each side for 3–5 minutes, or until they begin to blacken. Close grill lid in between turnings to create an oven.

4. Remove with tongs and place back in bowl with leftover oil and vinegar.

5. Toss with salt and fresh ground pepper to taste.

Other greens that work:
- collards, kale, and cabbage. These three will need a little more time than escarole and radicchio. They also need some indirect heat with the lid on to soften up.

Greens that don't work:
- mustard greens, Swiss chard, spinach, and lettuces. They wilt too quickly.

Grilled Polenta

Try this flavorful starch alternative with the Smoked Duck with Orange-Currant Glaze (pg. 69).

COOKING METHOD: Direct-Heat Grilling, Medium Heat

INGREDIENTS
1 cup water
1 cup milk
1 cup coarse cornmeal
1 teaspoon kosher salt
1 teaspoon dried thyme

TOOLS: Spray oil, spatula

STEP BY STEP
1. In a saucepan, bring water and milk to a boil. Stir in cornmeal. Add in salt and thyme and cook, while stirring, for 10 minutes, until thick.

2. Pour in a greased loaf pan and cool in refrigerator for 3–4 hours until set.

3. Make fire for direct medium heat. Once preheated, wipe grill grate with lightly oiled rag.

4. Pop out polenta from loaf pan and cut ½-inch slices. Lightly spray slices with oil.

5. Place pieces on grill and do not move around. Cover lid. Flip after 10 minutes with spatula and cook for another 4–5 minutes on second side.

Fire-Roasted Corn Salad with Lime-Cumin-Honey Dressing

COOKING METHOD: Direct-Heat Grilling, Medium-High Heat

INGREDIENTS
6–10 ears of corn (factor 1 ear per person)
Canola oil spray
¼ teaspoon chili powder
½ chopped red onion
1 whole red pepper, diced
Optional: ½ cup diced jicama
¼ cup fresh chopped cilantro

DRESSING
⅓ cup lime juice
½ cup olive oil
3 tablespoons red wine vinegar
1 teaspooon cumin
½ teaspoon chili powder
1 tablespoon honey
¼ cup orange juice
1 tablespoon lime zest
Salt and fresh ground pepper

MAKE AHEAD—Salad can be made up to a day ahead before serving, as the dressing does not wilt the corn. Or you can make parts of it ahead: Shuck your corn up to 3 hours prior to grilling. Grill corn up to a day ahead of making salad.

STEP BY STEP
    1. Shuck corn, lightly coat with canola oil, and sprinkle on chili powder.

2. Make fire for direct-heat grilling, medium-high heat.

3. Grill corn, turning frequently so it chars but does not burn, approximately 8–10 minutes. (As soon as corn kernels look "plump" or are soft, they are done.)

4. Remove from fire and cool in fridge for 1 hour.

5. While corn is cooling, chop onion, red peppers, and jicama.

6. Cut corn off cobs and add to chopped vegetables.

7. Combine all dressing ingredients. Toss with salad. Add fresh chopped cilantro just before serving.

STICK IT

It's a well-known fact in the country fair and festival world: Put anything on a stick and it sells. I think the skewer is part of the feminine domain. My husband hates them. Skewers send his blood pressure straight to Mars. I have no such reaction; in fact, I adore the skewer. I love satay, kebabs, and mixed veggie kebabs. I love fruit skewers. So did my catering clients, but I was once told by a chef that I would be fired if I sold one more damn fruit skewer for a party of 200. She had a point—they *are* labor intensive—but for the home griller, skewers can be made up ahead of time and take no time at all to cook.

 TIP: Skewers grill great on a hibachi. These perfect-for-high-heat mini grills will fire up quickly and use much less charcoal than a grill.

Ground Lamb Kebabs

Serves 3 for a meal, more as an appetizer

COOKING METHOD: Direct-Heat Grilling, Medium-High Heat

INGREDIENTS

½ medium onion, diced

3 tablespoons olive oil

½ teaspoon finely chopped fresh thyme

¼ teaspoon finely chopped fresh rosemary or marjoram

½ teaspoon finely chopped fresh mint

1 teaspoon salt

¼ teaspoon fresh ground pepper

2 garlic cloves, finely chopped

1 cup bread crumbs

1 pound ground lamb

1 egg

TOOLS: Soaked bamboo skewers or (12) metal skewers, spray oil

STEP BY STEP

1. Sauté onion in olive oil with herbs, salt, and pepper.

2. In a bowl mix chopped garlic, bread crumbs, and onion mixture.

3. Mix in ground lamb thoroughly with hands. Be careful not to overmix.

4. Whisk egg and add to lamb.

5. Roll ground lamb into 1½-inch-thick "logs." Firmly press onto skewers. (Makes about 12 logs.)

6. Spray kebabs with oil before placing on grill.

7. Place on grill directly over coals or medium-high gas grill. Leave for 5–7 minutes on covered grill; then turn when brown crust has formed on kebabs. Turn and cook for another 5–7 minutes on covered grill.

SERVING SUGGESTIONS—Serve with tzatziki sauce, grilled pita, tomato, and chopped lettuce.

Thai Chicken Satay with Peanut Sauce

Makes about 16 skewers
Serve this as an appetizer, or with other skewers for a meal.

COOKING METHOD: Direct-Heat Grilling, Medium-High Heat

INGREDIENTS
2–3 pounds boneless, skinless chicken breasts

MARINADE
6 garlic cloves, finely chopped
4 teaspoons grated or finely chopped ginger
¼ cup packed brown sugar
½ cup soy sauce
¼ cup lime juice
6 tablespoons canola oil
½ teaspoon fresh ground pepper
4 teaspoons ground coriander
¼ cup chopped fresh cilantro

PEANUT SAUCE
1 cup chunky peanut butter
1–2 teaspoons hot chili Thai sauce
4 tablespoons honey
¼ cup lime juice
¼ cup water
2 garlic cloves, finely chopped
½ teaspoon cayenne pepper

TOOLS: About 16 skewers, soaked for 30 minutes ahead

STEP BY STEP

1. Whisk all marinade ingredients together. Set aside ½ cup of marinade for basting.

2. Cut chicken breasts into ½- to ¾-inch-long strips. Place in marinade for 1–2 hours before grilling.

3. After chicken has marinated, weave strips on skewers, 1 piece per skewer.

4. Combine all peanut sauce ingredients and heat on low before beginning to grill.

5. Make fire for direct, medium-high heat.

6. Place skewers on grill directly over heat. Cook on one side for 2–3 minutes, until you see grill lines on chicken. Turn over; baste with reserved marinade. Close lid.

7. Cook for another 5 minutes, or until chicken has *just* lost pinkness in center.

8. Remove and serve with peanut dipping sauce.

Grill-Roasted Fingerling Potato Skewers

Serves 4

COOKING METHOD: Combination, Medium-High Heat

INGREDIENTS
1 pound fingerling potatoes (pick the chubbiest ones in the bin)
Juice from a large lemon or ⅓ cup lemon juice
⅓ cup olive oil
⅛ cup finely chopped rosemary
¼ cup sea salt

TOOLS: Flat metal skewers, 10–12 rosemary stems

STEP BY STEP
1. Cut potatoes in half lengthwise.

2. Soak potatoes in lemon juice and olive oil for at least 30 minutes.

3. Skewer with flat metal skewers, or, with a little more effort but great presentation, make skewers with rosemary stems.

> a. *To make with rosemary stem skewers*: Cut 10 woody stalks and remove all but the top greenery. Pre-score the holes in your potatoes with a flat metal skewer. To do this without stabbing your hand, place the flat side of the potato down on a cutting board, and place one hand on top of the potato to hold in place. Then run the skewer through the potato. Replace skewer with the rosemary stems.

4. Mix the sea salt and rosemary together. Roll the skewered potatoes in the mixture.

5. Grill on medium-high heat for 8 minutes, turning skewers every 2 minutes. Move to indirect side of the grill, close the lid, and roast for another 12 minutes or until done.

MAIN MEATS
Pretty Patty Makeover
The hairdo equivalent of the plain Jane burger is the ponytail. Get out of the rut and give that Patty a makeover. She deserves it. Like the endless variations of potato salad I've discussed in chapter 13, the burger is really a blank canvas for your creativity. Our fast food nation has given a bad name to burgers, which, when made by hand, can be tasty, healthy, *and* fancy. Here are some ideas plus a few tips on grilling these beauts.

HERB IT UP—Grate onion and add fresh herbs to the meat. Favorites are thyme, oregano, chives, and basil. Salt and pepper before grilling.

CHEESE-STUFFED PATTY—Place a 1-ounce cube of your favorite cheese in center and pat burger around the cheese. Add salt and fresh ground pepper before you grill.

CORNY GIRL PATTY—Southwest her up with corn, cumin, and a bit of chipotle paste mixed in the meat. Top with a grilled green chile and Jack cheese.

B-GIRL BURGER—Serve it up straight with a little barbecue sauce mixed in the meat, then brushed on top after you flip.

BLUE CHEESE PATTY WITH GRILLED ONIONS—Salt and pepper the meat; grill, and then melt blue cheese and pile on the grilled onions. Add a few slices of cooked bacon for further decadence.

CONDIMENTS—Let yourself break free of the three: ketchup, mustard, and mayonnaise. Add chutney, salsas, teriyaki sauce, and grilled pineapples. Flavor your mayonnaise with Worcestershire sauce, garlic, chipotle peppers, and fresh herbs; pile on the veggies, avocado, and cheese.

How To Make the Perfect Patty

Treat your meat with kid gloves. As gently as you can, pat ground beef into a patty shape. Don't squeeze or overmix because this will cause the meat to dry out and be tough. With your palm, smooth the ragged outer edges. Some other tips:

1. Make burgers larger than you think—they shrink. Shoot for a 6- to 8-ounce burger.

2. Aim for a thickness of ¾ inch or slightly thinner.

3. Put a thumb depression in center to combat bubble burger.

4. Use lean (80/20 or 23% fat) ground beef rather than extra lean for the best patties.

COOKING TIPS

1. Make your fire for direct medium heat.

2. Grill on one side for 5 minutes; then flip and cook for approximately 4 more minutes.

3. Don't press down on burgers to "make them cook faster." This just squeezes out the juices.

Turkey-Zucchini Burgers

Serves 4

I love these for a healthy and inexpensive alternative to beef burgers. They are also great cold the next day to take to the park with kids for a protein snack.

COOKING METHOD: Direct-Heat Grilling, Medium Heat

INGREDIENTS

1 small zucchini, grated (about 1 cup)
1 small onion, grated
1½ pound lean ground turkey (7% fat is best for consistency; the 99% fat free will fall apart)
Salt and fresh ground pepper
Fixin's—your favorites

STEP BY STEP

1. Make your fire for direct-heat grilling, medium heat.

2. Grate zucchini and squeeze out excess liquid. Grate onion and squeeze out excess liquid.

3. Add both to turkey meat, salt, and pepper. Make into patties.

4. Wipe grill with lightly oiled rag before placing patties. Turkey, because it is so lean, has a tendency to stick more than beef.

5. Cook for 4–5 minutes per side. Serve with your preferred fixin's.

STEAK CUTS

I don't know about you, but I spent years in steak confusion. I knew a few steaks I liked but was basically like Plato in the Cave, watching vague shadows of a cow dancing on the wall of my mind, not knowing where any of the steaks came from.

Here is the beef on beef. A cow is divided into primal cuts: the chuck, rib, and loin on the top of the cow, the round (which is the rump) and the shank, brisket, short plate, and flank on the lower half. While there are steak cuts in most of these sections, from two of these primal cuts—the loin and the rib—we get our most excellent steaks.

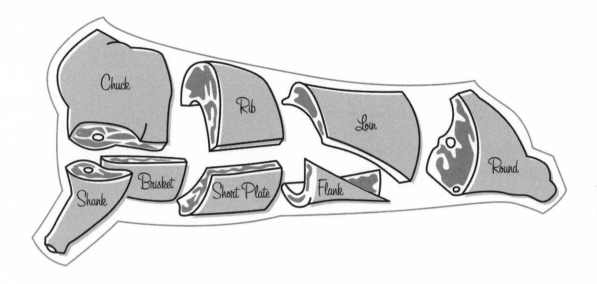

The rib gives us **prime rib** as well as one of my favorite steaks, the **ribeye.** A ribeye's marbling makes for a tender, juicy, and flavorful steak.

The loin produces the mother lode of steaks: the **tenderloin,** including **filet mignon** (the most tender of steaks); **New York strip steak** (king of steaks, cut from the center of the loin and well marbled), also called the **Kansas City strip steak**; the **T-bone** (New York strip on one side of the bone, the filet on the other); **porterhouse steak** (a larger T-bone), **top sirloin** (very lean cut); and the **tri tip** (a triangular steak from the tip of the sirloin).

The chuck is my favorite meat for burgers. It contains plenty of flavor and enough fat to make a good patty. The **flat iron steak,** known for its bold flavor, also comes from the chuck.

The brisket is of course best for barbecue. **Skirt steaks** come from the plate and are best marinated, then grilled fast on high heat, and from the round we get round steaks and roasts.

The flank gives us the delicious though tougher **flank steak.** Marinate the flank long and it makes for delicious eatin'.

Simple Pleasures Grilled Steak

COOKING METHOD: Combination, Medium-High Heat

A good steak needs minimal fuss. Rub with olive oil, kosher salt, pepper. Serve with savory herb butter or blue cheese butter.

STEAK—Ribeye, top sirloin, T-bone, porterhouse, or New York strip steak
RUB—Olive oil, kosher salt, and fresh ground pepper

STEP BY STEP

1. Make your fire for medium-high heat.

2. Lightly rub steak with olive oil, kosher or sea salt, and fresh ground pepper.

3. Put steak directly over fire and sear for 3–4 minutes. Turn 45 degrees on same side and cook for 1 minute to get crosshatch marks. Flip and cook on other side for 2–3 minutes.

4. Move to indirect side and check internal temperature with your instant read thermometer. Based on how you like your steak and how thick that steak was to begin with, remove if ready or continue to cook for up to 4–5 minutes on indirect heat with the lid down. Generally 130°F is rare, 140°F medium-rare, and 150°F medium.

Making Herb Butters

Finishing a steak with herb butter, also called Maître D' butter, gives it that steakhouse sheen and flavor. Herb butters are easy to make. Simply let butter stand at room temperature for 20–30 minutes to soften. Add in fresh herbs of your choice and a squeeze of lemon. With a rubber spatula, mix butter until herbs are fully incorporated. Mold into a roll and refrigerate. Extra butter can be frozen too. Cut off butter circles, and either heat on low and pour over steak or put the cold dollop of herb butter on top of the hot steak. For blue cheese butter, use ¼ cup crumbed blue cheese to 1 stick of butter.

TIP: To make those nifty crosshatch marks on your food just like the pros, rotate your food 45 degrees after 3–4 minutes of heat. You only need to make crosshatch marks on one side, the side that you will face up on the plate.

Kalbi Beef Short Ribs

Serves 4

COOKING METHOD: Direct-Heat Grilling, High Heat

Beef short ribs are the large, meaty ribs that come from the rib plate, not the long, skinny back ribs. Korean short ribs, also called the "Hawaiian cut," are sliced horizontally in strips, with the bone embedded. You can get them in most grocery stores with an onsite butcher, at your butcher shop, or any Asian market. Marinate 4 hours up to a day ahead to tender up the tendons.

INGREDIENTS
About 12–15 ribs (3–4 per person)
Kalbi Marinade (pg. 61)

TOOLS: Long-handled chef tongs, plastic sealable bags

STEP BY STEP
1. Marinate ribs in a plastic sealable bag, or a pan with marinade fully covering ribs.

2. Make a direct, high-heat fire with an indirect space on one side. If using charcoal, make coals 2 layers high.

3. Lift ribs out of the marinade and shake off excess. Put on grill, spacing them out a few inches. If fire gets too intense, move ribs over to your indirect space and cover lid until flare-up dies down. Ribs needs about 2 minutes per side. Serve with white rice and cucumber Oyi Namul salad (pg. 236).

Skirt for Skirts

COOKING METHOD: Direct-Heat Grilling, High Heat

I've always liked the inexpensive skirt steak for its flavor and superfast cooking. Fajitas are made from the skirt, and this chewier cut needs two things to make it just right: Marinate it for at least 4–8 hours, and cook it on high heat.

INGREDIENTS
6-ounce skirt steak per person
Easy Steak Marinade (enough for 4 steaks; pg. 62)

STEP BY STEP
1. Marinate meat for 4–8 hours.

2. Make your fire for high heat. If using *charcoal*, make coals 2 layers high. *For gas*, leave burners on high after you preheat.

3. When coals are red, or grill preheated, shake off marinade from meat and place directly over fire. Cook for 2 minutes per side. *Note:* Make this the last thing you do in your meal preparation.

SERVING SUGGESTIONS— 1) Add a spice rub after you shake off the marinade to give it a kick for fajitas. 2) Slice against the grain and put in a steak salad.

Bistecca Fiorentina

Serves 2

COOKING METHOD: Direct Grilling, High Heat

My first introduction to this mouthwatering juicy steak was in Florence, cooked by a Florentine, in a pit in his back yard. I had the real deal the first time, and none others have compared (I'm still talking about the *steak* here, gals, in case you got stuck on thoughts of "Italian," "dinner," "his backyard").

It didn't hurt that I was a poor college student studying on a semester abroad and that my usual fare was the "buy two, take three" grocery store pasta cooked by me in my tiny shared apartment. Most of the finer culinary delights were lost on me and my lack of funds and youth, but Italy did awaken my taste buds to fresh, local foods direct from the source. This has never been a fashion statement by the Italians, or one espoused by those who shop at Whole Foods—it is just done because food tastes better that way. This Bistecca, a batch of pesto made by a real Genovese *signora,* and roasted rosemary-lemon-olive oil chicken eaten at an out-in-the-country trattoria are just a few food memories cemented in my soul.

About the Bistecca Fiorentina: Tuscans like to keep it simple and let the flavors of the food be the feature of the dish. This steak embodies those principles. Cook it on very high heat without anything; then remove from fire and rub with olive oil, kosher salt, and fresh ground pepper.

INGREDIENTS

1 T-bone steak, 1½–2 inches thick (Often the steaks already wrapped in the grocery store are less than 1 inch. This just won't do. Talk to the butcher in the meat department to cut off a thicker T-bone for you, or buy your T-bone at a bona fide butcher shop. They will hook you up.)
Extra virgin olive oil, good quality
Kosher salt
Fresh ground pepper

BEST EQUIPMENT: Charcoal or wood-fired grill
TOOLS: Long-handled chef tongs, instant read thermometer, oil rag (*lightly* oiled with vegetable oil)

Party Planning Tips: Calculating How Much Meat To Buy

In my years of professional party planning and catering, I've had to come up with some unusual requests—from flying in 2,000 hot dogs from New York to buying tube socks for the Red Hot Chili Peppers . . . for a body part other than their feet. Most people start with the theme, the creative part of the party that will make their event stand out from their cousin's boring bar mitzvah or Aunt Rachel's third wedding. In reality, though, the key to successful party planning comes down to math. Math, you say? What a buzz kill. But before you order the ice sculpture or that 10-foot-tall cutout of George Clooney, the first tool you need is a calculator.

There are certain averages of food a person can eat. Yes, your cousin Bubba is going to put skinny Aunt Rachel away, if not eat her if she's not careful, but with a calculator we can plan the happy medium between the two. After the math, you can think about ordering the personalized temporary tattoos for your guests.

How much meat to buy? Most people overcompensate on food, with the exception of some family members, and you all know who they are. Meat portions are pretty standard.

Start with a base of 6 ounces finished meat weight per person. If you have two equal entrées, calculate 3 ounces of each per person. If this is a college football team, bump up the portioning to 10 ounces per person. If your crowd is older, diet conscious, mostly ladies, largely from another country, then reduce the meat portion to 4 ounces.

To calculate the total meat you need, figure this:

100 guests x 6 ounces = 600 ounces total ÷ 16 (ounces in a pound) =
a total of 37.5 pounds of finished meat per person.

What do I mean by *finished* meat? This is your yield after the loss of weight due to cooking and trimming. In the case of boneless, skinless chicken breasts, the loss is next to nil. If you are smoking an untrimmed whole packer brisket (you'll learn what that means in the Beef chapter), your raw weight will be 50% higher than your end weight. How do I know this? I've done yield tests. I don't expect you to, so I've given you yields on the meats that lose weight the most, namely pork butt and brisket, in those chapters.

For *ribs* start with ¾ of a pound per person and go up or down from there. Even big burly guys who boast they can eat a whole rack of spareribs won't eat much more than a pound to a pound and a half. Factor chicken by piece. Use ⅙ of a chicken per person as your base.

STEP BY STEP

1. *For charcoal*: Use lump charcoal, as it burns hotter than briquettes. Light a full charcoal chimney. When coals are red hot, pour into center of grill. Make a circle of coals a little larger than the diameter of your steak. Make the fire 2–3 layers high with coals. Add fresh coals on edges of circle if needed to fill the area. *For wood*: Make fire with about 6–7 pieces of wood. Burn down to red-hot coals. Follow the same placement as with charcoal.

2. Place grill grate and close lid for 10 minutes. Rub grate quickly with a lightly oiled rag.

3. Put steak directly over coals and cook for 2 minutes. Flip and cook for another 2 minutes. Flip again (ignoring my grilling tip #4, above) and place the thicker part of the steak in the direct-heat circle, with the thinner part, the filet, at the cooler edge. Flip again, keeping the filet at the cooler edge. This method combats the challenge with the T-bone—that when the filet is a perfect medium rare, the rest is too rare.

4. Check in the thickest part of the steak that the internal temperature reads 125°F for rare, 130°F –135°F for medium rare, 140°F for medium. Steak temperature will rise 5°–10° while the meat rests.

Grilled Rack of Lamb with Mint Pesto

COOKING METHOD: Direct-Heat Grilling, Medium-High Heat

INGREDIENTS

1 lamb rack or partial rack, cut up (factor 2–3 chops per person)

MARINADE
1 herbal mint tea bag, or 2 teaspoons dried mint
1 teaspoon dried thyme
1 teaspoon kosher salt
Juice from ½ large lemon
4–6 garlic cloves, chopped
2 tablespoons olive oil
Fresh ground pepper

MINT PESTO

1 ounce fresh mint leaves, or 1 cup of leaves, lightly packed

2 ounces grated Parmesan cheese

½ cup pine nuts

4–8 garlic cloves (about 1 clove per chop)

Juice from ½ large lemon

¼ cup olive oil

¼ teaspoon kosher salt

TOOLS: Food processor, long-handled chef tongs

BEST EQUIPMENT: Charcoal or gas grill

MAKE AHEAD: Make the mint pesto up to a day ahead.

STEP BY STEP

1. *For mint pesto:* With a food processor, chop mint; then add the remaining mint pesto ingredients. Mix on high until combined into a paste.

2. Rub chopped garlic into both sides of each chop.

3. *For marinade:* Mix tea bag, thyme, and salt together. Lightly coat lamb with olive oil; then rub with dry ingredients. Squeeze lemon over all, and add fresh ground fresh pepper. Be sure both sides of the lamb get covered. Let sit for 30 minutes.

4. Make your fire for direct-heat grilling, medium-high heat.

5. Once coals are red-hot or gas grill is preheated, put chops on grill directly over heat. After 2 minutes, close the lid (with top vents partially open), and cook for another 3 minutes. Turn meat over and cook for another 4–5 minutes with lid down. Check that internal temperature reads 130°F for rare, 140°F for medium rare, and remove when ready. Keep in mind the meat temperature will rise another 5° while it rests. Serve each chop with a dollop of mint pesto.

Grilled South Carolina Mustard Thighs

COOKING METHOD: Combination, Medium Heat

The South Carolina Mustard sauce on page 73 works great for direct-heat grilling because it is low in sugar. Use the cooking directions here for *any* marinated chicken thighs.

INGREDIENTS
South Carolina Mustard Sauce (pg. 73)
Chicken thighs, skin on, bone in or out (factor 1½ thighs per person)
NOTE: *If using boneless thighs, see adjusted cooking time in recipe.*

BEST EQUIPMENT: Any charcoal or gas grill
TOOLS: Long-handled chef tongs, instant read thermometer, spatula
MAKE AHEAD: Make the sauce ahead and marinate the thighs 3 hours to 1 day ahead.

STEP BY STEP
1. Marinate thighs in sauce 3 hours to a day ahead.

2. Make fire for direct-heat grilling, medium heat, with ⅓ of your grill space reserved for indirect-medium cooking.

3. Once coals are ready or gas grill is preheated, place thighs over direct fire, skin side up. Close lid and cook for 5 minutes. Keep top vents on your grill open about halfway.

4. Turn thighs and cook, skin side down, for 5 minutes. Close the lid while cooking.

5. Move thighs over to indirect part of grill, flipping them back to skin side up. Close the lid and cook for another 10 minutes, or until instant read thermometer registers an internal temperature of 155°F.

6. Remove thighs and let rest for 5–10 minutes. Your chicken temperature will increase to the recommended 160°F during this time.

TIP: Though this recipe does not require a glaze or "finishing sauce" in the last 10–15 minutes of cooking, for another recipe you may brush on your sauce or glaze when you move the thighs to the indirect side of the grill. The cooking method is the same, but the flavors can change. Try this recipe with the Pacific Rim Rub on page 52, finished with the Orange-Currant Glaze on page 69.

Donna Moodie's Jamaican Jerk Chicken

Serves 4
See chapter 8 for the **She's Smokin'** *side bar about this Seattle restaurateur. Originally from Jamaica, Donna shares her family recipe.*

COOKING METHOD: Combination, Medium Heat

INGREDIENTS
4 bone-in, skin-on chicken breasts, washed and rubbed with fresh lemon juice
2 tablespoons lemon juice
2 tablespoons canola oil
1 tablespoon honey
1 Scotch bonnet pepper (also known as habanero)
1 teaspoon allspice
1 teaspoon ground cinnamon
1 teaspoon ground nutmeg
2 teaspoons ground cumin
1 teaspoon ground cloves
2 teaspoons salt

BEST EQUIPMENT: Any charcoal or gas grill
TOOLS: Food processor, instant read thermometer
MAKE AHEAD: Let chicken marinate overnight in rub.

STEP BY STEP
   1. Blend the ingredients above in a food processor, and rub on chicken.

2. Grill until cooked*. Chicken can also be marked on grill and finished in the oven, or roasted on a rack over a pan in oven. Wonderful when accompanied by pureed sweet potatoes and hearty greens.

*Use an instant read thermometer to check that chicken reads 160°F internally. It will reach 165°F while it rests.
**Julie's suggestion: Grill for 7–10 minutes on each side over direct, medium heat. Finish on indirect medium heat with the lid down for an additional 10–12 minutes until done.

GRILLING SEAFOOD

Seafood lends itself to grilling, often requiring less than 10 minutes to cook. The key is to remove your fish before it is "done." It will continue to cook while resting. For meatier fish like halibut and swordfish, use the combination of direct-heat grilling and indirect medium cooking with the lid on your grill. This will let the top of your fish cook evenly with the bottom.

TIP: If you are cooking your own fresh-caught fish, it should not be cooked for at least one day after caught if possible. The intense adrenaline released in the fight to survive causes the meat to be bitter and tough. Resting a day will relax the meat and essentially drain out the adrenaline for a better taste.

Kiss of Smoke Grilled Fish

COOKING METHOD: Combination, Medium Heat

Though the cooking time is only about 7 minutes, your fish will carry a nice smoked flavor from the wood because of the combination cooking method.

INGREDIENTS:
Halibut fillets or steaks, or swordfish steaks. Choose a fresh, wild fish, 4-6 ounces per person
Olive oil (*not* extra virgin) or canola oil
Salt and fresh ground pepper
½ cup chopped fresh thyme

1–2 lemons

2–3 tablespoons butter

BEST EQUIPMENT: Any charcoal or gas grill

TOOLS: Spatula, long-handled chef tongs

PREFERRED WOOD: Grapevines, alder, or other mild wood

STEP BY STEP

1. Make your fire for a combination of direct- and indirect-heat grilling, medium heat.

2. Add your wood once your coals are ready or grill is preheated, and close lid for 10 minutes.

3. Rub your fish with oil; then sprinkle salt, pepper, and thyme.

4. *If cooking steaks*: Place fish directly over heat for approximately 2–3 minutes each side, closing the grill lid each time. Move to the indirect side and cook for an additional 2–3 minutes with the lid on.

5. *If cooking fillets*: Place fish skin side down on grill, directly over fire, for 3–4 minutes, with lid down. Move to the indirect side, close lid, and cook for another 5 minutes. Your time will vary according to how thick your fillet is. *Tip: If cooking fish on a Weber, you can just rotate the grill rack to the indirect side and avoid moving the fish.*

6. Just before removing fish from grill, rub butter over the top and squeeze a lemon over fish. Let rest for 10 minutes before serving.

 TIP: Extra virgin olive oil, while perfect for salad dressing, burns at a lower temperature than non-virgin oil. For grilling choose a second- or third-pressing olive oil—in other words, the cheaper stuff.

Grilled Oysters-'n-Greens Appetizer

COOKING METHOD: Combination, Medium Heat

This is a simpler and lower-fat version of Oysters Rockefeller.

INGREDIENTS
6 leaves Swiss chard
½ medium onion, diced
3 tablespoons olive oil
1 dozen fresh raw oysters
¼ teaspoon salt (Try smoked salt on these. Learn to smoke your own salt on page 58.)
Parmesan chunk (you will shave it rather than grate it)

TOOLS: Carrot peeler, oyster shucker, or flat-head screwdriver

STEP BY STEP
1. Sauté greens and onion in olive oil. Let cool for 10–15 minutes. Squeeze out excess liquid. Finely chop; then squeeze out liquid again. Set aside.

2. Shuck off flat oyster shell, leaving oyster in the "boat" shell. Spoon in 1 tablespoon greens mixture, and "nuzzle" next to oyster. Sprinkle salt lightly on oysters.

3. With a carrot peeler, shave a slice of Parmesan and place on top of oyster and greens.

4. Place shells directly on grill for 4 minutes with lid closed.

Grilled Fish in Cedar Wraps

COOKING METHOD: Direct, Medium-High Heat

I love placing delicate fish in "packets" of either cedar wraps or banana leaves. It guarantees you won't have fish falling through the grill grates, and it steams the fish inside. I also am *not* a fan of the cedar plank. I see these large slabs of wood for sale labeled as "one time use" and think there has got to be a better use of resources. The wraps impart as much flavor at only a fraction of the material used.

INGREDIENTS
Cedar wraps (1 per fish piece)
Salmon fillets or any whitefish fillets (4 to 6 ounces each)
Fresh thyme stems (4–5 stems per piece of fish)
1 green onion stalk

STEP BY STEP

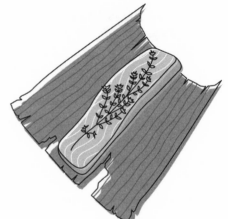

1. Pre-soak cedar wraps for 10 minutes. Place 5–6 stems of fresh thyme on top of fish. Roll fish and herbs in the wraps, and tie with a green onion stalk. The ends of the rolls will be open.

2. Make your fire for medium-high heat. Grill packets directly over flames, turning every few minutes for about 10 minutes or until done.

3. Remove from grill; unwrap and serve. The steam makes these super moist and in need of very few other flavors. You can brush with melted butter or serve with a sauce, but I like them simple and low fat.

VARIATION—Drizzle some teriyaki sauce over the fish before you wrap.

Grilled Pizza
....

Makes two 9-inch pizzas
Grilled pizza is fun once you get the hang of it, and it has the taste of authentic wood-fired pizza. Use your own favorite thin-crust pizza recipe or the one below. Here are some pointers about grilling pizza for the beginner.

COOKING METHOD: Combination, Medium Heat

1. Make your fire for combination cooking. Half of your grill, gas or charcoal, should be set or made for high heat, the other half reserved for indirect cooking.

2. Start with smaller pizzas. Initially, working with the dough quickly on a grill may be awkward. I know it took me three times before I felt comfortable making pizza on the grill and got a result I liked.

3. Use a lipless cookie sheet for moving and flipping pizza. Most of us do not have a pizza board as they do in pizzerias. Spatulas and tongs just don't give you the coverage you need, but you can slip a cookie sheet under the dough and shift it around easily.

4. Keep your toppings Italian style, not Chicago style. In other words, go minimal. There won't be enough time to cook heavy toppings before the crust starts to burn.

5. Be prepared. Grilling pizza is fast, so have everything at the ready before you begin.

CRUST
1 package dry active yeast
1 cup warm water
3½ cups all-purpose flour
1 tablespoon salt
Olive oil

TOPPINGS
It's your movie! Choose a sauce base (olive oil, marinara, pesto); add grated cheese and your other favorite toppings.

TOOLS: Lipless cookie sheet (in lieu of pizza board), oven mitts, pastry brush for olive oil

STEP BY STEP
1. *Making the dough*: Dissolve one packet of yeast in warm water (110°F–115°F) and let sit for 5 minutes. Add flour and salt, and stir until all the flour and liquid are incorporated. On a floured surface, knead

dough for about 10 minutes until it is elastic and smooth. Form into one ball. Set aside in bowl and brush a light coating of olive oil on the dough. Cover bowl and set in a warm part of the kitchen. Let dough rise to twice its size.

2. While dough is rising, prep all your ingredients for the pizza. Grate the cheese, get out the pizza sauce (or make it from scratch), chop toppings, and gather all your tools. Just before you are ready to punch down your dough and form the pizzas, make your fire or pre-heat your grill.

3. Make your fire for combination grilling.

4. Once dough has doubled, punch down the dough and split into 2 even sections. On a floured surface, knead the dough again, about 5–10 minutes, so that it is springy to the touch. Roll out to ¼-inch thick. Dough will shrink back—it's okay; just keep spreading it out as best you can. Don't worry about perfect shapes. Often rectangular pizzas work better in terms of grill space.

5. Now you are ready: Bring dough out on your lipless cookie sheet. Brush one side with olive oil, and place the olive oil side down directly on grill over hot coals. Close the grill lid for 2 minutes. Open lid and move pizza to the indirect side. For gas grills this may mean you will turn the middle burner down to low while you add your toppings.

6. Brush with olive oil; then flip. Add your sauce, cheese, and toppings. Close lid for 3 minutes. With your cookie sheet, move pizza around to direct heat side for a moment, then back to "safe." Do this as needed until bottom crust is done and toppings are melted.

7. Let pizza rest for 5–10 minutes before slicing.

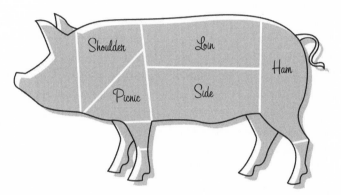

Chapter Six

Pork
First Barbecue

CAROLINA BARBECUE

Ah, pork. Since that first little piggy went to the market, American barbecue has bowed down to the plump porcine god as slow-cooked royalty. We have entire festivals, competitions, and more than a few bed-and-breakfasts out there that have gone way past cute with collections of all things pig.

In the Carolinas, discussions on every aspect of barbecue can escalate to longstanding feuds and published insults. They do agree on one thing: that smoking the whole hog over wood coals is the *definition* of barbecue. Most of us have neither the capacity nor the time to smoke the whole pig. Smoking a pork shoulder will get you pretty darn close and is acceptable in most parts.

I once threw a party and did a side-by-side taste test of pork butt smoked with charcoal and pork smoked on an electric smoker. I took notes in my journal, and here is a perfect example of why it's good to document everything: You never know when or how you will use the information.

TRIVIA: The full pork shoulder is made up of two sections: the upper part, most often called the Boston butt or pork butt, and the lower picnic shoulder. A Boston butt with the bone in will weigh 6–9 pounds, boneless about 4–7 pounds. Bone-in picnics weigh 8–10 pounds.

I used two boneless pork butts, rubbed them with a simple rub similar to the Basic Barbecue Rub on page 51, and basted on the hour with a mix of apple cider vinegar and red chili flakes.

Although it's sacrilege in some barbecue circles, I'm a fan of electric smokers both because they are convenient and because they burn less fuel and create fewer carbon emissions. There *is* a difference in taste, though I'm not sure it represents the vast planetary-scale chasm that those of the barbecue religion contest. The charcoal adds a sweeter, caramelized smoke flavor to the pork. In my taste test, both butts were juicy and tender because I smoked them for the whole day, slow and low. The charcoal butt cooked a bit faster on the kettle grill I used. I had to move it over to the top rack of the electric smoker to slow it down a bit so both would be ready at the same time.

After we pulled and chopped the pork, we separated the meat into three parts and tested three Carolina sauces: a basic eastern Carolina sauce, a Lexington "Dip" recipe inspired by Bob Garner's book *North Carolina Barbecue: Flavored by Time*, and our Smokin' Pete's Carolina Sour Sauce, which includes paprika and has a bit more kick to it. It was a three-way tie among the guests. (By the way, taste testing makes for a great party. Guests have fun pulling and chopping the pork, as well as casting their vote.) Choose your favorite. All three sauce recipes are noted in chapter 4.

Carolina Pulled Pork

COOKING METHOD: Slow and Low

TEMPERATURE AND TIMING

There are so many variables that can slow down or speed up your pork. Give yourself about 10–12 hours from start to finish for your pork butt. This means that you will have about an hour to rub your pork, light your coals, or get your electric or pellet smoker preheated. If you start at 8:00 AM, get the meat in by 9:00 AM, you can be serving chow at 7:00 PM. If you don't have this much time, there are shortcuts listed below.

Shoot for a temperature range of 200°F–250°F. My ideal is 212°F, the boiling point of water, but my Weber gravitates to 230°F. She likes it there, and I've accepted that. If you get sidetracked and the temperature dips down to 180°F for an hour because your coals got too low, don't sweat it. It's far easier to increase the temperature than to lower it.

If you are using a kettle drum grill, tending your fire to keep it low will take a little more finesse, but that doesn't mean you have to stand there for 10–12 hours. I often see a "comfy chair and case of beer" on the "equipment" needs for a pulled pork recipe, but you can still manage the kids, do the laundry, clean the house, and prep the rest of dinner during the cooking time. If you can sit down and drink a beer, by all means do it. If you have small children, it helps to have someone with you to "tag-team" between adding charcoal and playing chase, at least for part of the time. Here are some pointers on smoking butts in the kettle:

Smoking Pork on a Weber

THE MEAT: You may smoke 1–2 pork butts or a whole pork shoulder, bone in, on a kettle grill (like a Weber). Fresh pork is best.

THE RUB: Choose the Basic Barbecue Rub on page 51 or the Feisty Girl Rub on page 53.

THE MOP: I like to mop with a simple mixture of apple cider vinegar, any all-fruit juice in the fridge, and red pepper flakes. You may spray apple juice or cider vinegar with a clean spray bottle. When I'm using red pepper flakes in my mop, I drizzle it on carefully so the excess falls in the drip pan, not on the coals. For other mop recipes, see chapter 4.

It is often prescribed that you mop the pork every half hour. I think that is fussing too much and just a way to lose the stability of your temperature. You want a constant low temperature of about 200°F–250°F, so opening the lid every half hour is going to make this part of your work more difficult. Mop every hour.

- **CHARCOAL**—About one 5-pound bag

- **PREFERRED WOOD**—I prefer wood chunks to chips, but both work well. Hickory, or a mix of hickory and cherry, is a favorite. Have 10–15 chunks on hand, small enough to slip through the handle holes. You will need 3–4 cups of wood chips.

To Soak Or Not To Soak

Many advise soaking your wood chips prior to casting on the fire for two reasons: Damp chips won't flare up as easily in your grill, and the dampness creates more smoke. The best argument I've heard not to soak your chips is that they can actually put out your fire. Soak 'em if it makes you happy.

TOOLS: Chimney starter (if you have one), long matches or lighter, long-handled chef tongs, oven mitt, metal scoop or garden trowel for the coals, spray bottle for mop. A remote thermometer for checking internal temp of the grill and an instant read thermometer for checking meat.

MAKE AHEAD: Make rub days or weeks ahead if you want. You can rub your pork up to a day ahead.

STEP BY STEP

1. Rub your pork. If you are using a boneless butt, be sure to pat the rub in the folds.

2. *Make your fire:* Start with about 20 briquettes. Light in a charcoal chimney or make a pyramid/revised pyramid (review pg. 28) on one side of the bottom grill grate.

3. When coals turn gray, arrange into a compact pile on one side of the grill. Place an aluminum 10 x 10 drip pan on the other side, and fill ¾ with water or a mix of water and apple juice. Get your smoke on: Add two wood chunks on top of the coals, place your top grate on, and close the lid for 10 minutes. **Tip:** *If you can hold your hand over your grate for about 10 seconds, your heat is low enough to begin.*

4. Position the cooking grate so the side openings from the grill handles line up with the coals. Place the lid with the vents positioned near the meat, but not directly over it. This way the smoke will travel across the grill yet keep heat loss over the meat to a minimum.

TIP: Place a remote thermometer through the top vent, so that it hangs above the meat, or push the prong all the way through a potato and set it on the grill next to the meat. This way it won't sit on the grill, which may be hotter than the internal temperature.

5. Place the rubbed meat with the fat side up, directly over the drip pan. The fat will drip down and baste the meat.

6. Close the lid, and close the top vents almost completely; close the bottom vents about halfway. Leave it.

7. In 20 minutes, start 10 coals in your charcoal chimney or in a second grill (a small grill like a hibachi works great for your coal "feeder").

8. When the coals are *completely* ash gray, quickly add to your pile, sneaking them in through the holes by the grill handles and keeping the pile tightly stacked. Add a wood chunk if your first two are almost burned down. You can use tongs or a metal scoop or garden trowel to transfer the hot coals quickly. Repeat this step so that you are feeding new coals about every hour until done. Add 1–2 wood chunks with the new coals each time for the first 3–5 hours. *Tip: If you get tied up and don't get a chimney started in time, you can add fresh coals to the pile. They will burn hotter at first, affecting your overall temperature average. Add only 5–7 fresh coals to your pile at a time.*

9. After 2 hours, mop the pork every hour.

10. Halfway through the cooking time, rotate (don't flip) the pork so that the other side is closest to the heat.

HOW TO TELL IF IT'S DONE

First use science: Insert your instant read thermometer in the middle of the pork. The time between it being "done" for safety (160°F) and "done" for tender barbecue (180°F–190°F+) can often seem endless, so much so that it has its own term: "the stall." Your pork will just sit there, not budging a bit on the thermometer dial, and will feel noticeably resistant to the touch. It will "push back" when you poke it, and you don't want your barbecue to push back. At this point, you need to stop paying so much attention to the science and move on to your senses. **Tip:** *To soften a stubborn butt that has been on the smoker for long hours, wrap it in foil and place it in a preheated 250°F oven for an hour.*

THE FEEL TEST—When I touch the pork butt with my finger, I want to feel as if my finger will go through the meat if I push it. Of course, I won't actually do this, because it would burn my finger and put a hole through my nice crust, but you want to feel as if the pork will give in, not be a wall of meat.

During the stall, I stop reading the internal temperature of my grill and move my remote thermometer to the meat. Keep the lid on the grill as much as possible to help that butt "break on through to the other side" of tough. The finished pork should have a delicious crust on the outside, a pink smoke ring, and soft white inside.

THE FORK TEST—In general, you never want to use a fork to turn your meat on the grill. Puncturing holes will let the juices escape. When you are at or near the end of your pork butt journey, however, you can try the fork test to check what you already know in your gut—that it's done. Insert a fork, and if it twists (with *some* resistance), then your pork is done. **Tip:** *You can add a little more sauce or ½ cup of stock to liven up a drier butt. If there is some char on a spot where your butt sat too close to the fire, cut off this part before pulling or chopping it with the rest.*

PULLING THE PORK—Let meat rest for 15 minutes before you begin. Traditionally the pork is hand-pulled or shredded. Use thick kitchen gloves to keep from getting burned when hand-pulling, Some other methods: Shred the pork with two forks, or slice and chop it into more manageable pieces before pulling it apart. I like to chop most of it into smaller chunks with a cleaver (back side facing me); then pull apart the rest by hand. You want to mix the fat and the meat well and break up any chunks larger than an apricot. Don't you *dare* remove all the fat—it's not all that much, and you'll be taking the good moisture and flavor away. You have my permission to remove the one larger chunk of fat on the outside, but scrape off the nice crust and put that back in the pork.

CHOOSING A SAUCE—Try one of the Carolina vinegar sauces on pages 71–73. The tang of the vinegar and spice is a wonderful contrast to the smoke. You may be blasphemous and serve it up with any of your favorite tomato-based barbecue sauces. Or, better yet, try a Carolina sauce on half and your favorite tomato-based barbecue sauce on the other half to compare.

Recipe for Electric Smokers

Follow the instructions for the Meat, Rub, Mop, Preferred Wood, and Tools in the Smoking Pork on a Weber recipe, above.

1. Preheat your electric smoker for 15 minutes and "get your smoke on".
Add 2 wood chunks in between the elements.

2. Fill the water pan with half water, half apple juice or apple cider.

3. Smoke for approximately 10 hours. Add wood chunks every hour for the first 6 hours (electric smokers need wood longer than charcoal).

4. After 2 hours, mop your pork every hour.

5. Follow the How To Tell If It's Done and the Pulling the Pork instructions, above.

Recipe for Gas Grills

Gas is my least favorite equipment for pulled pork. I recommend the shortcut of finishing your pork in the oven. Follow the instructions for the Meat, Rub, Mop, Preferred Wood, and Tools in the Smoking Pork on a Weber recipe, above.

- Preheat your gas grill on high for 15 minutes. "Get your smoke on": If your grill does not have a smoke box, make a foil wood-chip pouch (see pg. 32) while the grill preheats.

- Once the foil pouch produces a good smoke, turn the center burner off and the side burners down to low. Place the pork fat side up on the grill and leave it for 1 hour. Add wood chips to your foil pouch after 1 hour.

- Mop your pork after 2 hours, and smoke for another ½ hour; then remove and follow the Finishing in the Oven shortcut, below.

SHORTCUTS

Here are a few shortcuts you can do when you want pulled pork but don't have all day.

FINISHING IN THE OVEN—Smoke your pork for 2 hours on any grill or smoker. On a medium-high stovetop, heat a Dutch oven or a large, deep cast-iron skillet with a lid. Preheat your oven to 325°F.

Add a thin coating of vegetable oil to the pan; then sear the pork butt for 10 minutes on two sides. If using a Carolina sauce, pour 2 cups over the pork; cover and bake for about 3 hours. For tomato-based sauces, thin 2 cups of barbecue sauce with 1 cup of water. Check both after 2 hours to be sure they have enough liquid.

Cooking Times and Temperatures for Pork *

CUT	COOKING TEMPERATURE	COOKING METHOD	WEIGHT
Boston Butt	225	Slow and Low	6-8 lbs.
Boston Butt	300-350	Indirect-Medium	6-8 lbs.
Whole Pork Shoulder	225	Slow and Low	12-16 lbs.
Spareribs	225	Slow and Low	2½-3+ lbs.
Spareribs	225	Slow and Low	4-5 lbs.
St. Louis Cut Ribs	225	Slow and Low	2½-3½ lbs.
Baby Back Ribs	225	Slow and Low	1½-2 lbs.
Baby Back Ribs	300	Indirect-Medium	1½-2 lbs.
Pork Loin	225	Slow and Low	4-6 lbs.
Pork Loin	300-350	Indirect-Medium	4-6 lbs.
Pork Tenderloin	225	Slow and Low	1-2 lbs.
Pork Tenderloin	300-350	Indirect-Medium	1-2 lbs.

If your Dutch oven isn't large enough, cut the butt in half and cook in two pots. This will cut down the cooking time by 30 minutes or more.

HOW TO TELL IF IT'S DONE—As with the shortcut on the previous page, first use your thermometer, then the Feel and Fork tests (pgs. 121–122). Transfer the pork to a new pan for pulling. Save drippings to add back into your sauce if you like. Drain off the top layer of oil, however, so your pork doesn't get greasy.

TIME	INTERNAL TEMPERATURE WHEN DONE*	NOTES
10-12 hrs	185-190	1-1½ hrs per lb.
4-6 hrs	185-190	about 45 min per lb.
14-18 hrs	185-190	1-1½ hrs per lb.
5-7 hrs	wiggle, bend test	
7-9 hrs	wiggle, bend test	
5-7 hrs	wiggle, bend test	
3-5 hrs	wiggle, bend test	
2-3 hrs	wiggle, bend test	
3-4 hrs	160	45-1 hr per lb., will reach 160° while resting
1¼-2½ hrs	160	20-30 min per lb., will reach 160° while resting
1-2 hrs	160	pull at 155°, will reach 160° while resting
30-45 min	160	pull at 155°, will reach 160° while resting

* IMPORTANT NOTE: Internal temperatures are based on USDA recommended minimal temperatures. Cooking times are estimated and may vary according to equipment, weather conditions, and other factors.

PRESSURE COOKER METHOD—My brother swears by this method. He's far off in the Czech Republic, and though the Czechs are masters of smoked pork, they don't have barbecue joints like we do. Rub the pork (pg. 119). Put the pork in a pressure cooker for 20 minutes; then smooch it with some smoke on the grill for about an hour. Be generous with your wood chunks or soaked wood chips, as it will only get an hour of smoky goodness. Pull, chop, and sauce afterward.

CROCK IT, BABY—Smoke pork for 2 hours in any of the above equipment; then go seventies style and break out the Crock-Pot. This works great for a daytime meal. Smoke your butt the night before; then put it in the Crock-Pot with either 3 cups of Carolina-style sauce or 2 cups of tomato-based sauce and 1 cup of water. Cook on high for 1 hour to get the internal temperature up; then cook on low overnight. In the morning, drain off the liquid; then pull/chop it and add another cup of sauce of your choice. Cook on low for another hour. Serve when ready.

RIBS, RIBS, RIBS

I love Carolina pulled pork, but for many of you out there, when you're talking barbecue, you're talking ribs. Whether you like the meaty spareribs or the spare but finger-lickin' baby backs, all cuts when done right will win you kudos at a party.

Rib Cuts

BABY BACK RIBS—These are the smaller back ribs from the top of the back rib cage. Though they are less meaty, their manageable size and smaller cartilage/fat ratio make them a favorite.

COUNTRY STYLE RIBS—The country-style ribs you see packaged in the grocery store are not ribs but instead cut from the blade end of the pork loin, or they are cut sections of a pork butt made to look like ribs.

KANSAS CITY CUT—A tighter trim than the St. Louis cut.

RIB TIPS—A tasty treat for those who don't have to gnaw on the bone. The rib tips are the end meat flap from the rib. Often these are cut off prior to smoking the rack because they cook faster and can get dry if smoked for the entire time. I like them smoked for about 4 hours, then sauced and put back in the oven to finish. Typically ordering the "tips" is slightly less expensive at a barbecue joint, but they are not always available.

SPARERIBS—The large ribs on the belly side of the rib cage. These have a large bone and a nice amount of meat and fat, which, when slow-smoked, are quite tender.

ST. LOUIS CUT—Spareribs with the top section connecting to the sternum trimmed off. The end tips are trimmed as well. Essentially the cut makes the ribs rectangular and visually similar to the more expensive baby back ribs.

Smoked Spareribs, Memphis-Dry Style

COOKING METHOD: Slow and Low

The goal of "meat falling off the bone" is a bit of a misnomer. If it's falling off, it's probably overcooked. You want a slight tug to your ribs—tender and juicy, but something you can bite into without losing half the meat on your shirt. This is particularly true with the larger spareribs. Baby backs may "fall off the bone" and be just right, but the meaty and fairly fatty spareribs need some tug.

INGREDIENTS
1 or more whole sparerib racks (about 3–5 pounds each)
Basic Barbecue Rub (pg. 51) or rub of your choice
Bone Sauce (pg. 65), optional. You may mop with plain apple juice or nothin'. In a
    charcoal or gas setting, I'd suggest a mop.

BEST EQUIPMENT: Any charcoal or gas grill, any smoker
TOOLS: Remote thermometer (if grill does not have external temperature reading), instant read thermometer, spatula and long-handled chef tongs, pastry brush for bone sauce
SUGGESTED WOOD: Hickory, oak, or cherry.

STEP BY STEP
    1. Remove the membrane on the rack.

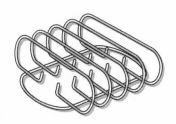

TIP: If you are smoking multiple racks and they can't fit over the indirect part of your grill, make a "rib rack" so they can smoke sideways. While you can buy one of these, if you have a roasting rack, you can simply turn it upside down and place the ribs in there. Leave a space in between so maximum smoke and consistent heat circulate in between the ribs. If your grill or roasting rack is too small, just cut the racks in half.

Removing the Membrane

Ribs have a thin membrane around them that acts as a barrier to your spice rub and has a slight chew to it when eaten. The membrane can be easily removed with a spoon and a paper towel. It's a bit like removing a sticker. On the back of the ribs, lift up the edge of the membrane with a spoon, a knife tip, or your fingernail. Once you have a piece of it, grab hold with a paper towel and slip it off. Needle-nose pliers also work, but sometimes I find they tear through the membrane, making extra steps.

2. Rub your rack with about 1 cup of rub per rack.

3. Make your fire for indirect, slow and low heat.

4. Once your grill is preheated, "get your smoke on." Place ribs on the grill; close the lid with top vents nearly closed, bottom vents open; and let it be. Put your remote thermometer next to the ribs (see tips above) and set it to 200°F–225°F, so it sounds the alarm if you are getting too hot. These babies need to cook slowly.

5. After 2 hours, mop with the Bone Sauce (pg. 65) every hour for about 5 hours. Add ready-to-go coals at this time (if using charcoal) and more wood as needed when you baste the ribs.

6. At 5 hours, check the internal meat temperature. Check every 45 minutes to an hour until it reads 160°F. If it reads 150°F, they may be done. The

temperature will continue to rise about 10° after you take them off. If they are hovering closer to 140°F, they definitely need more time.

Use two tests:

THE WIGGLE TEST—Grab a bone and wiggle it. It shouldn't just fall out (meaning the rib is overcooked) but should wiggle as if it may fall out of the meat with a good tug.

THE BEND TEST—Pick up the rack at one end. It should bend rather than stay straight.

7. Serve with your favorite table sauce, on the side. These are good 'nuf to eat plain, or dabbed in some sauce for some extra zing.

This Little Piggy . . .

I once had a job booking performing pigs for fairs. These little piggies would push shopping carts around a circle and count potatoes. You just can't get that kind of entertainment in places like New York or L.A. I booked other acts too—jugglers, magicians, hypnotists, and a trick bicyclist or two—but the pigs were by far the best clients. Compared to most entertainers, they were laid back. They didn't require an imported cheese tray in their own dressing room. Really, any old garbage would do.

Ego-Stroking Baby Back Ribs with Apricot-Zing Glaze

COOKING METHOD: Slow and Low

Whenever I make these ribs at a party, praise abounds (it's nice to have your ego stroked once in a while). Start with the Feisty Girl Rub, smoke them with hickory or maple, and finish with the Apricot-Zing Glaze, a variation of Karen Putnam's Apricot-Maple Glaze recipe in her book *Championship BBQ Secrets for Real Smoked Food*.

INGREDIENTS
2–4 racks of baby back ribs (factor ½ rack per person)
Feisty Girl Rub (see recipe pg. 53)

Apricot-Zing Glaze (see recipe pg. 70)
Apple juice for drip pan and spray bottle mop

BEST EQUIPMENT: Any charcoal or gas grill, or smoker
SUGGESTED WOOD: Fruit wood or hickory
TOOLS: Remote thermometer (if grill does not have external temperature reading), instant read thermometer, long-handled chef tongs, pastry brush for glaze
MAKE AHEAD: Make rub before starting your grill (or days ahead if you want). Rub ribs up to 2 hours ahead.

STEP BY STEP
Prepare your fire for slow and low indirect heat. Make sure your coals are fully ready and low or that your gas grill or electric smoker is fully preheated. Put apple juice in a drip pan (for charcoal or water smoker).

1. "Get your smoke on." When it is producing plenty of smoke, give an oil swipe to the grill. Baby backs can stick if you are sloppy with the glaze at the end.

2. While your fire is getting ready, prepare your ribs. Remove the membrane (see instructions above), and then add the rub. You may also do this step ahead.

3. Put your ribs meat side down, on the indirect side. Close the lid and leave 'em. Monitor your remote thermometer to keep heat at 200°F–225°F. For charcoal, start your chimney with about 10–15 coals after 30 minutes.

4. After 1 hour, flip ribs and drizzle or spray with fruit juice in a spray bottle. Check your wood and coals. Add your ash-gray-ready coals. Add wood as needed. Mop again every 30 minutes.

5. Prepare glaze. After the ribs have cooked 2½ hours, brush them with the glaze and close the lid. Cook for another 30 minutes or until you can tug at the bone and it starts to separate from the meat.

COMPETITION BARBECUE

The tent city slowly unfolds. Shiny trailers adorned with team names and huge black smoker rigs lie dormant. Cleaning crews fan out, sweeping the grounds for the coming hordes.

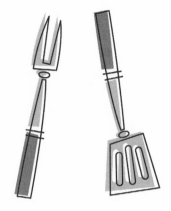

Folks set up their spaces with tiki lights, prep tables, coolers, and everything else they will need for three or four days of barbecue, booze, and babying their entries through the night. They come in fresh, a hop to their step, like the day with its morning chill still in the air. Their deliberate, almost ritual movements in the set-up let you know this is not their first time. Above them hovers the sun, about to descend to spread its heat across the barbecue competition.

When I first explained the barbecue circuit to my mom, she said, "Oh, it's a whole other world out there, kind of like dog shows." Yes, in a way, only much less uptight, and with plates of nicely browned meat, instead of, well, other things. The basics are this: Most teams start out at local competitions that may range from ten to thirty other competitors. These competitions are organized by a local barbecue association (see Resources for a list of association websites). Often a competition is tied to another community festival, like a county fair.

Typically teams load in on a Friday to set up their equipment, tents, and so forth in their paid-for, assigned spot. At night they start their smokers and put in their longer-smoking meats like brisket or pork butt. Depending on the competition, teams may enter a number of meat categories: Pork Butt, Ribs, Brisket, Chicken, plus regional specialty items like Sausage, Lamb, Mutton, or others. Usually competitions include some fun categories like Desserts or Appetizers. These don't "count" in the tally for team rankings, but they add spirit and camaraderie to the event, and they give team members who may not be the pit master a place to shine individually.

Team members take different shifts throughout the night to stoke the coals, mop the meat, and make sure the temperature remains steady. The next morning, the shorter timed meats will go in so that everything is ready at the designated "turn-in time." These are strict times when teams must present their categories to the judges. Usually the times for each category are staggered by 30 minutes: Chicken at noon, Ribs at 12:30 PM, Pork at 1:00 PM, and Brisket at 1:30 PM. Teams turn in what are called their "boxes," uniform 9 x 9 to-go boxes garnished only with green lettuce, or whatever that specific competition deems as acceptable garnish. Garnish is often optional, although almost universally used, and overgarnishing can lower the scores of a contestant. You can see what's important here. It's a meat competition. The turn-ins are "double blind" so the judges know only the meat in front of them, nothing about who dunnit, and vice versa. Teams don't know who judged their box.

Categories scored by the Kansas City Barbeque Society (KCBS) rules rate entries on a scale of 2 to 9, by "tables" of judges. With six judges to a table, each team must turn in six samples of its entry in the box. Judges consider three categories in their scoring: Appearance, Taste, and Texture/Tenderness. Taste counts for more than 50% of the overall score. The results are then tallied by team. Teams may win first place in one category and bomb in others. The team with the highest overall scoring in all categories wins Grand Champion. There are numerous other rules and regulations, such as the meat inspection, which verifies meat was not pre-cooked or pre-seasoned, to disqualifications for things like sauce "pooling" in the turn-in box, not including six samples, or garnishing an entry with $10 bills. Only wood, wood pellets, and charcoal may be used as fuel.

Go, Team!

As with any sport—although it's been argued that competition barbecue can't be deemed a sport because no calories are burned, and you can drink while you do it—the equivalent of playoffs and the World Series exists. The three big competitions in the United States are the Kansas City American Royal Invitational, the Jack Daniels Invitational, and Memphis in May. To get to the first two competitions, a team must win Grand Champion at an event sanctioned by the Kansas City Barbeque Society, or other sanctioning organization, and declared a state champion at an event that has twenty-five or more teams competing. Qualifying for "The Jack," however, still doesn't guarantee a spot. Since only about sixty-five teams go to the show, a lottery system picks the teams from the list of contenders. Those teams that have won at least seven Grand Champions in a competition year automatically get invited, as well as veteran teams that have been invited to the Jack ten or more times.

FANCY PANTS BARBECUE
Smoked Pork Tenderloin with Drunken Port Sauce

Serves 3-4

COOKING METHOD: Indirect Medium

I'm not sure who originated this recipe. My husband cooked this with roasted pork at a well-known Seattle restaurant. I *do* know that it is always a hit when either of us makes it for a dinner party. The rich sauce also complements the Smoked Stuffed Cornish Game Hens (pg. 227) or makes a great dessert sauce with poached pears.

Smoking the pork tenderloin adds another dimension to an already flavorful dish. I love the contrast between the sweet sauce and smoke flavor. Instead of cooking it slow and low, I prefer this recipe first seared on the direct heat side, then cooked indirectly at about 325°F–350°F. Because it is a lean cut, the faster time and higher temperature will keep it moist.

INGREDIENTS
1 pork tenderloin (about 1½–2 pounds)
Olive oil
Salt and pepper

SAUCE
2 cups port wine (cheaper variety)
1 cup heavy cream
¼ cup Craisins (or fresh figs when in season)
2 ounces Stilton or other blue cheese

BEST EQUIPMENT: Any charcoal or gas grill
TOOLS: Remote thermometer (if grill does not have external temperature reading), instant read thermometer, spatula and long-handled chef tongs, whisk for sauce
SUGGESTED WOOD: Cherry or other fruit wood

THE TENDERLOIN
STEP BY STEP
 1. Rub the tenderloin with olive oil, salt, and pepper.

2. Make your fire for indirect medium heat. If you are using charcoal, keep in mind you will only need about 20–30 coals to cook. Aim for a temperature of 325°F–350°F. For gas grills, preheat on high, turn off the middle burner, and turn down the side burners to 350°F.

3. "Get your smoke on": Add wood to the coals, or add a foil wood-chip pouch to gas grill while preheating. Close the lid for 10 minutes.

4. Place the tenderloin over the direct heat side for 3–5 minutes per side.

5. Move to the indirect heat side and close lid, and lower vents.

6. Check that your grill temperature maintains about 325°F–350°F. Cook the tenderloin for 30 minutes; check the internal temperature of the meat. If it registers 160°F, it is done. If not, close the lid and cook for another 10 minutes. Let rest 10 minutes before slicing.

THE SAUCE

My father-in-law became fascinated with cooking in his later years. He poured over recipes and tried new concoctions for us when we came to visit. When he first began, however, he overcame a large learning curve. In making a sauce similar to this one, he came to the point of the recipe that said to "reduce sauce by half." He promptly took out half the sauce he'd just made and chucked it down the sink. We all know (right?) that a sauce reduction requires us to boil half the liquid away so that we are left with a rich, thickened sauce. In this recipe, you are really making a caramel sauce, only with port. Be careful not to go too far, or you will scorch it and have to start all over again (the taste of scorch permeates and just can't be fixed).

STEP BY STEP

1. Using a heavy-gauge pan (sauce will be less likely to burn), heat 2 cups of port on medium high. You can do this on high, but the sauce tends to boil over, so first check that you have enough room for its expansion. Stir occasionally with a whisk. Reduce sauce for about 20 minutes until it starts frothing.

2. Add heavy cream and stir constantly until it gets back up to a boil and reduces further—about a third less in volume. One way to tell when you are "there" is that the bubbles, which start out quite large, start to get

tighter. This means the sauce is getting denser and heavier and is right where you want it.

3. Add the dried fruit, and stir for another 5 minutes. Take off the heat and drizzle it over your sliced pork. Crumble the Stilton or other blue cheese on top.

Smoked Pork Loin with Grilled Apples

Serves 6

COOKING METHOD: Indirect Medium Heat

A perfect recipe for those first days of fall. The Cocoa-Bliss Rub forms a spicy sweet bark to complement the pork. Because the pork loin is so low in fat, I like to first sear it on each side over direct heat, then cook it at indirect-medium for about 1 hour, or until it reaches 155°F internally. It will get up to 160 °F while you rest the meat. The higher heat seals in the juices for a moist and smoky meal. When you slice it, the interior meat will have a slight pink hue. Suggested sides: grilled apples, sautéed greens, and roasted potatoes.

INGREDIENTS
1 pork tenderloin (about 3 pounds)
Cocoa Bliss Rub (pg. 53)
2 medium apples, sliced in whole rings

BEST EQUIPMENT: Any charcoal or gas grill
TOOLS: Remote thermometer (if grill does not have external temperature reading), instant read thermometer, spatula and long-handled chef tongs, lightly oil-sprayed paper towels (for grilling apples at the end)
PREFERRED WOOD: Apple
MAKE AHEAD: Make the rub up to a few weeks ahead. Rub the meat before starting your grill (or up to a day ahead).

STEP BY STEP
1. Rub pork loin with Cocoa Bliss Rub. Give it a good, thick coating and pat in place. Let sit for 10 minutes; then apply more rub. Let sit for another 10–20 minutes.

2. Make fire for indirect medium heat.

3. When coals are ash gray, or a gas grill is preheated with middle burner turned off, "get your smoke on."

4. Place the pork loin on direct heat side for 2–3 minutes each side.

5. Move it to the indirect heat side, place a remote thermometer near the loin to monitor your heat (if your grill does not have an external dial), and close the lid. For charcoal, close the top dampers until your heat stabilizes to a range between 300°F and 350°F.

6. At 50 minutes, insert your instant read thermometer into your pork loin. You will want to pull the loin at 155°F.

TIP: Place a remote thermometer through the top vent so that it hangs above the meat, or push the prong all the way through a potato and set it on the grill next to the meat. This way it won't sit on the grill, which may be hotter than the internal temperature.

7. At 155°F, remove the pork loin and let it rest 15 minutes. While the meat is resting, grill apple slices over the direct heat side long enough to get grill marks on each side. Give the grill a quick swipe with an oil rag before placing the apples. Use tongs to turn so the apple slices don't fall through the slats.

SHE'S SMOKIN': Balancing the Diva and Supermom Within

I spoke with Danielle Dimovski, founder of barbecue team Diva Q, to talk about her quick rise to success on the barbecue competition circuit while raising three kids. Hailing from Barrie, Ontario, she had just been invited to the most prestigious barbecue invitational in the United States: the Jack Daniels Invitational. It's a big deal and was one of Danielle's goals when she started her journey into competition barbecue only two years ago.

Danielle's infectious enthusiasm will make you want to buy a rig, pack up the kids with a 50-pound bag of lump charcoal, and drive ten hours to set up a tent in a parking lot to stay awake half the night stoking the fire and mopping your meat. If it sounds sexy, it ain't. But it does connect you to a greater community, something I think appeals especially to women.

"I started almost two years ago," she explained of her move into the world of competitive 'cue. "I just had my son and I was getting stir crazy in the house after having three kids. I read about the Barrie, Ontario, competition, and my husband and I applied to be judges. I was accepted and he wasn't. I judged the Canadian Open and was *gobsmacked* on how good some of it was, and the rest I thought I could do better.

"I've always been passionate about cooking and food. This focused that passion. As soon as I got home I told my husband, 'I need to buy one of those smoker thingies.' Three days later I bought my first WSM [Weber Smokey Mountain]. I went crazy after that, reading and cooking different recipes. My learning curve has been very steep because I practice every single week, whether it's testing brines, rubs, or meat recipes."

Danielle practices mostly at night, after the kids get to bed. "My first priority is always my kids. Then it's my passion for barbecue. Besides, it's impossible to focus with a two-year-old and a four-year-old."

Since that first judging experience, where the first person she met was Dr. BBQ Ray Lampe, barbecue guru, chef, and cookbook author who "looks like Colonel Sanders on overdrive," Danielle jumped in with both feet and a pair of tongs. In her first full year of competition 2007–2008, she won a total of ten first places and four Grand Champions. She's smokin'! She attributes her success in part to taking classes from the greats: the Dr. Barbecue course, a Traeger pellet smoker course (one of the smokers she uses in competition), and a class taught by Ron Gray and Johnny Triggs. She voraciously reads, chats it up in forums such as barbecuecentral.com, continually practices, and then puts her own personal spin on it all.

The other component comes from her support system. "We have a great network of family and friends. Dad comes the Thursday before the competition so I can go shopping.

(continued on next page)

(continued from previous page)

Then we drop the kids off on the way to the competition," she said. For now they stick with events closer to home. As the kids get older, she hopes to do more, with kids in tow. Diva Q includes her "totally supportive" husband and another "amazing" couple. With all her successes, Danielle admits to "setting so many things on fire, it's funny. That's a lot of jerky I've made." She's knocked her water pan and put out her charcoal at 3:30 AM during a competition and even forgotten to bring the charcoal. "But a big part of the barbecue community is that someone always steps up to help you. No one wants to win because you didn't have something and couldn't do your best. It's a community of spirit, and it's not pretentious."

Her tip for women just starting to barbecue at home? "Take the tongs back!" she says. "You are doing all the work anyway—send *him* out for dessert and flowers. Secondly, just enjoy the whole process. Enjoy the fact that barbecue isn't just about food, it's about family and friends and putting love into the food."

Here is Danielle's Pork Loin recipe:

Diva Q East Meets West Pork Loin

Marinate a whole pork loin overnight in the following:

½ cup red wine
½ cup packed brown sugar
¼ cup red wine vinegar
¼ cup ketchup
¼ cup hoisin sauce
1 tablespoon Chinese five-spice powder
2 tablespoons soy sauce
1 teaspoon ground ginger
½ teaspoon salt
½ teaspoon pepper
3 garlic cloves, minced or finely chopped

The following day stuff with the following:

4 cups cornbread, crumbled
1 onion, minced and sautéed in 1 tablespoon of butter
A handful of fresh chives, finely chopped
1 teaspoon sage
Salt and pepper to taste

Mix in an egg and enough chicken stock to make it easy to spread. Smoke at 250°F–275°F until the internal temperature reaches 155°F, approximately 1½ to 2 hours. Let it rest 15 minutes before serving.

CAMP Q
Buried Jerk Pork
....

Take this recipe camping—not backpacking, mind you, but camping that allows you to dig a pit or that has a deep fire pit at the campground. You can do this at home, too, if you're willing to give up about 2 square feet of space in the garden.

Pit cooking is ancient. Burying food under hot coals is found around the world. Read chapter 10 on the Pacific Northwest Salmon Bake to learn about a Native American buried clambake.
Is it practical for a Tuesday-night dinner? No, but for a special-occasion party, start digging for your dinner—it's incredibly simple, and the result is well worth it. It's also really facho (that's the feminine of macho).

In Jamaica they cook their pork in steel drums converted into grills, on indirect heat. You can easily convert this recipe on a grill, exactly as you would the Carolina Pulled Pork, above. Jerk seasoning can either be a wet paste or a dry rub. I'm partial to the wet paste for this recipe, because it steams the pork inside the banana leaves. Banana leaves? Read on.

You will need the following:

- A shovel

- Chicken wire

- About 10 stones, the size of large russet potatoes

- About three grocery-store bundles of wood. This is for measurement purposes—don't actually buy grocery-store wood, unless you know for sure what it contains. Buy this quantity in hickory, cherry, or the Jamaican preference, pimento. If you are buying wood at the camp store on your way to the campground, make sure it is not an evergreen wood like pine or hemlock.

- 1–2 pork butts, bone out

- Some thin wire

- Heavy-duty oven mitts

- Fiery Jerk Paste (pg. 57). Recipe is enough for one pork butt; double it for two.

- Banana leaves (4 per butt). I find banana leaves frozen in my favorite Asian market. I realize that Seattle is different from, say, Ames, Iowa, in terms of demand for this item. Banana leaves are inexpensive at my market, about $2 per package of 8 leaves. I've seen this same quantity listed for $48 on the Internet! If you can't find them locally or for a reasonable cost via mail, soak corn husks for 30 minutes in water. Line a large sheet of foil with three layers of husks; place the jerk seasoned pork in the center and wrap (see complete instructions below).

DIGGING THE PIT—Your pit doesn't have to be huge, but if you are building one for your home, you want it big enough for future cookouts. Our pit is elongated with a small cooking area that is deeper and opens up to a larger fire pit for keeping a fire going to feed coals to the cooking pit (it's also nice for sitting around, talking, and roasting marshmallows after dinner). If you read the Salmon Bake chapter and want to host a clam or salmon bake someday,  use those same pit dimensions for this recipe. At minimum, your pit should be 2 feet by 2 feet by 1 foot deep to cook two butts. Once you dig the pit, line with the rocks.

BUILDING THE FIRE—Use about half of the wood on hand, on top of your rocks so that they get hot (for review on campfire building, see pg. 37). Let the fire burn down all the way to the coals. During this time, prepare your pork (see below). Once coals are ash gray, scoop half of them out with a metal shovel and put aside in a metal wheelbarrow or other fire-safe container. Wear heavy-duty oven mitts for safety. Sparks can and will escape during this extremely hot step. Keep children away from this area.

Keep a small fire going separate from your cooking area to keep feeding new coals. You may use the other end of a larger pit or use a second grill to feed the fire.

SLATHERING THE PORK—Slather your pork in the Jerk Paste (pg. 57) and let sit for 30 minutes before wrapping.

WRAPPING THE BUTTS—Open up the banana leaves and lay out 2 layers for each butt. Place the butt in the center and fold leaves as though you are wrapping a package. You want them fairly tight so the juices don't escape into the fire and cause flare-ups. Secure by tying metal wire crossways, like a present. Your 2 bundles are ready to cook.

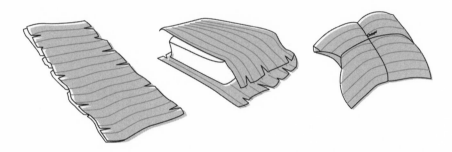

MAKING A CHICKEN WIRE CAGE—Once you remove half of the hot coals, lay down a layer of chicken wire so that it extends out of the pit. Place the wrapped pork "packages" in the center of the chicken wire, and place another sheet of banana leaves over the top. Fold the wire over the pork.

BURYING THE PORK—Shovel the coals on top of the butts and around them. Add 10–20 coals every hour or two. Your banana leaves will get charred, but they shouldn't ever be on fire. Douse them with a little bit of water and shovel off coals if flames do occur. Total cooking time will be about 6 hours (see illustration on pg. 142).

UNWRAPPING—Shovel off the coals and carefully remove the butts with your shovel and some long tongs. Wear oven mitts. Let sit out of the fire for 30 minutes in the package. Then carefully untie the metal and unwrap the pork. When you first open the banana

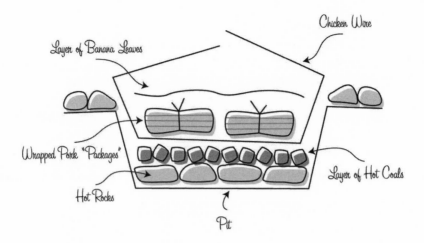

Chicken Wire

Layer of Banana Leaves

Wrapped Pork "Packages"

Hot Rocks

Layer of Hot Coals

Pit

leaves, escaping steam can cause burns. Use oven mitts. Let meat sit another 10 minutes in the open; then chop, pull, or slice and serve with sides below.

TIP: Bake sweet potatoes while you cook your pork. Oil sweet potatoes, wrap in foil, and bake in the coals for 1½ hours. Turn your potato packets to keep cooking evenly. When they're done, unwrap them and serve them with butter. Yum!

Some Favorite Accompaniments:

Grilled Pineapple (pg. 90)
Jamaican Festival—a sweeter style of hushpuppy (pg. 240)
Pit-Baked Sweet Potatoes (see tip above)
Island Slaw (p. 235)
Refreshing Fruity Drinks

Chapter Seven

Big & Beefy

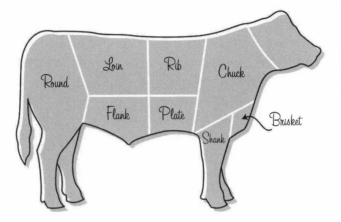

In Texas, barbecue means beef. Since cattle stampeded across that state, cowboys have been russlin' up some cow, slow-cooked over the coals. German and Czech immigrants slow-smoked brisket in their butcher shops, using old-world indoor smokers with large chimneys to the outside. Patrons bought the meat and ate it right off the butcher paper. Texans still like their brisket without a lot of fuss. At the most famous Texas barbecue joint, Kreuz Market, which began as meat market and grocery store, brisket is slow-cooked with nothing but salt and pepper. It is served on paper, without forks, sauce, or salads.

Brisket requires special attention to make it palatable and, because of this, presents bragging rights in barbecue. The tough cuts, from those muscles that the animal uses most, are full of flavor if cooked properly. Anyone willing to devote the 10–20 hours needed to subdue the sinews of a brisket deserves a nod, but if you can make that meat melt in your mouth, it gives you an amazing sense of accomplishment.

Not all cows are created equal. Choosing your beef from among today's choices can be daunting. As you know, beef labeled "natural" can mean a variety of different things depending on who's doing the labeling.

BEEF LABELING 101

AGED BEEF—It sounds like old meat, but beef toughens up 12–24 hours after butchering, and aging brings it back to tender. The meat is aged dry at low temperatures to prevent spoilage, usually for about two to three weeks. Dry-aging causes beef to lose weight from loss of moisture, a process that adds to the flavor of the meat but also the cost.

ANGUS CERTIFIED—Angus beef, advertised at steakhouses, refers to the genotype of the cow. Known for its desirable marbling, it is prized by beef eaters. In order for cattle to be Angus Certified, there must be proof of the Angus parentage, and it must be predominantly (51%) black.

BEEF GRADES—Beef grades mostly refer to the level of marbling in the beef, which enhances the tenderness and flavor. Marbling is graded by the visual flecks of fat dispersed in the lean tissue. From the top there are **Prime,** found mostly in fine steakhouses, followed by **Choice** and **Select,** the usual choices in your grocery store. Don't bother with the next levels down, from **Standard** (do *you* want to eat the government definition of "standard"?) to **Commercial, Utility, Cutter,** and **Canner,** which go into things like cheap-ass frozen patties, canned spaghetti, dog food, and military rations.[1]

CERTIFIED ANGUS BEEF—This designates the crème de la crème of the Angus herd, measured by meeting a higher grade on marbling and tenderness.

GRASS-FED—The grass-fed beef movement is growing by leaps and bounds. Studies show that grass-fed beef is higher in omega-3 fatty acids, lower in saturated fat, higher in antioxidants, and even lower in incidences of *resistant* E. coli, meaning that most E. coli found in grass-fed cows are strains that the cattle can easily fight with their normal immune system.[2] The "100% grass-fed" label means that cattle were raised exclusively on pasture and not grain-fed. We'll talk about cooking with grass-fed beef later in the chapter.

NATURAL—Why choose a natural beef rather than commercial-feed lot beef? At our restaurant we first happened upon natural brisket by accident. Our meat company sent us a different brand of brisket, because they were out of the "regular" brand. We were amazed by the difference. The taste difference rivaled that of your homegrown tomatoes versus the

You won't find Painted Hills at the farmer's market. Plenty of large grocery stores and major restaurants carry the brand to provide customers with a natural meat choice. On the continuum ranging from local farmer to commercial-feed lot, Painted Hills falls somewhere in between. I asked Will Homer, farm operations manager, why customers choose Painted Hills' higher-priced beef over the "cheap stuff" at a discount retailer.

"We fight the perception that 'meat is meat and cheaper is better' every day," he says. "What we come back to is our story. Raising beef of this quality takes more: more time, more energy, more care. In order to grow hormone- and antibiotic-free beef, producers must make the commitment to keep the animals longer than generic beef. It simply takes longer for the animals to grow to the choice grade level we sell, which adds cost." Homer notes that without the "safety net" of antibiotics, natural meat producers must rely on gentler handling practices to keep animals healthier. "You've got to let the cows do the work of growing," he says, explaining that forcing them to grow faster taxes their immune systems, thus requiring antibiotics to keep them healthy.

bland waxy things they sell at the grocery store. Ditto for the texture. It was terrific. "What is this stuff?" asked my husband. We looked on the box and discovered it was all-natural beef from Painted Hills in Oregon. Since then we've delved further into research about natural meats and seek out vendors with higher standards and better products. Choosing natural meats has become an integral part of our company philosophy.

ORGANIC—Organic beef is not necessarily grass-fed; grass-fed is not necessarily organic; natural is not necessarily organic. Organic beef follows the same guidelines as chicken or pork: The feed must be 100% organic, the animal must be raised without antibiotics or growth promotants, and it must have outdoor access.

Buying a Brisket

You may purchase just the **flat,** for a more manageable piece. Often whole briskets run 8–12 pounds, a flat only about 4–5 pounds. I prefer smoking the whole brisket, also called a **whole packer,** because the point is fattier and because the fat cap, which keeps your brisket moist, wraps around the point.

TEXAS BEEF BRISKET: AN IN-DEPTH STUDY

On the one hand, smoking a brisket is about as basic as it comes: Slow-smoke a big hunk o' tough meat until it is tender. Get two or more folks together, however, and each and every step along the way can be debated until red faces turn blue. Do you mop? Do you turn it? Do you wrap it halfway through? These are battleground points. In the spirit of bipartisanship, we'll examine the arguments, and I'll give you *my* two cents, for what it's worth. But first, some brisket background.

Anatomy of a Brisket

So what exactly is a brisket? It is the chest meat of the cow. Full of muscle, fat, and connective tissue, this meat needs some major work to make it fit to eat. Pastrami and corned beef are both made from the brisket, showing that many cultures take on the undesirable cuts and make it a symbol of pride in their cuisine.

A brisket has two parts to it: the "flat" (sometimes called the "plate") and the "point" (often called the "deckle"). The flat is aptly named because it sits, well, flat, while the thicker "point" tapers up like a little hill on the brisket. These two run almost perpendicular to each other, with a channel of fat connecting them in between.

Wrapping around the top is the "fat cap," a layer of fat perfect for insulating your brisket during the long cooking process. The challenge comes when carving the meat because you want to slice it against the grain, but the grain runs two different ways. We'll talk about how to carve a brisket at the end of the recipe.

....

TIP: Brisket Yield—Purchase slightly less than I pound per person for a 6- to 8-ounce portion per person. You lose about 50% from raw weight to serving weight due to trimming the brisket and shrinkage from smoking. Keep in mind this yield is on a whole packer, untrimmed. For a partially trimmed brisket flat, your loss will be only about 20%.

....

TIME TO SMOKE A BRISKET

Brisket is a time commitment. Period. It can take anywhere from 10 to 18 hours, depending on the size, smoking temperature, weather conditions, and that particular cow. Generally speaking, factor 1½ hours per pound; however, you cannot set the timer with a brisket to know whether it is done. We'll talk about target internal temperatures and how to feel if the meat is done. There are, of course, a few shortcuts, like the "Texas Crutch" on the opposite page.

Finding Inner Barbecue Peace

My husband and partner at Smokin' Pete's BBQ is a "rub it and leave it" kind of guy when it comes to barbecue. He's pretty much that way with most things—keep it simple, minimal fuss. In terms of the house, this translates into letting things go way beyond my threshold of mess. His inefficiency drives me crazy sometimes, like the fact that he just stares into space while the coffee is brewing, while I can unload the entire dishwasher before the ding. Like most women, I am in constant motion. Never go past the laundry room without swooping up clothes to throw in the pile. Call your girlfriends to catch up while you are doing that laundry. While this "efficiency" may be the key to our success and survival as women, when it comes to barbecue, we must resist the urge to fuss. Busyness, lists, and multitasking are not allowed within six feet of the smoker. Repeat after me: Let the heat and the meat do the work. Got it? Good.

THE "TEXAS CRUTCH"

Paul Kirk, the "Baron of Barbecue," coined the phrase "Texas crutch" describing a popular brisket shortcut. The Texas crutch follows a simple formula 3-2-1: 3 hours naked in the smoker, 2 hours sealed in foil or wrap with sauce or other moisture added, then finished unwrapped for 1 more hour. Wrapping with moisture speeds up the time, but the last hour brings back the bark to its original crunch. I'm not opposed to shortcuts, especially those that don't completely throw out the fundamentals. I do think, however, that one should always learn the fundamentals before experimenting with the form.

What you get for that time is a delicious piece of meat that will be devoured at a party, or as meals and leftovers at a relatively low cost. It's also low-maintenance cooking. You can go about your day, keeping an eye on the coals and temperature, but without any exact times or crunch moments.

The Great Brisket Debates

CONTENTION #1 TO TRIM OR NOT TO TRIM?

ARGUMENTS PRO	ARGUMENTS CON	MY TWO CENTS
The fat creates a barrier to the spice rub and smoke.	Though the fat will not baste your meat (nor make it significantly higher in fat), it will insulate the meat. This insulation is key to keeping your brisket moist, far more effective than mops or water pans. As for the smoke, after 14-20 hours in the smoker, that brisket has plenty of smoke!	I believe the trend in trimming the fat to be a result of competition barbecue. Teams only get to submit a small amount of brisket to the judges' table, so they want their rub to be featured prominently around the edge of those slices. They are forced, then, to highly manage the meat by mopping and basting in an effort to keep the meat moist. For home barbecue, we can relax and let the meat and fat do the work.

CONTENTION #2 SLATHER FIRST?

ARGUMENTS PRO	ARGUMENTS CON	MY TWO CENTS
While most agree in a generous application of rub, whether to first slather it in mustard or butter is a choice. A slather helps adhere your rub.	Slathering is not necessary; the rub sticks fine to a brisket.	I reserve slathers for when I am smoking just the flat. Because the flat is missing much of that good insulating fat, the slather adds a layer of moisture.

CONTENTION #3 SALT IN YOUR RUB?

ARGUMENTS PRO	ARGUMENTS CON	MY TWO CENTS
On a tour at the American Royal BBQ Competition, I heard barbecue guru Paul Kirk state when asked "Ninety-five percent of folks out there are using salt in their rub. Sure, it may dry it a little, but I like salt and sugar as flavor." I'm going with a Grand Champ on this one.	Much ado in the Barbesphere admonishes salt, especially if you rub your meat the previous day, saying that salt dries out the meat.	I like salt in my rubs, and in a side-by-side comparison, one brisket with salt and one without, I did not find any noticeable difference in dryness.

CONTENTION #4 ROOM TEMPERATURE OR COLD?

ARGUMENTS PRO	ARGUMENTS CON	MY TWO CENTS
Those in the "Cold Camp" profess that starting with a cold brisket will	The "Room Crew" notes that rub stays on the surface of the brisket	I'm diplomatic, splitting the issue down the middle. I agree that rub

take on more smoke than room-temperature meat. Since the brisket takes longer to heat up, it will slow down the smoking process, delaying the "bark" and increasing the smoke. The Cold Camp also hollers health codes stating that meat needs to reach 140° in four hours to be out of the "danger zone" for bacteria growth. The clock begins once that meat is removed from the fridge.

when it is cold. They encourage you to rub your meat, bringing it up to room temperature so it can absorb into the first layer of the meat before it enters the cooker.

needs a little time out of the fridge to set on the meat, but I think "room temperature" is far too vague for safety. I know plenty of folks who like their room at the toasty temp of 80°, and also know that in the hotter locales, flies and other critters can be a problem. Rub the meat a day to an hour ahead. While your coals are getting hot, take out the brisket and let it set the rub, about 20-30 minutes max.

CONTENTION #5 FAT SIDE UP OR DOWN?

ARGUMENTS PRO

Placing brisket on the grill fat cap up allows the fat to drip down over the brisket. While it may not actually baste the meat, placing fat furthest from the heat will minimize flare-ups and allow the smoke to penetrate the meat side better.

ARGUMENTS CON

Fat-side-down folks argue that the fat acts as a barrier between the heat and the meat, keeping that temperature low.

MY TWO CENTS

I'm a fat-side-up gal.

CONTENTION #6 TO MOP OR NOT TO MOP?

ARGUMENTS PRO

Mopping keeps the brisket moist during the long smoking process.

ARGUMENTS CON

Rub and leave it. Mops don't really affect the end product.

MY TWO CENTS

I like to mop, but as I've said before, I tend to be a minimalist. See page 64 for a basic beer mop you can put in a spray bottle.

CONTENTION #7 TO TURN OR NOT TO TURN?

ARGUMENTS PRO

Some turn over their brisket halfway through the cooking process for even cooking.

ARGUMENTS CON

Not necessary.

MY TWO CENTS

I don't turn, but I do rotate the meat at the halfway mark, to ensure even cooking.

TIP: Never use a fork prong to turn a brisket, or any other cut of meat, lest you pierce the meat, allowing juices to spew forth. Heavy-duty industrial rubber gloves work best for turning that bad boy.

(continued on next page)

(continued from previous page)

CONTENTION #8 TO WRAP OR NOT TO WRAP?

ARGUMENTS PRO	ARGUMENTS CON	MY TWO CENTS
The "Wrap Pack" postulates that either wrapping in film or foil will soften your brisket to a perfect tenderness. Within the ranks of Wrap Packers, a fault line divides them between foil and film. Foil reacts to acids in vinegars and tomatoes, so if your mop contains any acids, choose film. Temperatures under 250° will not melt the film. Further cracks in the Wrap Pack contingent occur on when to wrap: some wrap right before the "plateau," others during or after. Plenty of big-time barbecue folks are in the Wrap Pack, so you'll have to decide for yourself which side you fall on.	Naked Brisket: I keep my brisket naked for two reasons: I want a crunchy bark on the outside, and a definable slice. Brisket that gets too soft will just mush. Then it's only good for chopping up and dousing with sauce to hide the fact it is overcooked. Wrapping opens the door for both of these. I also swear I can taste foil or film on the meat. Maybe it's psychosomatic, but there you go.	Gals, I am decidedly a non-wrapper. The only time I wrap is when I have to "hold" a brisket for a length of time for a catering, or because the brisket finished early.

How To Tell If It's Done

More indicative than the clock is the internal temperature of your meat. Shoot for a temperature of 185°F–200°F. Other important timing tips and factors:

THE FEEL TEST—If you pick the meat up (with heavy-duty rubber gloves), it should feel pliable but not fall apart.

THE VISUAL TEST—Often juices begin to pool on the surface, letting us know that the connective tissues are breaking down.

"THE STALL" OR PLATEAU PERIOD—Steven Raichlen, author of *The Barbecue Bible*, among a host of other books and a popular TV show, *Barbecue University,* says, "Love your plateaus! . . . This is when all the good stuff is happening." This slowdown period is when all that tough collagen is melting into the meat. Meat will stall at about 150°F–160°F for hours. Just let it be. When the temperature starts rising again, you know you are getting close.

RESTING PERIOD—Thirty minutes? Two hours? Resting a brisket can be a challenge with hungry mouths surrounding you and sneaky hands picking at the bark. But cutting into a brisket you've just smoked for 12–14 hours without letting it rest is like running the marathon and giving up with the finish line in sight. Heat has pushed the juices to the surface. The juices need the time to flow back into the meat. Resting the brisket will take off the final "edge" of resistance, so that it cuts like butter. Here are a few meat-resting methods:

> **METHOD #1**—Some just rest the meat on the platter for at least 20–30 minutes before cutting. It's such a large piece of meat that it won't get cold in the center.

> **METHOD #2**—A popular resting technique is to warm up an ice chest with hot water, then dump the water and place the wrapped brisket inside to rest for up 2 hours. This softens the meat further, but at some loss of crunch to the bark. I like my bark, which is why I rest meat by continuing with . . .

> **METHOD #3**—Let the coals in the smoker die out, and rest the meat in the smoker. Folks are also less apt to snitch on a brisket still in the smoker.

So now you've read through the arguments, pondered your affiliations, and are ready to put your meat where you stand on the issues. Here is a simple brisket recipe to get you started.

Texas Two-Step Brisket

COOKING METHOD: Slow and Low

I call this "two-step" because you just rub it and mop it. There is no wrapping, no finishing sauce, and no resting in warm snuggly coolers at the end.

INGREDIENTS
1 whole packer brisket
Basic Barbecue Rub (pg. 51) or your preferred rub
Really Basic Cheap Beer Mop (pg. 64)
Optional: Mustard Mummy Slather (pg. 54) Apply this mustard slather before the rub if you are smoking a brisket flat vs. smoking the whole packer.

BEST EQUIPMENT: Any charcoal grill or smoker, or electric smoker (see gas-powered recipe, below)
TOOLS: Heavy-duty rubber gloves, spray bottle for mop, remote thermometer, instant read thermometer
SUGGESTED WOOD: Blend of hickory and oak

STEP BY STEP

1. Rub your brisket one hour to a day ahead of time.

2. Make your fire slow and low, and "get your smoke on": Feed hot coals to the fire, rather than fresh coals, to keep a consistent heat (review pg. 33). *TIP: How much charcoal? How much wood? Depending on weather conditions, you will use about 10–12 pounds of charcoal. For quantities of wood chunks or chips, factor about 1 cup per hour or 1–2 chunks per hour for the first 3–4 hours. If you're using an electric smoker, continue adding chunks of wood for the first 6 hours. If you are using wood as your fuel, you will use 12–20 pieces, depending on the size of your smoker. I recommend mixing wood with charcoal to avoid oversmoking your meat.*

3. Place a water pan in the indirect side, under your meat.

Water Panology

Water pans have two uses: to put moisture into the cooking chamber, combating the drying nature of smoking, and to regulate the temperature. Water holds heat well, with little variation, which is why ocean temperatures vary so little. Brisket especially benefits from water pans. Think of your brisket as a guest. You'd offer your guests some refreshment if they were hanging out all day, wouldn't you?

4. Take the brisket out of the refrigerator 20–30 minutes before smoking to allow the rub to stick best to the meat.

5. Once your coals are ready, or your smoker is preheated, place your meat on the indirect side of the grill. Close the lid. Leave it.

6. After 30 minutes, if using charcoal, start about 10–15 coals in your charcoal chimney starter. Add when ready. Repeat this so that you are feeding hot-and-ready coals to your fire about every 45 minutes to an hour. Add wood as necessary every 1–2 hours.

7. Make your mop, and spray your brisket every hour. If you must open your grill lid to feed coals, mop at the same time to minimize the number of times you are opening the lid. Monitor your remote thermometer to ensure you are keeping a consistent 200°F–250°F.

8. After about 6 hours, take an internal temperature in a thick part of the meat. Do this every hour as well to check doneness. See the above tests on doneness to know when the meat is ready.

Gas-Powered Brisket

Cooking a brisket on gas, while not ideal, can be done with this shortcut method.

INGREDIENTS
1 whole packer or flat brisket
Mustard Mummy Slather (pg. 54)
Basic Barbecue Rub (pg. 51)
Basic Beer Mop (pg. 64)
Texas All-Nighter Sauce (pg. 75) or your favorite sauce

TOOLS: Foil wood-chip pouch (review pg. 32)

STEP BY STEP
1. Read through the Great Brisket Debates above, as all apply for gas-powered brisket. Because the gas-powered brisket is better prepared "wet" rather than "dry," first rinse and pat dry your brisket, apply the mustard slather, and then your rub. Let set for 30 minutes to 2 hours ahead in refrigerator.

2. Preheat your gas grill on high for 15–20 minutes. "Get your smoke on" by adding your foil wood-chip pouch to the burner. Once it starts smoking fully, turn the middle burner off and the side burners to low.

3. Place the brisket on the grill and smoke for 2 hours, mopping on the hour. Shoot for an internal grill temperature of 200°F–250°F.

4. Add a new foil pouch with wood chips after 1 hour. You may need to turn up that burner to get it to smoke. As soon as it does, turn it back down.

5. Preheat your oven to 300°F. Place the brisket in a heavy-gauge pan and drizzle with 1 cup mop mixed with 1 cup barbecue sauce. Make a foil "tent" over the pan by sealing the foil all around the pan, folding it in the middle. Put the brisket in the oven for 3–4 hours, depending on the size of the meat (see chart). Check that your internal temperature reads 185°F–190°F.

6. In the last 30 minutes to an hour, baste with sauce and take off the foil.

HOW TO CARVE A BRISKET

As we discussed in The Anatomy of a Brisket, above, a whole brisket has two distinct sections: the flat (or plate) and the point (or deckle). The point sits on top of the plate at about a 60-degree angle, which means the direction of the grain on these two sections is dramatically different. When carving a brisket, you need to carve *against* the grain of the meat for tender slices. Carving with the grain, cutting in the same direction as the meat runs, will result in tough, stringy

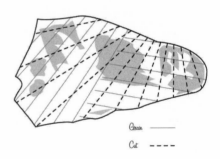

Grain ———
Cut - - - -

slices that fall apart. The challenge is to find your starting point and to deal with the crossed paths of these parts.

There are two methods that work: One is to separate the two parts and carve them separately. The other is to start out at one angle and fan out as you go so that when you get to where the two sections cross, you hit both at an acceptable angle. I will explain both.

Separating the Brisket and Carving

1. Set your whole brisket on a large cutting board with the fat cap up. Underneath, if you turn over the brisket and look, the flat is obvious

because it sits like a kite-shaped plate and has considerably less fat on it. Position it so that the "point," or wavy, thicker section, is closest to you, and the tip of the flat is on the upper right. Notice that the "hump" of the brisket facing you contains the channel of fat connecting these two sections.

2. Run your knife along the curve of this fat channel. There will be very little resistance in cutting the fat, so if you hit resistance, you are hitting meat. Once you get in a little, lift up the piece and you will see the fat layer between the two sections. Cut along this until the layers are mostly separated.

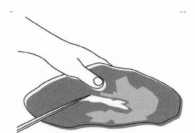

3. At the end of the fat layer, you will find the spot where the point meets the flat and curves over it. Turn the brisket over and cut along this curve to finish separating the pieces.

4. First carve the flat. Start at the angled tip and cut off a small triangle of meat. Continue at this angle all the way through. Make your slices about ¼-inch thick, or the thickness of a pencil.

5. Next trim the fat off the top of the point to help you see the grain of the meat. With the highest part of the point positioned in your upper left

corner, slice straight from the right-hand side. You will know if you are cutting against the grain because the slices will look like this:

Carving the Whole Brisket at Once

1. Set your whole brisket on a large cutting board with the fat cap up.

2. Underneath, if you turn over the brisket and look, the flat is obvious because it sits like a kite-shaped plate and has considerably less fat on it. Position it so that the "point," or wavy, thicker section, is closest to you and the tip of the flat is on the upper right (see illustrations on pg. 155).

3. Trim off some of the fat cap so you can see the direction of the grain on the point section.

4. Starting at the tip of the flat, cut off a small triangle piece of meat and continue slicing at this angle through approximately ¼ of the brisket. Cut your slice at about ¼-inch thick, about the width of a pencil (see illustration above).

5. Once you are approaching the thicker middle, start to angle your slices in a wider smile pattern (illustration pg. 154). When you get to the middle where the two pieces overlap, you will be at the bottom of the smile. Keep curving up as you get to where the flat underneath ends and the point continues. Halfway through, you will want to stop slicing and remove the inner core of fat that runs between the sections, rather than trim out each individual slice. Cut it out, and then finish the slicing.

NOTE: For both methods, carving a brisket is messy! Carve in the kitchen, not at the table. Wear an apron, wash your hands before and after, and make sure you have two or three rags on hand for clean-up.

Burnt Ends

Burnt ends are the yummy crispy bits at the ends of the brisket. Heavily spiced and far more cooked than the rest of the meat, these are prized by some and disdained by others. I'm a burnt end eater. Often restaurants offer burnt ends as a dish. Since there is no way they could keep these in stock, because only two small portions are created by a whole brisket, restaurants "make" burnt ends by chopping, re-spicing, and re-smoking the fattier parts of the brisket. We don't advertise burnt ends at Smokin' Pete's BBQ. If someone asks, I'll begrudgingly give mine up.

Jamaican Jerk Dino Bones

COOKING METHOD: Slow and Low

This is one of my husband's dishes. He serves up beef ribs every Friday but changes how he prepares them. His jerk ribs are a favorite. These monstrous bones have a kick; serve them up with some plain rice on the side and Aunt Sandra's Three-Week Slaw on page 234. Beef short ribs are the meaty ribs that come off the rib plate, not the long, skinny back ribs. They are the same ribs that are cut horizontally into cross-section strips for Kalbi Beef Short Ribs (pg. 103).

INGREDIENTS
1 rack beef short ribs, cut into 2–4 bone sections (factor 1–2 ribs per person)
4 tablespoons dry mustard
Fiery Jerk Paste (pg. 57)
Apple juice for mopping

BEST EQUIPMENT: Any charcoal, electric, gas grill, or smoker
PREFERRED WOOD: Blend of mesquite and another wood of your choice; if it's available, use the Jamaican favorite, pimento wood (see Resources chapter)
MAKE AHEAD: Make Fiery Jerk Paste ahead; slather and apply wet rub to ribs 2–4 hours ahead. Reserve 1 cup for mop.

RIBS
STEP BY STEP
    1. Take the meat out of package, rinse, and pat it dry with a paper towel.

She's Smokin': Squeal of Approval

The all-gal team Squeal of Approval didn't start out that way. Originally Betsy Masters and Lana Hall started the competition barbecue team with their husbands. Betsy's sister, Allison Verman, joined after both couples unfortunately parted.

"I had always joked with my husband that if we ever split up, he'd get the ring and I'd get the smoker," said Betsy. She did, in fact, get the smoker and recipes in the settlement, and in the women's first *all-female* version of Squeal of Approval, they won third place overall in a competition. Four years later, their list of firsts and Grand Champions is long. Their biggest thrill was being chosen for the *All Star Barbecue Showdown* television program.

"They had two professional teams and chose one amateur team for 'local color' on the show. The producers saw all of our pink (even their smoker trailer is painted pink) and chose us. The show format pits teams against the unknown: Teams do not know what equipment or ingredients they'll be given until the start.

"On one show a team had to first build a smoker out of cinderblocks, so we were pretty scared. We thought, 'Oh, god, what if we have to cook a whole hog,'" said Betsy. Squeal gals wound up beating out one of the professionals and went on to the finals, in New York. They were flown, all expenses paid, to compete once again under a shroud of mystery. This time they were lucky to get a Backwoods smoker for equipment and pork ribs and butt for the meat. The pro teams included big-time circuit champions Lotta Bull and Ray Lampe, the Dr. of Barbecue. Thrilled just to be there, but amazed at how tiny the New York hotel rooms were, Squeal of Approval won the competition and the $25,000 prize money.

When asked how their time as an all-female team differs from their experience with men, Betsy piped in, "We're much more organized!" They also share, rather than divide, the work. "If the chicken didn't place, then it was that guy's fault who did the chicken. We have different roles, but we all cook the entries together. That way if we win, we all win, and if we don't, well, we all try to improve for the next time."

All three women have enjoyed watching their kids compete and win in "Kid Q" events, created largely for competitors' kids. Betsy's daughter started grilling at age five. "We got a baby Weber and started her out on hot dogs. Anything that can roll is a good start for kids."

Allison encourages women to have the confidence that they can cook great barbecue. "Women just need to find out they can do it. We weren't taught that way," she said. Allison is no stranger to being a woman in a man's world—her "day job" is on the police force. "I never wanted to be the 'the girl' in the police department," she admitted. "We're self-conscious as an all-female barbecue team and don't want to rely on help because we're 'girls.' We're in it to compete." What both sisters love about the barbecue community? "It's about friendship, old and new."

Allison: "In today's age of the Food Network and cooking shows, just keep it simple. Pork should taste like barbecued pork. Sauce should taste like sauce."

Betsy on brisket: "We like to butter our brisket rather than slather with mustard. Other than that, we just rub it and smoke it."

2. Rub with dry mustard; then coat with Fiery Jerk Paste and refrigerate for 2–4 hours.

3. Make your fire or preheat your grill for slow and low cooking." Get your smoke on." Place a drip pan underneath the indirect part of the grill and fill it ¾ full with water. Once your grill is good and smoky, place ribs on the grill over the drip pan and close the lid. Leave it for 1 hour.

4. Replenish coals as needed with hot-and-ready coals. Add wood every hour or so for the first 3–4 hours (charcoal) or up to 6 hours (electric or gas). For gas grills, replenish wood chips to your foil pouch or add a new pouch.

5. After 2 hours, mix paste with 2 cups of apple juice and mop ribs every 45 minutes to an hour.

6. Smoke for approximately 6 hours at 200°F–225°F.

Cooking Times and Temperatures for Beef *

CUT	COOKING TEMPERATURE	COOKING METHOD	WEIGHT
Brisket, whole packer	225	Slow and Low	8-14 lbs.
Brisket, flat	225	Slow and Low	4-6 lbs.
Brisket, grass fed	225/300	Combination	2-6 lbs.
Brisket, short cut	225/300	Combination	8-14 lbs.
Beef Tenderloin	225	Slow and Low	3-4 lbs.
Beef Short Ribs***	225	Slow and Low	4 lbs.

Prime Rib: See Holiday chapter for Prime Rib cooking times.

*** These are the meaty ribs from the rib plate, not the long, skinny back ribs. Each rib weighs about 1 lb.

Grass-Fed Beef Brisket

Serves 2–6

COOKING METHOD: Slow and Low, Finished in Oven

One of the benefits of buying grass-fed brisket is that it is smaller than commercial briskets, so you can cook brisket for less than a crowd. This can also be the challenge: Grass-fed beef is so much leaner than grain-fed that the longer temperatures needed to make it tender can dry it out. A 2-hour smoke, finished in the oven, works well for grass-fed beef.

INGREDIENTS
1 grass-fed brisket (2–4 pounds)
Feisty Girl Rub (pg. 53)
Apple juice in spray bottle for mop
No Fail-Barbecue Sauce (pg. 66) or your favorite sauce

TIME	INTERNAL TEMPERATURE WHEN DONE	NOTES
10-18 hrs	185-210	1½-2 hrs per lb.
5-12 hrs	185-210	1½-2 hrs per lb.
2½-4 hrs	160**	Slow and Low/Oven finished
5-6 hrs	185-210	Slow and Low/Oven finished
3-4 hrs	130-150	130 rare, 140 medium rare, 150 medium
5-7 hrs	160	

*Internal temperatures are based on USDA recommended minimal temperatures. Cooking times are estimated and may vary according to equipment, weather conditions, and other factors.
**Grass-fed beef, because it is so lean, requires a lower internal temperature to avoid drying out.

BEST EQUIPMENT: Any charcoal, gas, or electric grill or smoker
TOOLS: Spray bottle for mop, pan and foil for oven
PREFERRED WOOD: Blend of hickory and apple

STEP BY STEP

1. Rub brisket 20 minutes up to a day ahead.

2. Make fire for slow and low barbecue; then "get your smoke on."

3. Place brisket fat side up on indirect cooking side. Close the lid and leave for 1 hour.

4. If using charcoal, after 30 minutes, light 10–15 coals in charcoal chimney starter or second grill. Add to the coal pile when ready.

5. After 1 hour, spray with apple juice, add coals if using a charcoal grill, and add wood to the fire if needed.

Interview with a Grass-Fed Beef and Lamb Farmer

A good college friend of mine went on to get her PhD in horticulture and now teaches at the University of Idaho. I just call her Professor Potatoes. Her family began a potato farm, Olsen Farms, in Colville, Washington, after our undergraduate days. The farm has now branched out to grass-fed beef and lamb and is a true family farm. Her mom acts as the "nerve center" of the farm, taking orders, managing the potato packing, fielding the phone calls and e-mails, and keeping the farm running while everyone is at market. Her brother Brent is the full-time farmer. When he's not in the fields, he's traveling between the many farmer's markets at which they sell in both Seattle and Spokane and managing the staff, inventory, and restaurant accounts. Nora, though she doesn't live on the farm, brings her scientific expertise and has created a state-of-the-art potato storage facility. She brings hubby and the kids to help with harvest most years too.

What is striking about the small farmers is that they are as busy as any top CEO, more so because they have to wear so many hats, without the private jet, the BlackBerry, or the personal assistant.

I chatted with Brent at Seattle's University farmer's market to talk about the grass-fed meat movement.

"This biggest surprise about adding grass-fed beef and lamb to our farm was the overpowering demand. People really want to know their local producers," he said. Adding the "meat" to their potatoes developed naturally. "We had the infrastructure already, the land, the barns, plenty of pasture—it just made sense." Everything the animals eat they grow on the farm, and the manure from their animals fertilizes the farm. While the cows and lamb are pasture fed, they also eat leftover potatoes. "They come running when they hear my truck because they know I usually have some potatoes for them," said Brent. He loves the sustainability of the farm, and though they will let it grow, it will be in keeping "in balance with the hay pile." In other words, they will only grow the herd according to how much pasture and hay the farm can produce.

Brent sells at farmer's markets in Seattle and Spokane year-round. "It's a challenge to do all your direct marketing and selling while being a full-time farmer. I joke when I get a call that I should say, 'Hold on, let me get the PR director,' then pause and get back on the phone." As I watch him greet customers with "Hey, how are you? I missed you last week. How did your lamb shanks turn out?" I see that as much as customers want to know their producers, the feeling is mutual, making the hard work worth it.

6. Spray with apple juice every ½ hour for the next hour.

7. After 2 hours, remove from grill and place in a glass baking pan. Spray apple juice again and pour ½ cup of barbecue sauce over brisket. Cover in foil and bake on 250°F for another 2–4 hours until tender.

Smoked Gouda Burgers

Serves 6–8

COOKING METHOD: Indirect Medium

These smoked burgers topped with smoked Gouda cheese will make you forget about going out for burgers. You can make them so much better at home. Keep in mind that smoked burgers cook evenly throughout and will be medium when done, rather than rare or medium rare.

INGREDIENTS
1 tablespoon salt
1½ teaspoon fresh ground pepper
1 cup chopped onion
3 pounds quality natural ground beef (not lean or extra lean)
2 tablespoons finely chopped fresh thyme
½ to 1 ounce smoked Gouda per burger
Toppings and condiments of your choice and a good-quality bun. I like kaiser buns and think dill pickles, garden tomatoes, and mixed greens complement the double-smoked flavors of these burgers. Avocado and radish sprouts make these extra-fancy burgers.

BEST EQUIPMENT: Any charcoal or gas grill or smoker
PREFERRED WOOD: Hickory, oak, apple, or a blend
MAKE AHEAD: Smoke the Gouda yourself (pg. 204).

STEP BY STEP
1. Make your fire for indirect medium cooking. Mix the salt, pepper, onions, and fresh thyme thoroughly in the ground beef. Make 6- to 8-ounce patties, as even in thickness as you can. Refer to page 99 for Making the Perfect Patty.

2. Once your grill is hot, "get your smoke on." Aim for 325°F. Place burgers on indirect side for 10 minutes; then flip and cook for another 10 minutes.

3. In the last 5 minutes, place sliced Gouda on the top to melt. Serve with your favorite condiments and toppings.

NOTE: The meat will have a slight pink hue due to the smoke. This is not the same color as a raw pink, nor does it indicate the burger is rare (a smoked pink hue does not get pinker in the middle). To know for certain whether your burgers are done, stick an instant read thermometer in the middle and pull the burger when it reaches 155°F. It will increase about 5° or more while it rests to reach the USDA-recommended 160°F.

Not Your Mama's Smoked Meatloaf

Serves 8–12

COOKING METHOD: Slow and Low

If your mom's meatloaf was ground beef with onions, cooked with ketchup, as mine was, this recipe will change your opinion of the loaf. For many of you, whose mamas did just fine in the meatloaf department, the smoked flavor will kick it up a notch. This recipe makes 3 medium meatloaves—I like leftovers for sandwiches the next day or for future freezer meals. Halve it if you just want enough for tonight for 4–6 people.

INGREDIENTS
2 cups fresh bread crumbs (grating a fresh baguette heel works nicely)
¾ cups whole milk
½ pound bacon, cut up
½ cup olive oil
2½ cups finely chopped onions (about 2 medium onions)
6 garlic cloves, minced
2 celery stalks, finely chopped
2 carrots, finely chopped
3 cups sliced mushrooms
4 tablespoons Worcestershire sauce
4 teaspoons kosher salt or 3 teaspoons table salt

3 teaspoons fresh ground pepper

2 tablespoons apple cider vinegar

4 pounds lean ground beef. (*Note:* Lean works better than extra lean; however, this recipe works great with grass-fed beef.)

½ pound pork sausage

4 large eggs

⅓ cup finely chopped thyme

BEST EQUIPMENT: Any charcoal or gas grill, any smoker

TOOLS: Cookie cooling rack, food processor (not essential), instant read thermometer, large skillet, large spatula

SUGGESTED WOOD: Blend of hickory and apple, or oak

STEP BY STEP

1. Make a slow and low fire, or preheat your grill/smoker. "Get your smoke on."

2. Soak bread crumbs in milk.

3. Heat up a large skillet and cook bacon until it's starting to brown but not crispy. Remove bacon, but leave drippings in pan. Finely chop bacon or pulse in the food processor.

4. Add oil to bacon drippings. Sauté onion for a few minutes; then add garlic, celery, carrots, and mushrooms over medium heat. Stir occasionally and cook for 5–7 minutes.

5. Remove from heat and add Worcestershire sauce, vinegar, salt and pepper, bacon, and bread-crumb mixture.

6. With your hands, mix ground beef and sausage thoroughly into above ingredients. Add thyme and eggs and mix evenly into meat.

7. Form into 2–3 rectangular loaves. Take time to smooth out the ends and any lumps or obvious "cracks" in the loaf.

8. With a large spatula and your hands to guide, carefully transfer loaves onto a cookie cooling rack, faced perpendicular to bars.

8. Put rack on top of grill rack so that rack lines are perpendicular as well.

9. Smoke for 3 hours or until instant read thermometer reaches 155°F internally and the meatloaf has a nice, browned exterior.

10. Let rest for at least 30 minutes so that loaf sets well before you remove it from cookie cooling rack. Slice and serve.

Find tips on grilled steaks, burgers, and Kalbi Beef Short Ribs in the Grilling Basics chapter. For Smoked Prime Rib turn to the Holiday Barbecue chapter.

Chapter Eight

Birds for Birds

The restaurant business seems to attract those of us who do not fit into the 9–5 business model. While some of us are just not made for corporate life with its meetings and pantyhose, there are others who would never make it past the front desk. As an employer, I've ceased being surprised by what walks in: A gal arrives to apply for the job with her best foot forward . . . in pajamas and flip-flops, another guy shows up drunk to the interview, and a new employee robs me two hours into her shift (missed the gut check on *that* one).

Still, these days are tame compared to the early years of my career, when I saw just about everything occur on the job, much of which should not be printed. One of the strangest job performances I witnessed was when a fellow employee brought a live chicken to work. We were catering backstage at The Gorge Amphitheater, an outdoor concert venue, so it wasn't as if the chicken was roaming around the office, but it did scuttle around our feet while we prepared hundreds of meals. We worked out of a tiny trailer kitchen connected to an outdoor deck that functioned as our prep room. A few feet from this area was a large yurt that served as our banquet room. The entire backstage area perched on a cliff that overlooked a desert landscape, funneling down to the mighty Columbia River Gorge.

The city boy who brought the chicken was getting grief from his neighbors about his urban flock, so he thought he'd just release the poor thing into the wild. The Columbia River Gorge is no farm. It's a harsh desert climate complete with rolling sagebrush and rattlesnakes. That domesticated chicken wouldn't last a day.

A not-to-be-named, rather high-strung production assistant ran from the yurt into our catering area and hysterically screamed, "I just saw a chicken walking around here! A chicken!" Instinctively, we all played dumb.

"Chicken? Are you sure? I mean, how would a chicken get here?"

Throughout the day, she periodically stormed in, exclaiming she'd seen that chicken again. Lucky for us, the chicken played along with our ruse and sat under the trailer whenever she came by. This production assistant had tormented us an entire summer with unusual demands and petty problems, causing a stress level that just didn't match the quiet, rolling beauty of the river gorge before us. The chicken was our revenge. We continued the farce, treating her gently as you would a crazy person who was hallucinating free-range chickens. By the end of the day she avoided the catering area, to our relief. We didn't know how long a chicken could keep a joke. (Fortunately, one of our staff's family farm was in the area, and he whisked the chicken away in his pickup before the dinner rush.) The production assistant "took a break" from work shortly after the chicken incident, and though we felt slightly guilty that we may have played a hand in it all, we welcomed the few weeks of peace.

The city kid with the chicken went on to study at Stanford and later married a Brazilian soap opera star. (We're not sure what became of the chicken.) Just goes to show that plenty of functioning people out there operate without any common sense. It also points to a disconnect with the natural world and the food we eat. The fact that his chicken, bred for egg laying in a cushy coop, had about as many skills as *he* had for survival in the wilderness never crossed his mind; he imagined it would live happily ever after, roaming free and pecking for bugs in the dust.

We are so removed from our food source that we rarely even buy whole chickens in the grocery store but prefer nicely cut pink shapes with all bone, skin, and fat removed. In 1962, 83% of chickens sold were whole. Today, only 9% are sold whole, 44% are cut up, and 47% are "further processed."[1] You may be like a catering client of mine, who confessed that as the last of seven girls in a family of great cooks, she somehow missed the cooking gene: "I look at a whole chicken, and I think, 'Yeah? So what am I supposed to do with this? Take it to a butcher to cut up?'"

Many cookbooks start with a chicken recipe: "Cut up a whole fryer . . . " If you get stumped on this first step, or need to improve upon your current method of cutting up a chicken, try one of the three ways to cut a chicken that follow. If you think there is no need for this because the grocery story sells pre-cut fryers, consider this: Cut-up fryers are Frankensteined parts. Bruised or damaged birds are cut up, and the good parts get mixed with others to make a whole bird. The bruised or damaged parts then go down the line for further processing and turned into products such as chicken fingers, cat food, or frozen "fajita pita" meat. A whole bird is also more economical, plus it gives you stock fodder.

HOW TO CUT A CHICKEN

There is more than one way to skin a cat, and the same goes for chicken. As someone who massacred chickens for years, when I finally decided to learn the proper way to cut up a whole chicken, I turned to Julia Child. I love that Child, in her great book *The Way to Cook*, tells us to first carve a chicken in the privacy of our own kitchen, with no one looking.[2] Too true. The same goes for cutting up a raw chicken. Another great teacher is repetition. Here are three ways to slice your bird, of varying degrees of finesse. I call them the Cave Woman, the Bird Quarterly, and Madame Butterfly.

The first thing to realize is that a chicken is much like you: a biped with wide hips. Look at your own body and think of where your joints are between your limbs; think about your backbone and pelvis, and your breastbone. You aren't so much going to cut the chicken as you are going to dismember it. Be a surgeon. While that concept may get lost in the Cave Woman method, it's certainly true for the other two.

The Cave Woman

You will need a sharp, heavy knife for this one.

1. With breast side down, grab one side of the neck with your hand. Cut along the other side, and cut down from there to remove the back. When you get to the pelvis about two-thirds of the way down, you will use some muscle (yours) to firmly cut (a.k.a. hack) down the middle.

2. Open up the bird. Cut along the other side of the back to remove it. Scrape out the giblets.

3. Score the breastbone and cartilage with your knife point. Lay your knife down and press down with both thumbs just above the breastbone to pop it out.

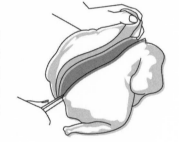

4. Pull the breastbone and cartilage out with your fingers (you might have to dig in a bit to yank it).

5. Slice down the middle. You now have two half chickens. Howl to the chicken god and get your fire ready.

The Bird Quarterly

Not nearly as coarse as our gal above; you might be inclined to put on some Pavarotti.

I like to slow-smoke whole chickens but prefer to grill half or quarter chickens with indirect medium heat. You can easily take this method one step further and cut up the chicken for frying.

1. Lay the chicken in the missionary position. Tug at one leg and slightly pull away from the body. Lightly cut the loose skin between the joint to expose where you will cut. Score meat along the thigh, keeping knife butted against the breast cavity bones, until you hit the joint.

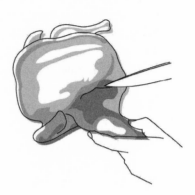

2. Place your hand behind the chicken hip, and pop it up to expose the joint. Cut the joint (be careful that your hand is out of the way of your knife) and slice the skin until the quarter is removed.

3. Repeat on the other side. You may want to turn the chicken around and cut from the other direction, as this will be your non-dominant hand.

4. Flip the bird over to remove the back. Grab one side of the neck with your hand, and cut along the other side. Cut to the hips and open up the bird cavity.

5. Score the breastbone and cartilage with your knife point. Lay your knife down and press down with both thumbs just above the breastbone to pop it out.

6. Cut through the wishbone and down the center of bird to halve it.

7. Cut off the remaining backbone and use for stock.

8. Cut off the wing tips, if desired.

NOTE: You now have two leg/thigh quarters and two breast/wing quarters. You can continue to cut at the joints to cut up the bird for frying. Just find the joint between the leg and thigh, for instance, and slice through it. For smoking or grilling, keep them quartered for cooking; then cut them up smaller when serving if desired.

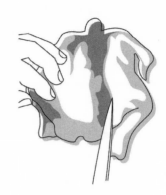

TIP: Love them love handles! The one thing that can get missed in this method is the delicious "oysters" of meat located above the hip bone. I call these two little pockets of meat the "love handles." Once you've mastered the basic quarterly method, you can save these morsels from the stock pot. Find them first before you start the leg/thigh removal. Make an incision around them and stop. When you start to cut out your leg/thigh quarter, connect that cut with the incision you made to include the love handles. It will be a cut that looks like this:

Madame Butterfly

With a butterflied chicken, also called "spatchcocked," you are creating a flat, whole chicken. The advantage of leaving it whole (rather than slicing through to make two halves) is that you can get grill marks and browning on the whole bird. I've seen huge pits with birds smoking this way, on giant skewers. It presents nicely on a platter too.

1. Lay bird breast side down. Score skin along backbone, and peel it partially away to expose the bone.

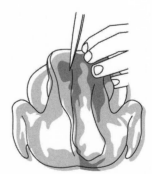

2. Cut along one side of the backbone. When you get to the "love handle" (see note above), dig out around it with your knife, then continue down.

3. Using the backbone as a guide, score meat away from the back with the top half of your knife to expose the hip joint. Cut through the joint.

4. When you cut through, be careful not to cut all the way to the other side, nicking the breast meat.

5. Open up the cavity. Cut the backbone out from the other side, keeping the knife against the edge so as not to cut out flesh.

6. Score the breastbone and cartilage with your knife. Lay your knife down and press down with both thumbs just above the breastbone to pop it out.

7. You now have a whole bird, flattened. You of course can easily cut through if you want two halves.

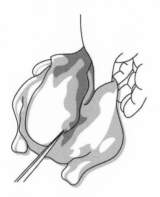

Simple Barbecue Half Chickens

COOKING METHOD: Slow and Low or Indirect Medium

We serve up our chickens "dry" at our restaurant, but I also like my birds saucy. You can't go wrong with this smoky saucy chicken. If you use a dedicated smoker, smoke these at 200°F–225°F for about 2½ hours. The faster indirect heat version, 300°F–350°F, takes 1 to 1¼ hours. If your chickens are the smaller broilers (often the case with organic chickens 3 pounds and under), figure one half chicken per adult eater. For larger broilers, 4 pounds and up, divide the number of guests by 3.25 to get your chicken count.

INGREDIENTS
1–2 whole chickens
Basic Barbecue Rub (pg. 51)
No-Fail Barbecue Sauce (pg. 66)
Fruit juice for mopping
Olive oil

BEST EQUIPMENT: Any charcoal grill or smoker is best for either method. Gas grills can accomplish the recipe via indirect-medium, electric smokers via slow and low.

TOOLS: Remote thermometer (if grill does not have external temperature reading), instant read thermometer, spatula and chef tongs, paper towels

SUGGESTED WOOD: Hickory, apple, or other fruit woods

MAKE AHEAD: Make rub before firing up your grill (or days ahead if you want).

STEP BY STEP

1. Rinse your chickens under cool water. Pat dry with paper towels. Halve your chickens using the Cave Woman method, above.

2. Start coals in a chimney or preheat your gas grill to indirect medium heat. You will need about ¾ of a chimney for two halves, a full chimney plus for four.

3. Rub a light coating of olive oil on the chicken, inside and out.

4. Dry-rub chicken with Basic Barbecue Rub. Let stand for about 20 minutes.

5. *Charcoal:* Once coals are hot, pour them on one side of your grill, add a drip pan, and fill with water. "Get your smoke on." *Gas:* Follow the directions for indirect medium heat and add a foil wood smoking pouch to "get your smoke on."

6. Place half chickens, breast side up, on grill. Cover grill and leave alone for 40 minutes. After 40 minutes, turn halves and mop with fruit juice. I use whatever is in the house—apple, pear, or my son's favorite, mango-peach.

7. After 20 minutes of cooking, flip and then baste all over with the No-Fail Barbecue Sauce or your favorite sauce. Check your instant read thermometer in the thickest part of the thigh to determine whether it's done (165°F).

Cooking Times and Temperatures for Poultry *

CUT	COOKING TEMPERATURE	COOKING METHOD	WEIGHT
Whole Chicken	225	Slow and Low	2½-3 lbs.
Whole Chicken	225	Slow and Low	3-4 lbs.
Whole Chicken	300-350	Indirect-Medium	3-4 lbs.
Half Chicken	225	Slow and Low	1-2 lbs.
Half Chicken	300-350	Indirect-Medium	1-2 lbs.
Duck	225	Slow and Low	2½-3 lbs.
Duck	225	Slow and Low	3-5 lbs.
Duck	300-350	Indirect-Medium	2½-3 lbs.
Whole Turkey	225	Slow and Low	10-14 lbs.
Whole Turkey	300-350	Indirect-Medium	10-22 lbs.
Cornish Game Hens	300-350	Indirect-Medium	1-1½ lbs.

Safe Cooking Temperatures for Chicken

Chicken should reach an internal temperature of 165°F during cooking to safely eliminate any bacteria. Typically the internal temperature rises about 5°–10° after you remove from heat. I factor that in when checking my meats with an instant read thermometer, so I don't overcook the meats. Be sure your thermometer is calibrated (see chapter 1) so you don't get a false reading.

TIME	INTERNAL TEMPERATURE WHEN DONE*	NOTES
2½-3 hrs	165 in thigh	
3-4 hrs	165 in thigh	
1-1½ hrs	165 in thigh	
2-2½ hrs	165 in thigh	
1¼ hrs	165 in thigh	
3-4 hrs	165 in thigh	
4-6 hrs	165 in thigh	
2½-3 hrs	165 in thigh	145° for rare (not USDA recommended)
30 min per lb.	170 in thigh	leg moves easily, juices run clear
15 min per lb.	170 in thigh	leg moves easily, juices run clear
45-50 min	170	time is for a stuffed hen

* **IMPORTANT NOTE:** Internal temperatures are based on USDA recommended minimal temperatures. Cooking times are estimated and may vary according to equipment, weather conditions, and other factors.

TIP: A word on handling raw chicken. I almost hesitate to mention this because there has been so much media hype about the dangers of raw chicken. People are scared to touch it. True, many chickens contain small amounts of salmonella and other bacteria that are safely sterilized through cooking. When handling raw chicken, or any other raw meat, it is important to wash your hands for about 20 seconds with hot soapy water. Dry your hands with paper towels and discard them so you don't transfer any contaminants to a towel that will be used throughout your cooking process. Be sure that you don't use unwashed utensils, platters, or bowls for raw and cooked or "prepared" foods.

Smoked Beer-Can Chicken & Smoked Corn

COOKING METHOD: Indirect Medium

This well-known recipe is great for the beginner: It's easy and makes almost no-fail tender chicken on the grill. The basic idea is that you steam a whole chicken with a can of beer (or juice) on the grill. I like the inexpensive beer-can chicken stands you can buy seasonally at most grocery stores. They keep the can and chicken stable to minimize tip-overs, the one risk of this recipe. Smoke the corn with the chicken because it takes about the same time to cook.

INGREDIENTS
Basic Barbecue Rub (p. 51)
1 whole chicken
Olive oil
Finishing sauce optional, use your favorite
4 ears of corn, silk removed, husk on
Optional: Serve with grilled veggies. See chapter 5 for recipe.

BEST EQUIPMENT: Any charcoal or gas grill. If you're using a dedicated smoker like an electric water smoker, your temperature will be lower. Chicken will take about 2½–3 hours.
TOOLS: Beer-can chicken stand (recipe can be made without one), remote thermometer (if grill does not have external temperature reading), instant read thermometer, spatula and chef tongs
SUGGESTED WOOD: Hickory, oak, or pecan
MAKE AHEAD: Make rub before starting your grill (or days ahead if you want). Peel back corn husks, remove silk, then close back up. If serving with grilled vegetables, prep your veggies ahead.

STEP BY STEP

1. Prep your chicken in the kitchen: Remove giblets. Rinse chicken with warm water and pat dry with paper towels. Rub with olive oil and any spice rub of your choice. You can use the Basic Barbecue Rub or a commercial mix in your pantry. Rub and oil the inside cavity as well.

2. Take any inexpensive beer, pour ⅓ of it into your drip pan, and poke two holes in the top with a church key. Insert the can into the cavity of the chicken (or in the beer-can chicken holder) so that the chicken "stands up."

3. Plug the neck of your chicken with half of a garlic bulb, a small potato, or a quarter of an onion.

4. Prep your corn: Peel back husks enough to remove the silk. Spread a light coating of olive oil, salt, and pepper on the corn; put husks back to cover.

5. Prepare your fire for indirect-medium heat. Light your coals in your chimney starter or preheat your gas grill. When your coals are ready, pour into grill and spread them to one side for indirect cooking. Place your drip pan with the beer and some water in the middle of the coals and "get your smoke on." *For gas grills*, preheat at least 15 minutes on high. Turn off the center or side burner and turn down the other burner(s) to 300°F. Place beer-can chicken standing up on grill.

6. Place your corn around your chicken, on the indirect part of the grill.

7. Put lid on tight and leave it for 30 minutes. After 30 minutes, check it and slip in 5–6 new coals around the edge of the fire. Close lid and cook for another 30 minutes. During the second half hour, I like to cut up thick slices of zucchini, eggplant, and peppers to grill on the direct part of the grill. Drizzle with olive oil, balsamic vinegar, and salt and pepper.

8. Check the temperature of the chicken with an instant read thermometer. It should reach 165°F in the meaty part of the thigh.

9. Grill veggies over direct heat. The fire will be low enough that you can close the lid on the veggies and roast them for 5–8 minutes, then flip for about 3–5 minutes on other side.

10. Removing the chicken is the only tricky part. Have a platter close or have someone hold it. Take two pairs of chef tongs and lift onto the platter. Be careful not to tip it, as the beer inside is extremely hot.

11. If you have used a stand, I suggest having someone hold the stand (using hot pads) while you lift the chicken up with tongs.

Finishing Sauces: Experiment with your favorite finishing sauce the last 15 minutes of cooking. Baste your sauce on the outside, and then close the lid until the sauce caramelizes. I'm a big fan of sweet sauces with chicken. Try the Plum-Bourbon Barbecue Sauce on page 67.

FANCY PANTS BARBECUE
Smoked Duck with Orange-Currant Glaze

COOKING METHOD: Indirect Medium or Slow and Low

Served this with Grilled Polenta and Grilled Balsamic Greens (see chapter 5).
You can cook duck by indirect-medium heat for about 2–2½ hours. Slow and low in the smoker will take approximately 3½–4 hours, depending on size.

INGREDIENTS
1 duck, 2½ to 3 pounds
Rice wine vinegar and soy sauce for drip pan
Feisty Girl Rub (pg. 53)
Orange-Currant Glaze (pg. 69)
½ cup orange juice

BEST EQUIPMENT: Any charcoal grill or smoker, gas grill, or electric smoker.
TOOLS: Remote thermometer (if grill does not have external temperature reading), instant read thermometer, spatula and long-handled chef tongs, pastry brush for applying glaze
SUGGESTED WOOD: Maple or fruit woods
MAKE AHEAD: Make rub before starting your grill (or days ahead if you want). Prep greens and polenta ahead (see recipes).

STEP BY STEP
1. Rinse duck under cool water and pat dry with paper towel. Pat Feisty Girl Rub all over duck, including inside cavity. Let sit while making fire. "Get your smoke on."

2. Fill a drip pan with a mix of half water, half rice wine vinegar, and a little soy sauce. Once it's in place and your unit is preheated, place duck breast side up directly on the grill over the drip pan, and close the lid.

She's Smokin': Donna Moodie Sets the Mood

Seattle restaurateur Donna Moodie has the foodie thing in her blood. Her mom was the quintessential hostess, so when Donna named her restaurant Marjorie, after her mom, she paid homage to her hostess heritage.

"My mom loved cooking and entertaining, and her dinner parties were very diverse, with simple and well-prepared food. She'd cook Jamaican, Italian, Southern . . . I'm sure it was exotic for the times. Her nature of being inclusive, seeking good ingredients, and being a good host carried through me," says Moodie.

The diversity at her mother's dinner parties was exotic for the neighborhood, too. Donna's family moved from Jamaica when she was five years old, into an incredibly segregated neighborhood on the South Side of Chicago. "The domino effect was in full force. As soon as one black family moved into a neighborhood, that whole neighborhood changed."

Upon opening Marjorie, her third restaurant but first solo venture, Donna wanted to get out of the kitchen more and get back to what her mom did, focusing on the front of the house and the atmosphere. The menu features simple ingredients from around the world—you'll find Indian-inspired dishes next to a seasonal local fish. Bold, warm colors invite you in. "Trends come and go, but it really is the feeling you get when you enter a space and how your palate is made to feel, whether you leave happy and full, or whether you question how you feel," says Donna.

Her favorite part about owning a restaurant? "Contact with people and sense of community you can have and share with people," she says. One way she shares with the greater community is being a part of the Central District forum, Food Is Art fundraiser for the past five years. "It is a huge gala event with twenty tables of black chefs and restaurateurs. You go around and fill your plate with really great food. It challenges the assumptions about being black in America. Not all black chefs cook barbecue or southern food."

Her least favorite part? "The 24/7 aspect of the work. I don't mind the commitment for that. But having a child and being a single mom means you both have to pile into the car at 2 AM to lock up because the bartender forgot his keys."

Donna's tips for gals at the grill is to "get really good ingredients, set yourself up well, and cook mindfully." She also encourages women to "Trust your instincts. Often our level of expertise is questioned. Be confident in what we bring to the table—we have a lot to give."

Donna shares her family jerk chicken recipe, straight from Jamaica, on page 110.

What the Duck?

The size and type of duck you buy will affect your recipe time, and the end product. Technically you will be buying ducklings, raised seven to eleven weeks. Here are U.S. ducklings defined:

WHITE PEKIN DUCK—Also called the Long Island duck; most ducks you buy will be this variety. Harvested young at about seven weeks, this duck has a mild flavor, lean meat, and is tender. The above recipe time is based on the White Pekin.

MUSCOVY DUCK—The larger Muscovy duck is prized for its breast and is leaner than the White Pekin. These are raised to eleven weeks and are excellent for barbecue if you can find them. Try your butcher shop.

MOULARD—A cross between the White Pekin and the Muscovy.

WILD DUCK—Wild duck will be much gamier and tougher due to their diet and extreme exercise. Some mallards are now being farm raised. I would not recommend wild ducks for barbecue, but smoke-roasting them on indirect medium heat is fine.

Ducklings under eight weeks old are called "broilers" or "fryers." Older ducklings, eight to twelve weeks, are called "roasters," because they are higher in fat. Roasters are excellent barbecue, but both work well. Grade A ducks have the most meat.

3. Keep vents set low. Leave it for 45 minutes.

4. Make your glaze. Whisk until sugar in glaze is dissolved. Split into two portions—one for basting, the other to make a finishing sauce.

5. At 45 minutes, brush glaze liberally on duck, inside and out. Glaze again at 45 minutes. *Note:* I usually glaze only in the last 30 minutes, but I find the duck needs more than that. Be careful not to spill glaze into fire or use so much that it will drip off in chunks. This will cause flare-ups.

6. Prepare Grilled Polenta and Grilled Balsamic Greens (pages 91–92). If using an electric smoker for your duck, fire up a charcoal or gas grill for medium direct heat to be hot 20 minutes before duck is ready.

7. *Finishing sauce:* Mix rest of glaze with ½ cup of orange juice and heat in saucepan. Drizzle over carved duck or let guests serve themselves.

Tuscan Grilled & Smoked Turkey Legs

Serves 6

COOKING METHOD: Combination

INGREDIENTS
3–4 turkey drumsticks
1 large lemon
Rub olive oil in skin of drumsticks. Sprinkle with salt, fresh ground pepper, and rosemary.

BEST EQUIPMENT: Any charcoal or gas grill, or smoker
TOOLS: Remote thermometer (if grill does not have external temperature reading), instant read thermometer, spatula and long-handled chef tongs
SUGGESTED WOOD: Grapevines or fruit woods

STEP BY STEP

1. Make fire for indirect cooking and "get your smoke on." Grapevines are a nice touch.

2. Grill turkey legs on direct medium heat, at 350°F, for 20 minutes total (turning every 5 minutes) to sear the meat. Then move to indirect fire. Squeeze a lemon over the drumsticks. The turkey legs are fairly low-fat, so a drip pan is optional. Slow-cook at 200°F for two hours. Squeeze a little more lemon at serving.

Smokin' Hot Wings

COOKING METHOD: Indirect Medium Heat

INGREDIENTS
Jumbo Wings. Factor 2 per person for an appetizer, 6–7 for a meal

Hotter'n Heck Wing Rub (pg. 52)
Hot Wing Tossin' Sauce (pg. 71)
Serve with celery, sliced cucumbers, and blue cheese dip.

BEST EQUIPMENT: Any charcoal or gas grill, or smoker.
TOOLS: Remote thermometer (if grill does not have external temperature reading), instant read thermometer, spatula and long-handled chef tongs, 2 mixing bowls
SUGGESTED WOOD: Hickory

STEP BY STEP

1. Toss wings in the Hotter'n Heck rub on page 52.

2. Make an indirect medium fire and "get your smoke on."

3. Place wings on grill and cover for 40 minutes. If using a slow smoker, smoke for an hour. *Note:* Time is for the meaty jumbo wings. If using small wings, smoke for about 20–25 minutes.

4. While wings are smoking, make your Hot Wing Tossin' Sauce in a mixing bowl.

5. Throw your hot-off-the-grill wings in the bowl and toss until coated. Serve with cool celery and cucumbers, and blue cheese to cut the spice.

See the Holiday Barbecue chapter for Smoked Turkey and Stuffed Cornish Game Hens. See the Grilling chapter for some high-heat chicken and turkey recipes.

CHICKEN DEFINITIONS: BUYING NATURAL, FREE-RANGE, PASTURED, OR ORGANIC CHICKEN

According to the National Chicken Council, Americans each consume an average of 81 pounds of chicken a year.[3] While over 97% of those chickens were produced by large commercial operations, the margin of free-range, organic, and pastured poultry is growing.[4] The USDA has specific definitions in its labeling, but to the end consumer those labels can be confusing. Read chapter 9 for a more in-depth discussion about labeling issues. Here is a breakdown of those labels in the grocery store and farmer's market.

NATURAL—Chicken labeled "all-natural" can legally be pumped up with a broth of up to 15% salt water, phosphates, and other ingredients in processing. "Natural" denotes that nothing "unnatural" was injected into the birds in postmortem processing. What is unnatural? Plastic wrap? Bubble Tea? What those little chickies ate before processing is, well, quite variable.

FREE RANGE—The USDA definition of "free range" is that poultry have access to the outdoors. This can be as little as limited access to an outdoor pen. Though all organic chickens must be free-range, free-range chickens do not need to be organic.

While the definition of "access" allows commercial poultry operations to qualify as free-range by installing outdoor pens next to their poultry house (little used because the food and water remain *inside*), there are many free-range poultry producers that exceed the USDA standards. These align with the European standard of stocking 400 chickens or 100 turkeys per acre. Compared to commercial poultry operations, which raise chickens in *less than* 1 square foot of space each, that's a lot more home on the range.

PASTURED—Chickens are housed in mobile coops, called "eggmobiles," and moved a few times throughout the day. Pastured poultry and sustainable farming guru Joel Salatin, at the forefront of this movement, states that one of the most compelling arguments for purchasing free-range or pastured poultry is that the birds consume valuable minerals, vitamins, and a variety of bugs from the pasture. His "whole farm" philosophy challenges the commercial mono-crop farm operations to a different way of doing business, one based on sustainable practices. In the poultry world this comes down to chicken shit and what to do about it.

In Salatin's model, it takes the same amount of land to pasture the chickens as it does to raise the grain they eat. The manure they make is then naturally spread, by the chickens, to fertilize the soil that grows their feed. It's a sustainable cycle. The limitation is of course that you can only raise X number of chickens on Y amount of land. If you try to raise too many chickens, the land will not support the manure, feed, and so forth, and the cycle is broken.

I asked Salatin about the commercial argument that there is no way we could meet the demand for the 81 pounds of chicken consumed per capita in the United States each year if we raised all chickens on pasture. He thinks otherwise, although he acknowledges that "people would have to live in close proximity to chickens and other livestock."

ORGANIC—Organic chickens are raised sans antibiotics or growth promotants, eat organic feed, and are given access to the outdoors. Some vaccinations are allowed. Organic certification is a lengthy and costly process, so some of the smaller farms may be raising chickens organically but lack the official stamp.

Chapter Nine

Julie's Soapbox

Okay, now let's have a little chat about your meat. Barbecue, after all, is first about meat. It's not the sauce, it's not the spice, it's not even the wood you choose. Those are just window dressings to the meat. The meat you find wrapped in uniform packages at the grocery store or butcher shop may *look* the same, but the differences are vast. We need to get real about the quality of the meat, as how it is produced affects our bodies, our environment, and our future generations. The meat industry is slowly waking up to this fact, but until they get out of bed and drink some coffee, we have to take the reins in our consumer hands. Sorry, but the USDA and the FDA are so bogged down in bureaucracy that they actually hinder the process rather than help it.

I'm no scientist, but if a scientific study can't find a problem with feeding cows plastic pot scrubbers[1] or old unsellable gum still in the wrapper[2], and can even *recommend* these two items as a substitute for roughage in a cow's diet, then there is something either wrong with their methodology or they have an incorrect definition of "acceptable." Come on! While these may seem more absurd examples of what commercial feedlot cattle have been fed, they are actually more benign than the loads of chemicals, antibiotics, and questionable ingredients being pumped into our animals to grow them big and fast.

Whether a cow is fed on green pastures or plastic pot scrubbers *does* make a difference in terms of nutritional value, health to *you*, the consumer, and our trust in the industry. I'm tired of commercial meat operations and associations repeating the mantra that "there is no difference . . . there is no difference . . . nothing has been proven . . . nothing has been proven . . . " A long list of research studies find definitively that what an animal eats and how that animal is raised directly affect the end product that we consume.[3] Commercial operations cry, "Untrue!" and point to numerous studies that show that antibiotic-free animals have the same or higher incidence of bacteria like E. coli and salmonella.[4] My unscientific response? In most of these studies, these "natural" animals were raised under the same conditions as the feedlot cows and commercial chicken houses. It's the whole system that is flawed. The animals raised under commercial operations *need* all those chemicals pumped into them to handle the stress of extreme proximity to other animals, noxious air quality, and feed not suited to their biological needs. Raising animals without antibiotics and other enhancements, within the same environmental criteria, will produce the same result, or worse.

Let's first talk about how it is now, and how it is changing.

"Natural" labeling came under fire in 2005 when the USDA Food Safety and Inspection division opened up the definition to include chemical preservatives and synthetic or artificial ingredients. They changed the rules because over the years companies had petitioned for exemptions on specific ingredients, for reasons of preservation and "food safety" of the product. A hearing in December 2006 questioned the new natural label rules. Though the petition referred to the *processing* label "natural," many commentators at the hearing pointed that the petition, and the FSIS, did not address the *real* problem with the "natural" label: Because "natural" referred only to postmortem processing, even the most unnaturally and inhumanely raised meat could be later labeled as "natural." This, stated numerous ranchers, farmers, and processors, was the true lie to the consumer, who as a whole defines "natural" as being "from farm to fork."[5]

As of now this is still being "reviewed." Granted, changing a label definition as big as this will cost millions to the producers in terms of changing their product, their labeling, advertising, on down the line. That the government follows the line "We can't be too hasty, precious!" makes sense, but mark my words—the longer it takes, the more watered-down and inefficient the end result will be.

WHAT CAN YOU, JANE CONSUMER, DO?

#1 UNDERSTAND WHAT IS AT STAKE.

Why buy natural foods? They cost more at the grocery store, and if it is all a sham, why do it?

One of the main reasons to choose meats raised without antibiotics is that strains of salmonella and E. coli are becoming increasingly resistant to antimicrobial drugs used in commercial production. One study found that almost 50% of the strains of salmonella and other bacteria in pigs were antibiotic resistant. The risk, of course, is that human consumption of resistant bacteria will make fighting the bacteria at the human end more difficult.[6]

A second reason to buy naturally raised and/or organic meat is for sustainability practices. Sustainability gets thrown around more than a baseball these days, but when we're talking animals and sustainability, we're mostly talking about poop. Commercial farms are monochromatic, so one crop doesn't support others. A sustainable farm uses the manure waste from the pigs, chickens, or cows to fertilize the crops and pasture that feed the same pigs or chickens. It's a supportive system. Farms that naturally raise their animals, by limitations of what that means, *must* practice sustainability.

The third reason to choose naturally raised meats is for animal welfare. Animal welfare is a *huge* can of worms, but how an animal is raised does affect the meat we eat. Reducing the animal's stress with open air, a healthy environment, and proper handling enables producers to keep that animal healthy without drugs like antibiotics.

#2 KNOW WHO RAISES YOUR MEAT.

Plenty of individual companies and cooperatives are dedicated to doing better than the minimum requirements. In speaking to a number of smaller farms, farm cooperatives, pork processors, and organizations like the National Pork Board and national and regional beef councils, it became painfully clear: It really is up to the producer to define "natural," create its own guidelines, or adopt an association's guidelines for the farms that participate in its program, and to set up and pay for their own internal monitoring system. Unless you do the research as a consumer, shopping in the "natural" section of your meat department can be a crapshoot. Some grocery stores do the research on their vendors and publish information about them in newsletters.

#3 KNOW WHAT THE LABELS REALLY MEAN.

ALL-NATURAL—As I've said, a chasm exists between what the consumer considers "natural" and how the USDA currently defines it. The label merely refers to processing. In other words, even if that pig ate potato chips, drank cheap beer, and sat in front of the TV all day, as long as nothing "unnatural" was pumped into the meat postmortem, a producer may slap a "natural" label on the package. Seek out those companies that walk the walk. I'll leave you with some books and websites in the Resources section of the book.

ORGANIC—There are great companies raising animals organically. This means all their feed is 100% organic, that the animals are given outdoor access, and that they receive no antibiotics or growth promotants. Keep in mind, however, that there are companies out there taking advantage of the higher price point rather than having a true commitment to the organic movement. They push the definitions of what is legally acceptable. According to Joel Salatin, a leader of the pastured poultry and sustainability farming movement, the regulations for labeling a chicken organic are vague and therefore slippery.[7] While many of our natural food markets may do the research, I like to sleuth myself. I look up the company's website and give them a call.

NATURALLY RAISED—Though meant to be a more stringent designation than "all-natural," the "naturally raised" label is no longer a safe haven. This was supposed to be the answer to the all-natural dilemma. It was *supposed* to signify that animals were raised without antibiotics or growth promotants, were given significant outdoor access and fed a vegetarian diet, and also that the farms had a documented animal welfare policy in place. At the writing of this book, the USDA's new official "naturally raised" label now includes cloned or genetically engineered animals, and has dropped both the animal welfare language and the outdoor access requirements. Now "naturally raised" means this: Animals have been raised without growth promotants and without antibiotics, and they have not been fed animal by-products. In essence, this is just another "greenwashed" marketing label.

PASTURED AND GRASS-FED ANIMALS—These animals are raised on their natural foraging diet. The health benefits for grass-fed beef, for example, are pretty astounding. Not only is the meat extremely lean, it contains much higher amounts of vitamin E, omega-3 fatty acids, and a number of antioxidants, to name just a few.[8] Pastured poultry could also be called "true free-range" as chickens are housed in moveable "eggmobiles" and rotated on different fields in order to ingest a variety of pasture, but also to spread their "fertilizer" around the farm.

For the animal to be truly "grass fed," the label needs to state 100% grass-fed or pastured. There are many producers who do a mix of grass-fed, then grain-finished. Proponents of the grass-fed movement may be against this, saying grain dilutes the health benefits, but I am more concerned with the overall practices of a farm.

FREE-RANGE—True free-range chickens spend most of their time foraging outdoors. The USDA definition is that chickens only have "access" to outdoors. Commercially raised chickens will tend to stay close to their food and water source rather than stray from the chicken pens. In a pastured model, chickens *do* have food and water outdoors, so they forage naturally in the open. Two independent studies in 2005 and 2007 by *Mother Earth News* found that pastured poultry eggs, or "true free-range" eggs, contained three times more vitamin E, half to a third less cholesterol, and three to seven times more beta carotene, among other health differences.[9] This was in direct response to the commercial stock line stating there is no difference. Again, as is true of many of the swine studies, the commercial studies aren't testing true free-range eggs but rather those from chickens that have limited "access" to the outdoors, housed under commercial conditions.

#4 ASK YOURSELF—ARE YOU PREPARED TO PUT YOUR MONEY WHERE YOUR MOUTH IS?

Time and again, in speaking with local farms producing natural meats, the same comment echoed: People want to see "natural" on the label, but they don't want to pay for it.

"When it comes down to the price they can't afford five times the cost of Wal-Mart. People say they want it until they have to pay for it," says Jake Burns of Carleton Farms in Oregon. He isn't being cynical, but he recognizes with today's rising food costs, price *has* to be an issue. I know lately I regularly drop my jaw at the checkout stand (What did I just buy?!) and that I don't always put my money where my soapbox stands. It's a fact that it costs more money to raise an animal naturally. They grow slower and so need to be fed, housed, and cared for longer. Each animal requires more space, since they aren't housed in confined pens. They also *have* to be handled more gently in terms of their environment and care, because they can't be given a quick fix of antibiotics. Higher staffing costs, more land per animal, higher feed costs, and lower production make it impossible for these growers to compete with the mentality that "meat is meat and the cheaper the better."

Most barbecue restaurant owners and experts agree that starting out with good-quality, fresh meat (not frozen) is key, and most agree that the less food must travel to you, the fresher it is. "The beginning is the most important part of the work," said Plato. Okay, soapbox over. All this talk has gotten me hungry. Hungry for some wild salmon. Turn to the Resources section at the end of the book for some good reading material and websites about sustainability and natural meats.

Chapter Ten

The Pacific Northwest Salmon Bake

Many summers during my childhood we packed up the car and headed out to Arletta on the Washington coast for the annual family salmon bake. The drive seemed endless, despite the fact that it was only about an hour and a half, but as kids we couldn't wait to jump out to Aunt Cookie and Uncle Dick's fantastic beach house. We'd run past the front-yard volleyball net and right through their neat little house to the magical land on the other side: the beachfront. The beach side of the house looked nothing like the proper front of the house. Double doors opened to a wide staircase made of embedded stones, seashells, and bones scavenged from the beach. Down the staircase you walked on paths made of a mix of broken shells and gravel. A winding buffet line on the right made of the same embedded stones and shells snaked around places that would soon be filled with steaming food. All this with the Puget Sound sprawling in the backdrop, the sounds of gulls fighting over mollusks, and the moist salt air penetrating your pores. To the left you first whiffed, then noticed the curl of smoke rising from Uncle Dick's opus—the Salmon Pit.

Uncle Dick remained permanently stationed around the preparation of the feast. I'd see him shoveling coals, laying down corn husks, and buttering huge salmon that would later be plattered and happily gobbled. As a kid I didn't pay much attention to how involved this was, but I did know one key ingredient to the process: seaweed. As kids our job was to wade into the brisk (numbing) waters of Puget Sound and harvest the widest "leaves" of seaweed we could find. With these the adults would wrap the salmon, sealing in the natural sea salts. We took our task seriously. I remember my extreme disappointment one time when we arrived at Cookie and Dick's too late, and I missed the seaweed gathering. The food just didn't taste as good without having participated.

While the salmon slow-cooked in the pit with corn, potatoes, and clams, Aunt Cookie and the other aunts tossed salads, filled deviled eggs, made dips, and set up the rest of the banquet. The kids passed the time hunting for shells and driftwood on the beach, chasing cousins, playing volleyball, and, best of all, sneaking into the living room to look at Aunt Cookie's shell collection. This wasn't off limits, per se, but her collection was one I've never seen matched, so we looked at it with a hushed awe. Inside, an enormous lacquered cabinet housed tiny drawer after tiny drawer filled with shell specimens from around the world. Aunt Cookie found most of her shells washed up right on her beach, but she also traded with others, and she shell-hunted on family vacations. We furtively picked them up and touched the smooth spotted ones, the prickly ones, or the day-glo pink ones that didn't seem real.

A bell called us to the feast. We grabbed tin trays and lined up to follow the curving line to load our plates with roasted corn, slaw, pit-smoked potatoes, clams in butter, salad, and fresh rolls. The salmon carried a salty smoke taste that beat the "regular" broiled salmon any day of the week.

Both Dick and Cookie have passed away. The new owners of the property bulldozed the pit and what was probably an out-of-date seventies outdoor landscape. I asked Dick and Cookie's kids —my mom's first cousins, Drew and Charlyn—about the family salmon bake. I wanted to know first what really had gone on, cooking-wise, and they each gave me specific instructions. This was no casual operation, and Uncle Dick oversaw the preparation like a commander-in-chief. I was also curious about the roots of this family tradition. Where did it begin? When? I found out far more than I bargained for. To my surprise, I found a direct link from our salmon bake to a Puyallup Indian tribe member and larger-than-life personality named Jerry Meeker, founder of the largest community salmon bake of its kind at a place called Browns Point.

THE BROWNS POINT SALMON BAKE

My great-uncle Andrew homesteaded a place at Browns Point near Tacoma, Washington. A beautiful country on the waterfront, this had been a favorite summer place for many tribes to gather and reap the bounty of the sea. In this area, once part of the Puyallup reservation, lived Jerry Meeker, who had been instrumental in helping Native Americans secure property rights for Indian lands. As tribal members sold off plats, white settlers moved in to build summer homes or permanent residences. The community grew and wanted to have a community space before it all became private land. Meeker, a storyteller, businessman, and community developer, hosted renowned clambakes for the local people. Our family pit and salmon bakes were based upon his clambake. In later community salmon bakes he would cook staked salmon on high racks, also traditional to the Coast Salish people[1], which I'll explain in more detail below.

In 1919, the community formed the Browns Point Improvement Club (BPIC), with the goal of raising money to put back into the community in different forms. My great-uncle became the first president of the club, and the salmon bake became the fundraiser that the club relied upon and continues today to rely on to raise money for the BPIC.

It was the first and still is the largest public salmon bake that mirrors traditional cooking techniques. Let me tell you, the grub is good! Today 2,500–4,000 folks line up to feast on alder-cooked salmon and enjoy the band and the bar. Dick Collins, the current head salmon-bake chef, is one of only three head chefs over the sixty-two-year

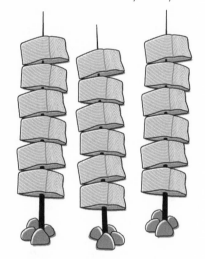

tradition. That continuity keeps this completely oral tradition alive. "There is no manual. I don't know of anything written down. It's just in your genes," said Collins. Many in the crew are third-generation salmon bakers, like him, and all have family roots in the area. While there is no secret society, there *is* the secret sauce. All swear to keep the recipe mum and will clam up if asked. Once a reporter put some in his hand to taste and the contents were slapped down by crew members. "He got a little too close," chuckled Collins.

The salmon is cooked high over brick-lined pits with a mix of green and seasoned alder. They fillet the wild Coho salmon right on site. Pieces are skewered on long, flat, hand-carved cedar stakes, then cooked flesh side down, hung over bars with a chicken-wire catch. Different from the original pit clam-bake methods, this method mirrors traditional Native American staked salmon, adjusted somewhat for large volumes.[2]

I stumbled on this salmon bake by accident, my brother having just moved to the area. He had read about it the day before, and we decided to check it out. A classic case of the younger generation losing touch with family history, my brother and I had no idea he had moved within five minutes of an old family homestead (now gone), or that our own family tradition had grown out of this. The question arises whether somehow we are drawn to these sites from something deep in our cells, like salmon returning to their spawning grounds.

Pit-Cooked Salmon—My Family Style

This won't be something you do for a weeknight dinner, but for a family reunion or other special occasion, the process makes the party. The method derives from Pacific Northwest Coastal Native American clambakes. After digging clams in the early morning, they would dig pits right on the beach and "bake" them with summer bounty like camas bulbs, nuts, roots, mashed berry cakes, and potatoes. Cooking with coals on top, rather than bottom, is the same as pit-cooking whole hogs that are "buried." Many cultures cooked by similar techniques, for lack of cooking pots.

STEP BY STEP

1. Dig a pit approximately 5 feet long x 1½ feet wide x 1½ feet deep. Line with 4–6 inches of fist-size to russet-potato-size rocks.
2. Build a fire. (For review on campfires, see pg. 37.) My family used 4-foot pieces of driftwood off the beach because it was available and because the salt-soaked wood burned "hotter," according to family lore. Most of us do not live on a beachfront, nor is it environmentally correct to burn driftwood anymore. *I suggest a mild wood like alder or apple.*

How much wood depends on how large your pit is and the quantity of salmon you are cooking. Mound the wood in the pit and burn it down to the coals. If you don't have quite enough wood, supplement with charcoal, preferably lump hardwood.

- For 10–20 pounds of salmon: the equivalent of 3 grocery-store bundles of wood, or 18 small to medium sections of cut wood.

- For 20–30 pounds of salmon: the equivalent of 5 grocery-store bundles, or about 30 small to medium sections of cut wood.

1. Gather "layering material": *If* you are on the beach, *and* the waters aren't terribly polluted, *and* it's still legal to do so, gather seaweed—the large ribbon kind works great. Otherwise, a combination of banana leaves and soaked corn husks works great. You will need enough to line the entire pit on the bottom, on the sides, and on top. It's a wet process.

Next use 2–3 soaked sheets to wrap around the salmon and layer between the salmon and the coals: Fill up a tub with about 3 inches of water, pour in a cup of salt, and soak 2 old sheets in the water. You won't be able to use these sheets on your bed again, but you can use them for future bakes. (Buy some used sheets at your local thrift store, first washing them in a mild detergent free of fragrance, bleach, or dyes.) Keep a bucket of salt water near the pit to add if the layering material is too dry as you are lining the pit.

2. Once wood is burned down to coals, shovel coals out into a steel wheelbarrow or bucket. Sweep out the ashes. Leave the hot rocks! Making the fire and burning it down to coals with the large driftwood pieces took from about 8:00 AM to 1:00 PM at the family bake. As you will be using smaller pieces of wood, give yourself 2 hours for this step.

3. *Prepare salmon*: Split down the middle to open up salmon. Coat with light layer of sea salt inside and out. Put slices of butter, lemon wedges, and fresh herbs inside. Close it back up, as you will cook them whole.

4. *Prepare corn and potatoes:* Foil-wrap potatoes. If very large, pierce with fork in a few places. For the corn, remove all but the outer husk. Save the removed husks for layering in the pit.

5. Line the bottom with wet seaweed or wet banana leaves. Place potatoes next. Then place a soaked sheet. Place prepared salmon in the center of the sheet. Wrap each salmon in a layer of seaweed; then fold the sheet on all sides to cover the salmon. Around the sides of the pit, place the corn, clams, and anything else you want to roast in the pit (covered with foil). On top of these layer the second sheet.

6. Layer more seaweed, or banana leaves and soaked corn husks. (Jerry Meeker included ferns and leaves at his bakes, so if you are well enough

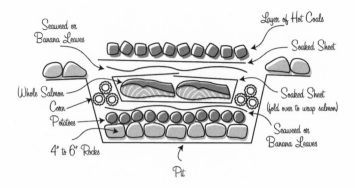

Layer of Hot Coals
Seaweed or Banana Leaves
Soaked Sheet
Whole Salmon
Corn
Potatoes
Soaked Sheet (fold over to wrap salmon)
Seaweed or Banana Leaves
4" to 6" Rocks
Pit

versed in botany to know which ones are edible, go for it.) Add more cups of salt water if any of the layering material seems dry.

7. Put hot coals back on top and spread evenly on the pit.

8. After 2 hours, check under the sheet. My uncle stated it took 3 hours to cook, but how much food you are cooking will vary the time. I also think we like our fish a little rarer than they did in those days. Once fish is done, remove coals, sheets, and layering and pull out the food. Serve immediately.

Hot Rock Tea

Lacking metal pots, Native Americans boiled water and cooked stews in baskets by heating up stones in the fire and placing them in water-filled baskets. As the stones cooled, they would be replaced with new hot rocks from the fire.

Salish-Style Salmon

The Coast Salish people cooked their bounty often right on the beach, in fire circle pits, dug pits, or on the high wooden racks like their East Coast counterparts used. I took the trip to Tillicum Village, a touristy "traditional" salmon bake and show on Blake Island near Seattle. Though clearly made for boatloads of tourists (their numerous references to the gift shop throughout the day were one tip-off), the salmon technique was pretty spot-on traditional.

Doing It Yourself: A Coast Salish–Style Salmon Feast

The Coast Salish people may have developed this style of cooking by using what they had, but the end result is still some of the best salmon you'll eat. It's also festive and a great way to cook salmon for a beach party or communal cookout.

TIP: Before you try any recipe or new technique, read through the entire directions at least twice.

MAKING THE STAKES

You may easily make the cedar stakes for your own Coast Salish–style salmon for about $3 yourself. The stakes can be used over and over again—perfect for beach parties, camping, or a temporary conversion of a back-yard sandbox into a Coast Salish salmon pit.

WHAT YOU WILL NEED:

- Untreated cedar pickets, 1 per salmon you are cooking. Purchase 1–2 extra just in case.

- Square, ¼-inch hardwood dowels. Each dowel makes 2–3 cross sticks. You will need 6–8 cross sticks per salmon you are cooking.

- Circular saw with rip guide, or table saw

- Vice grips or wood clamps

- Knife for whittling cross sticks to a point

Purchase cedar pickets at most home improvement stores or lumber stores. Make sure they are untreated! You don't want to cook with varnish. Each picket cost about $1.25, and you will need one stake set-up per salmon you are going to cook. Purchase ¼-inch dowels—square is preferred.

Secure pickets in vice grips. Remove any staples. Measure 24 inches from the flat end of the picket. Measure to find the center and mark in two spots; then draw a line from the

Hood Canal Kukbuk

The practice of cooking salmon on cedar stakes is documented in a number of local publications. While I based my method on observation, and trial and error, I found some of these explanations wonderfully straightforward, like this entry from a local 1970s cookbook, *Hood Canal Kukbuk*. Hood Canal runs between the Olympic Mountains and Puget Sound, some of the most beautiful land of Washington. The Skokomish people called it home before white settlers took their lands and they moved to the reservation in 1855.

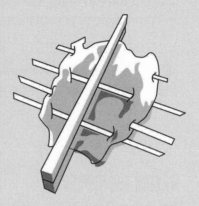

Salmon Sluitum: John Robinson

"Split salmon down the back, cutting along both sides of backbone. Lay open in one piece. Cut a green vine maple or hazel pole about an inch in diameter and 5 feet long. Split the small end down 2½ feet, tying with wire at lower end to prevent splitting. Prepare thin cedar strips as long as a width of the salmon and sharpen at both ends. Insert on alternate sides about 4 inches apart, piercing the skin on each side. Season and insert the salmon between the split halves of the pole and secure with wire above the fish. Stick pole into ground about 2 feet from a bark or alder fire, allowing salmon to tilt toward the fire. Cook from a back side until salmon is slightly pink. Then turn to front side and cook for a total cooking time of 45 minutes. Remove skewer sticks; pour melted butter and parsley over the fish and serve."[3]

The recipe immediately after this one states you can do this indoors with the stakes leaning into your fireplace and a drip pan underneath. This won't work with most modern fireplaces, especially those with carpeting surrounding them, but if you have a country house with a large old fireplace, give it a shot.

24-inch mark to the flat end. Measure ¼ inch on either side of the center line. Draw these lines down. You will cut out this center part, making a narrow prong.

Line up your circular saw on one of the side lines, using a rip guide. Most circular saws come with a rip guide. It is basically a piece of metal that inserts perpendicular above the blade and hooks on to the edge of your wood, guiding the saw along. When you are going across the grain of wood, it is called "cutting," but when you cut with the grain, as you are with these pickets, it's called "ripping." If you have a table saw, this step will be easier because the saw is stationary.

Cut along both interior lines you've drawn. You can punch out the center piece or drill the end out. Using the drill will make it pretty and smooth.

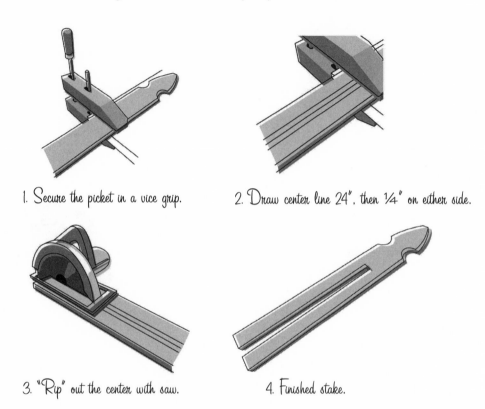

1. Secure the picket in a vice grip.

2. Draw center line 24", then ¼" on either side.

3. "Rip" out the center with saw.

4. Finished stake.

THE CROSS STICKS—Cut your standard-size dowels into three equal parts. If your salmon is large, cut one of your dowels in half. You want the dowel pieces to be at least as wide as the open split salmon. Whittle a point on one side of each dowel piece. This will help the skewer slide across the salmon skin.

BUILDING YOUR FIRE PIT

First—don't reinvent the wheel. Ground fire pits like the kind you find at campgrounds, parks, and beaches work great. You'll want to cook where your party is, however, so you can serve the bounty hot off the fire. In most of these you will need to push your stakes in the ground outside the pits, leaning over.

Dig a 3½-foot circle in diameter, 1 foot deep. Leave about half the dirt in the circle, but tilled so that you can easily push a stake in place. Line a 2-foot circle inside the pit with a row of rocks, for safety.

MAKING YOUR FIRE

Stack wood as if building with Lincoln Logs. Remember those? You place two logs down, then two more on top, in opposite directions, "log-cabin style." Stack about 5–6 rows high. Stuff plenty of newspaper and small-stick kindling underneath, and light. Let fire blaze down to coals and rake in center. While the fire burns to coals, prepare your salmon.

HOW TO BOOK-CUT A SALMON

Native Americans would actually cut the salmon from the back, removing the backbone and opening this way. While it is a more efficient method, unless you are catching the salmon yourself, you won't find a whole uncut salmon in the store because they are all split open to clean.

Your local fish store will book-cut your salmon for you. If you go this route—and no judgment if you do—be clear that you specify "book-cut, not filleted." It *is* satisfying to do yourself, and you get a free salmon burger in the process. Free salmon burger, you say? Read on.

The basic idea of a book cut is to remove the backbone while keeping the skin intact. The salmon will lay flat when open. It is very similar to filleting a fish, but without cutting all the way through.

1. Cut off the head above the collar or have that part done for you. Slit the collar to open up the salmon. Pressing your knife against the bones

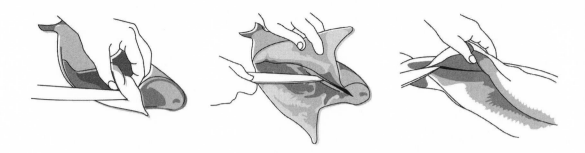

running along the center backbone, cut down the middle, being careful not to cut all the way through. Cut away the bones that connect to the backbone, keeping the knife pressed up against the backbone. Tentative cuts will mangle the flesh. It is better to make a decisive cut all the way down to the tail.

2. Cut down the second side of the backbone. Hold the backbone down while cutting against it, with knife slightly angled up into the backbone.

When you get to the tail, hold up the backbone and cut it out, removing the tail with it. You now will have a backbone with tail, with some good bits of salmon clinging to it.

Free Salmon Burger!

Plenty of salmon bits remain on the bones and parts you cut off. You can easily scrape these off with your knife (scrape as you'd imagine a frontier woman scraping a hide) and get enough salmon to make into a patty. Mix with onions and herbs, and coat with breadcrumbs. Freeze it for another day, so you can pan-fry it for a yummy meal. Salmon is too precious these days to waste a bit of the pink flesh.

PLACING SALMON ON STAKES

1. Lay salmon out flat. Carefully slide the salmon into the cut cedar picket. Keep in mind that the point of the picket will face down—so slide the head end first, so that the smaller tail end will be at the top, farthest from the fire.

2. With the flesh side up, slide 3–4 dowels across the salmon—top, middle, and bottom. Three skewers on each side will be plenty for most 5- to 10-pound salmon you purchase. For extra-long fish, use a fourth pair. Leave enough space between dowels to weave the same number of skewers on the opposite side.

3. Flip over to the skin side and put the next 3–4 dowels in spaces between opposing sticks. The tension of the opposing sticks will hold the salmon in place.

4. Secure the top with wire.

5. Lift the entire rack and take over to your fire. Place it about 1 foot outside of fire. If you have a very large pit with many coals, back your stakes as far as 2 feet. Push picket point into the sand or dirt at a 45-degree angle or slightly less, and tap in place until secure. I first tried this around the fire with pretty hard-packed dirt around. A sledgehammer worked very well, although a large rock could have done the trick in a pinch.

6. If you are worried that the ground is too soft and the racks may slip forward, secure it with rocks and make a Y bar to hold it in place.

COOKING THE SALMON

Place your salmon meat side to the fire. Smoke-roast the salmon for about 40 minutes. Turn and roast with the skin side to the coals for 5–10 minutes. This is just to loosen the meat from the skin. If salmon starts sliding off, remove it immediately. Take the entire rack to a platter. Undo the wire at the top of the stake; then carefully slide the entire salmon off the stake. Remove the cross sticks. Tug them gently to loosen them from the salmon, and then slide them off. You may need to hold your hand over the salmon to keep the cross sticks from ripping the meat. After all cross sticks are removed, brush the salmon with melted butter and a squeeze of lemon.

Chapter Eleven

Smokin' the Kitchen Sink
Cheese, Veggies, Spreads & Seafood

I remember sitting with my Grandma Ruth, in her small Birmingham kitchen that smelled permanently of burnt black-eyed peas and air-conditioned air. Because of an auto accident in her forties, she struggled with a speech impediment. That, combined with a thick Alabama accent, to which I was exposed only every other year for a few weeks, made understanding her difficult for my young northern ears. It always took the better part of a week for me to really *hear* what she was saying. Being early in the visit, we sat there like two foreigners trying to understand a common second language.

She carefully and deliberately unwrapped a box that had arrived in the mail. She was older than my other grandma, with snow white hair, slower movements, and that *feel* of old. But she was far more *there* than my other grandma. For one, she knew how to really laugh. Her laugh began deep inside her belly, traveling outward until her whole body shook, and ended in a coughing spell. When she told a joke, however, she could beat most comedians in a deadpan contest.

Grandma Ruth opened the box and pulled out something that at eight years old I'd never seen before. It was a small covered cheese plate. She turned it around slowly, examining it, then cleared her throat.

"Thirty years," she said. "I've been banking with this comp'ny for over thirty years." She paused, looking up at me. I nodded, looking pleased with this item that certainly looked neat but whose function I hadn't figured out. She looked straight at me, her eyebrows arching just a hair. "And they sent me this . . . fine . . . *cheese* tray." I may not have understood most of what she said, but at that moment I heard the subtle shift in her speech to know that the bank did not impress Mrs. Smith with its gift.

To Grandma Ruth, I dedicate the cheeses of this chapter. May they dress up even the most lowly of free bank gifts. Cheese isn't the only thing—you really *can* smoke it if you've got it. Once you get the bug, you'll want to throw everything next to a pile of coals. Here are a few of my favorites that are versatile. They can be enjoyed as is or used as a part of other recipes.

SMOKED CHEESES, DIPS & SPREADS
Hot-Smoked and Cold-Smoked Cheese
The first time I tried **hot-smoking** cheese, I called out, "Honey, looks like we're having fondue tonight." In other words, I let the temperature get too hot and found a lovely pan of smoked melted cheese goo. It *did* make a tasty snack scooped up with some crusty bread, so I decided to continue my efforts. Most of the hot smoked cheese recipes I'd read recommended a temperature of 200°F–225°F. Since my first fondue  fiasco occurred at 228°F, I shot for 165°F the second time and got decent results. Hot smoking does change the cheese, though. It sweats out the oils and gives the cheese a waxier texture. Over time I've realized I prefer the results from cold-smoking most cheeses, and I reserve hot smoking for low-fat cheeses like Queso Fresco, low-moisture mozzarella, and braided Mujaddal cheese. These don't melt like the higher-fat cheeses do, and they're delicious.

Cold-smoking cheeses will give you results that are like the smoked cheeses in the grocery store, only better. They retain their shape and fundamental texture. Designated cold smokers make the process a snap; however, cold-smoking cheeses on home equipment like a Weber, a charcoal water smoker, or an offset smoker can be done. It just requires more fire management to keep the temperatures in the target range of 60°F–100°F.

Hot-Smoked Cheese

INGREDIENTS

Semi-soft, low-fat cheese like Queso Fresco, low-moisture mozzarella, braided Mujaddal, or feta

BEST EQUIPMENT: Bullet water smokers (charcoal or electric), offset smokers, any charcoal or gas grill.

TOOLS: A remote thermometer is a must-have for this project. Also be sure to fill a water pan with ice to keep temperatures low.

PREFERRED WOOD: Hickory for cheddar is nice; nut woods like pecan are also excellent, or any mild wood

TARGET TEMPERATURE: 120°F–165°F

Electric water smokers, even the low-end Brinkmann, can be managed at low temperatures by turning them off and on. Once you reach about 120°F and have a good smoke going, add your cheese and turn it off for 30 minutes. As soon as it dips down to 90°F, replenish with 1 chunk of wood and turn the heat on for 20 minutes or so until it hits the target again. Keep this up for 2 hours.

Gas grills can be managed the same way as electric smokers. Get one side burner preheated on high, and put a soaked wood chunk directly over that flame. Once smoke is going strong, turn the burner down to low and put your cheese on the other side without any flame. Better yet, if your grill has an upper rack, put the cheese there, as far away from the one low burner. Keep the lid down and vents nearly closed. Continue to turn gas on and off to maintain temperatures. Smoke cheese for 2 hours.

For **charcoal** make your fire small, about 7–10 briquettes or lumps at a time, with 2 small chunks of wood. Keep the fuel pile stacked tightly together in one corner; put your cheese as far apart from the fire as possible. Keep the lid closed and your vents nearly closed. Replenish with ash-gray coals from a secondary fire.

Cold-Smoked Cheese

Try cold-smoking if you have a charcoal smoker like a bullet water smoker, an offset smoker, or, with vigilance, a Weber grill. If you are lucky to have a cold smoker or better model of smoker in which you can set the temperature digitally to hold a temperature under 100°F, then you can easily cold-smoke. Gas grills and most electric smokers will not get low enough for cold-smoking.

INGREDIENTS:

8-ounce chunks of cheese: Try cheddar, Gouda, Havarti, farmer's cheese, mozzarella, or plain Jack

Olive oil (optional)

You may brush or spray your cheese with olive oil to avoid the brown, slightly rubbery skin that occurs when smoking. My husband likes this skin, but I tend to cut it off because some stronger woods, like hickory, can leave a slightly bitter aftertaste on cheese.

BEST EQUIPMENT: Any charcoal smoker like a bullet smoker, an offset smoker, or, with vigilance, a Weber grill

TOOLS: A remote thermometer is a must-have for this project. Fill a water pan with ice to keep temperatures low.

PREFERRED WOOD: Hickory for cheddar is nice; nut woods like Pecan are also excellent, or any mild wood.

STEP BY STEP *(for both Hot- and Cold-Smoked Cheese)*

1. Make your fire for slow and low, indirect heat. Make your fire tiny, about 5–7 briquettes or lumps at a time. Add 2 small chunks of wood. Keep the fuel pile stacked tightly together in one corner; put your cheese as far apart from the fire as possible. Replenish with ash-gray coals from a secondary fire and wood on the hour.

2. Brush your cheese with olive oil (if desired). Put firmer cheese directly on rack, semi-soft cheese in metal pan or in a "foil boat." If smoking a large piece of cheese, cut it up into smaller pieces to get greater smoke coverage.

3. Smoke for 2 hours, checking your thermometer every 15–20 minutes to manage your heat. Let cheese cool while you let your fire die out.

Once the cheese has cooled, put in a covered container. Cheese can store for up to 4 weeks, but it will most likely be eaten long before this. Use in salads, dips, sandwiches, on Grilled Pizza (pg. 114), Smoked Gouda Burgers (pg. 163), or on the Smoked Cheesy Mac.

Smoked Cheesy Mac

Serves 6

Kids and adults will gobble up this mac, which is a perfect application of the smoked cheese above.

INGREDIENTS

12 ounces elbow macaroni
½ stick butter
4 tablespoons flour
2½ cups milk
½ cup heavy cream
2 teaspoons salt
1½ pounds smoked cheddar cheese, grated. (Reserve 1 cup for top if desired.)

STEP BY STEP

1. Cook elbows in salted water. Rinse under cold water and let sit in colander to drain while you make your sauce.

2. *Smoky cheese sauce*: Melt butter and stir in flour. Cook on medium-low heat, stirring, for about 5 minutes or until flour taste is gone. Heat milk and cream in separate pan (do not scald or boil). Add in a little of the warm milk at a time to the butter-flour mixture (called tempering). Cook for 5 more minutes on medium low, stirring. After 5 minutes, making sure there are no lumps, add salt and smoked cheddar.

3. Take off heat. Stir until cheese gets melted in. Add elbows. You may serve it right out of the pot, or pour it into a baking dish, sprinkle the top with 1 cup of reserved cheddar, and bake at 350°F until cheese is melted and bubbly.

Simple Three-Cheese Artichoke Dip with Diced Green Chilies

COOKING METHOD: Slow and Low

The eighties overdid the artichoke-cheese dip, just like sundried tomatoes and pesto. The thing is, though, it's a tasty dip. Rather than throw the baby out with the bathwater, here is a smoked and piquant makeover of that classic.

INGREDIENTS
1 can artichoke hearts, drained and chopped
3 ounces Parmesan (about ½ cup grated)
3 ounces medium to sharp cheddar (about ½ cup grated)
3 ounces mozzarella (about ½ cup grated)
½ cup mayonnaise
½ teaspoon kosher salt
1 4-ounce can diced green chilies
½ cup chopped onions

BEST EQUIPMENT: Any electric smoker or gas grill. For a charcoal grill, make this while smoking a longer meat recipe.
TOOLS: Foil mini loaf pans, olive oil pan spray
PREFERRED WOOD: Nut wood like pecan or walnut

STEP BY STEP

1. Make fire for slow and low cooking and "get your smoke on."

2. Mix ingredients together thoroughly.

3. Scrape into two foil mini loaf pans. Lightly spray top with pan spray oil.

4. Smoke for 1½ hours.

5. Transfer to serving dish. Serve warm with bread or crackers.

Smoked Onions

COOKING METHOD: Slow and Low

Make these when you are smoking longer cook-time items. Smoked onions taste great topped on a steak, chopped in potato salad, or made into the smoky onion dip that follows.

Prepare your fire and "get your smoke on" in a dedicated smoker, charcoal, or gas grill. Halve onions and place on grill, indirect from the heat source. Smoke for approximately 1½ hours.

Smoky Onion Dip

Enough for a party; halve for a smaller group

INGREDIENTS
1 smoked onion (see above)
1 cup mayonnaise
1 cup sour cream
2 tablespoon Worcestershire sauce
1 teaspoon salt
1 teaspoon fresh ground pepper

STEP BY STEP
　　1. Finely chop smoked onion in food processor or by hand. Mix all other ingredients together with the onions.

　　2. For a variation, add 3 tablespoons horseradish.

Smoked Romesco Sauce

....

Enough for a party; halve for a smaller group

COOKING METHOD: Slow and Low

This is one of my favorite sauces. From Tarragona, in the Catalonia region of Spain, it is good simply spread on grilled or toasted bread; it's also good served with a meaty white fish like halibut or with prawns or as a base dressing in a pasta salad. Traditionally the ingredients are oven-roasted, but I like the added layer of smoke. It's also easier—everything can be smoked together, then peeled and ground in the food processor. Roasting requires numerous steps since the almonds, onions, garlic, etc., roast and toast at different times.

INGREDIENTS
¼ cup olive oil
1½ medium tomatoes
6 garlic cloves
½ large yellow onion or 1 small white onion
2 red bell peppers
1 cup cubed firm white bread like baguette, Italian bread, or slightly stale sandwich bread
½ cup raw almonds
1 smoked poblano or ancho pepper (smoke them yourself; see page 54, or purchase dried peppers in the specialty section of your grocery store)
¾ teaspoon kosher salt
⅛ cup red wine vinegar, divided

BEST EQUIPMENT: Any charcoal, electric, or gas grill or smoker
TOOLS: Food processor
SUGGESTED WOOD: Pecan, alder, or grapevines
MAKE AHEAD: If you are smoking your own hot peppers, make these two days to two months ahead.

STEP BY STEP

1. Make fire for slow and low, indirect heat and "get your smoke on." Aim for 200°F–225°F.

2. While it is preheating, pour half of the olive oil in a 9 x 9 or half-size aluminum pan so that it coats the bottom. Arrange your tomatoes, garlic,

onion, bell peppers (cut off tops so they stand up straight), bread cubes, and almonds. Drizzle remaining olive oil over all.

3. Place pan on grill rack, cover, and leave alone for 2 hours, checking only for temperature.

4. While this is smoking, reconstitute your *dried* pepper (smoked peppers are fine as is). Put pepper in a bowl and pour boiling water over it. Let sit, covered, for 30 minutes. Put a small plate on top of the pepper at first, because it will float. After 30 minutes, let cool slightly.

5. Remove pepper stem and seeds. Tear into smaller pieces; then chop finely in food processor or with a knife.

6. Once the remaining ingredients are smoked, cool them slightly; then puree with the hot pepper, salt, and half of the red wine vinegar until you have a thick, textured spread. Add remaining red wine vinegar as you go to thin as desired.

Smoked Eggplant Baba Ganoush

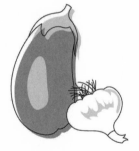

COOKING METHOD: Slow and Low

The smoked eggplant in this tasty Middle Eastern spread adds another dimension to a classic dip.

INGREDIENTS
2 medium eggplants, halved
4 tablespoons tahini
2 large or 3 small garlic cloves, minced
Juice from one large lemon, or 4 tablespoons lemon juice
2 tablespoons olive oil (plus about ¼ cup to coat eggplant prior to smoking)
½ cup toasted pine nuts (optional)
2 tablespoons chopped parsley
¼ teaspoon kosher salt

BEST EQUIPMENT: Any charcoal, gas, or electric smoker
TOOLS: Food processor
SUGGESTED WOOD: Mild wood like grapevine, alder, or apple
MAKE AHEAD: Smoke the eggplant a day before assembling the Baba Ganoush. You can make the entire dip 2–3 days ahead.

STEP BY STEP

1. Make fire for slow and low cooking, shooting for a temperature range of 200°F–225°F. Add just 1 chunk of wood, or ¼ cup soaked wood chips. The eggplant absorbs smoke easily.

2. Halve eggplants and generously coat with olive oil. Place face up on grill, indirectly from heat, and close the lid.

3. Smoke for 1½ hours; remove from heat and let cool for 20 minutes.

4. While eggplant cools, mix tahini, garlic, lemon, 2 tablespoons of olive oil, and salt. Toast pine nuts and chop parsley.

5. Once eggplant is cool, spoon out flesh, discarding skins.

6. Puree eggplant in food processor. When it is halfway done, add the remaining ingredients and process until smooth. Serve with bread or toasted pita, or top crostini for an appetizer.

Christine's Nirvana Smoked Tomato Bruschetta

By Christine Gaffney

....

Serves 4
This is a wonderful starter for a good barbecue. You're firing up the grill anyway, so it just works, and damn—it's so good and takes so little time for such a power flavor opener.

INGREDIENTS

Tomatoes, best you can find. Homegrown, vine grown, or organic.
Hearty crusty baguette, French loaf or ciabatta, cut on a ⅓-inch angle
1 garlic clove
¼ pound Gorgonzola
Olive oil

She's Smokin': Christine Gaffney, What's Smokin' on Your Phone?

My friend Christine formerly owned Christine's Catering Inc. in Seattle where she catered for rock stars and their crews backstage at venues all over town. For years she barbecued backstage at an outdoor desert concert venue called The Gorge Amphitheatre. She did it because the crew loved it but also because she had to: The tiny one-oven trailer kitchen couldn't produce 400–1,000 meals a day without plenty coming off the grill and smoker.

Her ribs once made a pack of Muslim Egyptians traveling with Led Zepplin fall off the no-pork wagon. "They kept sneaking into the catering tent, looking around, then helping themselves to another rib. It finally dawned on me that their religion forbade it and I'd just caused them to sin."

After leaving Washington State she returned to her beloved city of New Orleans (pre-Katrina) and was catering chef for Mat and Naddies, Michael's Catering, where she catered high-end society parties to whole pig roasts for thousands. Her screen saver on her phone? A very large smoked pig with tin-foil ear guards.

"I'd been catering these huge conventions here, and after smoking more than a dozen of these pigs—one at a time, mind you—I needed a souvenir. When I tried to retrieve my lost phone at a car rental place, they asked, 'What's on your screen saver?' I told them, 'A smoked pig with tin-foil ears.' 'Yeah, you right, here ya go, darlin'.' I think it made him hungry." Christine's husband, Shawn, has a crispy smoked quail salad via Susan Spicer from Bayona on his phone screen saver. What's on yours?

Christine, now just smokin' at home, is the chef at The Grill, New Orleans Lawn Tennis Club.

TOOLS: Veggie grill basket or screen to place over grill
PREFERRED WOOD: Mesquite

STEP BY STEP

1. Smoke sliced tomatoes on a grill using a veggie grill basket for about 20 minutes. I use my Weber and just throw some soaked mesquite chips on the fire, slice up those pretty tomatoes, spray my veggie griller with oil, and let them smoke until they get right.

2. Meanwhile, slice your bread of choice and run your pastry brush with olive oil over both sides.

3. Once tomatoes are smoked, take them off the grill and put them aside.

4. Briefly grill your bread on both sides. Turn ¼ inch to make those nifty crosshatch marks on your bruschetta. Remove and take ½ garlic clove and rub each side.

5. Place smoked tomatoes on each slice and top with crumbled Gorgonzola.

6. Return to grill and cover for about 2 minutes until the cheese is all melty. *Smoked tomatoes add a nice touch to salsa, tomato sauce, or chilled and mixed with a fresh shrimp salad.*

NOTE: I call this **Christine's Nirvana Smoked Tomatoes** because she made the best smoked tomato salsa I've ever had, when she catered backstage at the *MTV Live and Loud* taping in 1993. Pearl Jam's Eddie Vedder was too sick that night to play, but the rest of the band members joined Cypress Hill onstage for a jam. The highlight of the evening, though, was an amazing set by Nirvana. I remember not wanting their performance of "Lithium" to end. Though I doubt Kurt Cobain ever tasted the salsa, the roadies scarfed it up with enchiladas that Christine and I had made in the wee hours of the night. So did we, as I recall, washed down with pints of Guinness for breakfast.

Thai Smoked Baby Leeks

By Christine Gaffney

Serves 4

COOKING METHOD: Combination

INGREDIENTS

2 bunches baby leeks or 2 bunches green onions

MARINADE
¼ cup soy sauce
¼ cup rice wine vinegar
½ cup vegetable oil
¼ cup chopped fresh cilantro
1 teaspoon sugar

STEP BY STEP

1. Clean leeks thoroughly.

2. Soak in marinade for as long as possible, up to a day.

3. Make your fire for combination direct-heat grilling and indirect-medium. "Get your smoke on."

4. Shake off excess oil and grill for 3–5 minutes, turning while grilling. Move to indirect side and close lid for 2 minutes.

Smokin' Tofu

COOKING METHOD: Slow and Low

Often my veggie friends complain that there isn't anything for them to eat at barbecues, save for sides or store-bought veggie burgers. They miss out on that charcoal and wood-fire taste to their food. While most of you have probably put some veggies on the grill, try smoking vegetarian dishes to bring out that flavor you miss. This smoked tofu can be eaten as is, added to stir-fries, or skewered with veggies and quickly grilled.

INGREDIENTS
Thai Satay Marinade (pg. 62)
Pressed tofu, refrigerated unwrapped overnight.

 TIP: If you can't find "pressed" tofu, buy extra firm tofu and press it yourself. Just place tofu between two towels on a cutting board, and gently press down to remove excess moisture. Repeat with dry towels once more.

MAKE AHEAD: Leaving tofu to air-dry in the refrigerator overnight will help it keep its shape on the grill. Marinate it 2 hours before smoking.

STEP BY STEP
1. Marinate tofu for 2 hours.

2. Make fire for slow and low heat and "get your smoke on."

3. Place tofu pieces on indirect side of grill and smoke for 2 hours.

SEAFOOD

Seafood readily takes on smoke so even the short cooking times required for fish and shellfish give plenty of smoke flavor. See chapter 10 for Alder-Smoked salmon. Here are three simple recipes that let you practice smoking seafood.

Smoked Clams & Mussels

COOKING METHOD: Slow and Low

Clams and mussels are about the easiest seafood items to smoke. Make these as an appetizer to nibble on when smoking larger cuts of meat. Eat the clams and mussels as is, or add to other recipes like clam chowder, seafood stews, or a chilled smoked seafood salad.

INGREDIENTS
3 pounds clams and/or mussels
Melted butter, if desired, for dipping
½ large lemon, sliced

BEST EQUIPMENT: Any charcoal grill or smoker, electric smoker, or gas grill.
TOOLS: Long-handled chef tongs
PREFERRED WOOD: Alder or any mild wood

1. Make fire for slow and low heat, or preheat gas grill. "Get your smoke on." Keep in mind that you will only get 10–15 minutes of smoke on these, so don't be shy with the wood. Use 3 wood chunks or 1 cup of woodchips. Close lid for 10 minutes until good smoke fills the chamber.

2. Rinse shellfish, discarding any mussels that don't close shut. Remove beards from mussels.

3. Place shellfish directly on grill grate. Close lid for 10–15 minutes. Open lid and put all open shellfish in serving bowl. Discard any that haven't opened. If a lot have not, then give them another 5 minutes and see what shakes awake. Serve with melted butter and a squeeze of lemon. These are good enough to eat plain.

Smoked Trout with Cherry Tomatoes

COOKING METHOD: Indirect-Medium

This trout has so much flavor, I like to serve it with a simple starch like plain couscous or Grill-Roasted Fingerling Potatoes (pg. 97). Make extra and serve the leftovers with eggs at breakfast.

INGREDIENTS
1 whole trout, book cut (see pg. 200 for instructions or have fish market do it for you)
10–15 cherry tomatoes
1½ teaspoons kosher salt, divided
Chopped fresh rosemary (about 2 teaspoons)
Lemon wedges

BEST EQUIPMENT: Any charcoal or gas grill, or any dedicated smoker
PREFERRED WOOD: Alder or grapevines

STEP BY STEP
1. Book-cut trout (see pg. 200 for instructions).

2. Sprinkle 1 teaspoon kosher salt on inside of fish.

3. Make fire for indirect-medium heat and "get your smoke on." Aim for a slightly lower medium heat of 275°F–300°F. Place fish, skin side down, on indirect side and cook for 40–45 minutes with the lid down. Cut cherry tomatoes in half; toss with ½ teaspoon salt and chopped rosemary. Spread on top of the fish. Serve with squeezed lemon.

See the Grilling chapter for more seafood recipes, including the Kiss of Smoke Grilled Fish on page 111.

TIP: Fresh-caught fish should not be cooked for at least one day after caught if possible. The intense adrenaline released in the fight to survive causes the meat to be bitter and tough. Resting a day will relax the meat and drain out the adrenaline for a better taste.

Smoked Sugar-Cured Salmon

COOKING METHOD: Slow and Low

Sugar- or salt-cured fish done traditionally requires no cooking, but I like the combination of lightly curing and smoking the fish. This is a favorite at family brunches.

INGREDIENTS
2 salmon fillets (total about 3 pounds)
2 tablespoons kosher salt
4 tablespoons brown sugar
1 teaspoon chili powder or Cajun spice mix

BEST EQUIPMENT: Any dedicated smoker or charcoal or gas grill
PREFERRED WOOD: Apple or alder

STEP BY STEP
1. Rub inside of fillets with half of the sugar-salt-chili powder mixture.

2. Close the fillets together like a book, flesh to flesh, and wrap with plastic wrap or a plastic sealable bag with as much air removed as possible. Refrigerate for 1 day.

3. Unwrap and discard juices that have expelled from the salmon. Re-apply the remaining mixture. Wrap and refrigerate for 2 more hours.

4. Make a slow and low fire and "get your smoke on," aiming for a temperature of 200°F–225°F. Smoke salmon for 1¼ hours. Serve hot or chilled as an appetizer.

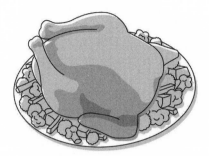

Chapter Twelve

Holiday Barbecue

My Grandma Alida used to love to tell this story:

A mother teaching her daughter how to cook a pot roast instructs, "Cut off both ends and stuff the cut ends around the roast."

"Why do you do that?" asks her daughter.

"Oh, my mother always did," replies her mother.

"We should ask her why," says the daughter, and she does the next time she sees her grandmother.

Her grandmother only shrugs her shoulders. "That's just how my mother taught *me*. We should ask her when we visit her in the nursing home next week."

The following week the three generations of women visit the ancient great-grandmother, bedridden in the nursing home.

"Mother!" shouts the grandmother. "Why do you cut off the ends of the pot roast?"

"Eh?" says the great lady.

"The pot roast, Mother. You always cut off the ends. What is the reason?"

"Ah," nods the great-grandmother. "Because I didn't have a pan large enough to fit a roast!"

It can be difficult to try new recipes at holiday times. You might hear family grumbling and feel your own resistance to changing a steadfast family tradition. You might also be surprised to find that many family members are tired of the same old thing and will welcome something new. If you haven't tried smoking a turkey, a prime rib, or lamb shanks, try it this year. You can mix in new recipes with old to hedge your bet.

Brined Smoked Turkey

INGREDIENTS
One 10- to 12-pound turkey
Citrus & Clove Brine (see pg. 63)

SIMPLE TURKEY RUB
6 tablespoons dried sage
4 tablespoons kosher salt
2 tablespoons fresh ground pepper
2 tablespoons lemon pepper
1 cup olive oil
½ cup butter and ½ cup canola oil for basting
Fruit juice for mopping

BUYING YOUR BIRD—Fresh is best for flavor and juiciness. Order your turkey well in advance (in early October) from your local butcher shop or meat department to be guaranteed a fresh one. Choose a turkey free of additives, moisture added, or flavor enhancers. We are going to brine our bird so we don't want any water or salt solutions already in the turkey. The flavor of organic, free-range turkey is amazing if you can spend the extra bucks.

HOW BIG A BIRD TO BUY—Generally you need 1 pound per person. For plenty of leftovers, factor another ¼ to a ½ pound per person.

For smoked turkeys it is recommended to use smaller birds, under 14 pounds, because of the time it takes for the turkey to reach past the "danger zone" (over 140°F) when cooking on such low temperatures. If you're feeding a larger crowd, smoke more than one turkey.

HOW TO THAW A TURKEY—Thaw turkey in refrigerator, allowing 1 day per 5 pounds of a bird. If you get caught with less time than that, immerse your turkey in cold water (with the wrapper still on) and run cold water over it. Allow 30 minutes of thawing time per pound of bird with this method.

THE PRACTICE RUN
Smoked turkey is great any time of year, so I would encourage you to try it once or twice first, before Thanksgiving Day. You want to work out the bugs and be relaxed when cooking for a crowd.

Step # 1: Brining the Bird

A brine is a combination of water or other liquids, with salt and usually sugar. The saline solution will cause your meat to swell and take on the additional moisture. This will not only make your bird juicy, it will get flavors inside the meat rather on just the outside. To be most effective, you must submerge your turkey fully in the brine for a minimum of 1 hour per pound, and a maximum of 48 hours. I usually brine one full day ahead.

Try the Citrus & Clove Brine or the Basic Brine on page 63 in chapter 4.

Remove the giblets and rinse turkey. Fully submerge meat into brine. Place the turkey, head side down, in a plastic bucket with the brine (you may have to remove a shelf in your refrigerator) or place the turkey and brine in a large food-grade plastic bag and close it securely. Place the bag in a roasting pan for stability. In the first 5 hours, dunk your meat and slosh the brine around to make sure the meat gets covered completely. You may need to place a pot or plate on top of the turkey to keep it submerged.

Step # 2: Preparing the Bird

THE RUB

Remove turkey from the brine and pat it dry. Rub entire turkey, inside cavity and outer skin with olive oil. Rub inside and out with the Simple Turkey Rub above or your favorite rub. You can simply rub with kosher salt and pepper too.

Adding rub under the skin: Turkeys have thick skins, so your rub won't really penetrate into the meat. I like to gently take up the skin and add rub underneath. This technique will also help combat "rubber turkey skin syndrome" in smoking as you will read below.

Starting at the large cavity of the turkey, gently slide your fingers between the skin and the flesh of the breast and legs to loosen skin, being careful not to tear skin. Spread the rub, making sure to shake out any clumps.

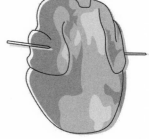

TRUSSING THE WINGS

If your turkey doesn't come "pre-trussed" as many now do, simply push a long skewer from elbow to elbow to pin back the wings.

STUFFING THE BIRD

Due to the low cooking temperatures, stuffing is not recommended because it will slow the inner temperatures. You may, however, stuff aromatic herbs and orange wedges inside.

Step # 3: Making Your Fire

CHARCOAL—Make you fire for slow and low. "Get your smoke on" (see note below). You may also choose to smoke your bird at a higher temperature of indirect-medium (see recipe variation below).

ELECTRIC—Preheat your electric smoker for 15 minutes. "Get your smoke on" (see note below).

GAS—Preheat on high for 15 minutes and "get your smoke on" (see note below). Turn off two burners, and turn the third burner down to 300°F. Place turkey in a roasting pan on top of indirect side of grill.

CHARCOAL AND ELECTRIC—Fill a water pan, and add in ¼ the amount of orange juice if desired. Place the bird, breast side down, directly on the grill.

EASY ON THE SMOKE

A common mistake is oversmoking your turkey. You want to be able to taste the meat, not creosote. Too much smoke will also turn the skin almost black. I use smaller chunks than usual or only ¼ cup of soaked wood chips at a time for the first 3 hours. If you are cooking with charcoal, often this adds enough flavor without added wood. Try it light in your practice run, and add more if you want for the big day.

Step #4: Basting the Bird

After 2 hours, baste the bird in a melted mix of ½ butter and ½ canola oil and brush it on the skin. Thirty minutes later, spray fruit juice like apple or peach juice, and continue to do so every 30 minutes. For gas grills, baste turkey with juices in roasting pan. Baste quickly, as every time you open the lid, you slow down the cooking time.

CRISPING UP THE SKIN

Smoked turkeys notoriously have one fault—rubbery skin. I am an avid skin-picker; here are my tips for crisping up that skin.

1. Separate the skin slightly from the meat. You did this when adding your rub.

2. Butter your bird (also noted in Step #4).

Temperature and Cooking Times

WEIGHT	COOKING TEMPERATURE	TIME	GENERAL RULE
10- to 12-lb. turkey	200-225	5-7 hrs.	30 min per lb.
10- to 12-lb. turkey	275-300	2½-3 hrs	15 min per lb.

WHEN IS IT DONE?
Place an instant read thermometer in the thickest part of the thigh for a reading of 170°F. This will ensure that the breast reads the minimum USDA reading of 165°F after resting.

3. *Cheesecloth butter method:* Cover the entire top of the bird with a butter-soaked cheesecloth. This will help crisp up the skin and keep the color to a nice golden brown. Do this by slightly melting a stick of butter in a sauce pan and adding in 2 layers of cheesecloth. Put the whole pan in the refrigerator until butter hardens. Pull the cheesecloth up and lay over top of bird. A few notes on this method: (1) It slows down the cooking time as much as 1 hour and (2) It's best if you cook it at a slightly higher temperature, 250°F–275°F.

4. Cook the turkey above 250°F. Cooking the turkey at a temperature of 275°F–300°F will give better skin and speed up your cooking time. The downside is you have to be careful not to dry out the bird.

LETTING THE BIRD REST
Rest turkey for 30 minutes before carving.

CARVING THE TURKEY

Having a game plan before you carve a turkey will yield more slices and reduce your stress level. As always, start with a sharp knife. Also use a carving fork.

1. Start with the drumsticks: With the drumsticks facing right (if you are right-handed), hold one leg and cut down between the thigh and body. Use the fork to gently pull the drumstick away from the body as you cut through the joint and skin.

2. Place the drumstick on a serving platter. Cut it in half at the leg-thigh joint. Holding the leg bone, slice meat off the drumstick for dark meat pieces. Cut slices off the thigh as well.

3. Remove the wing. Use the fork to pull wing away so you can see the joint to slice.

4. Before you begin slicing the breast, cut through the breast horizontally until you reach bone. This way your slices will fall away as you cut down.

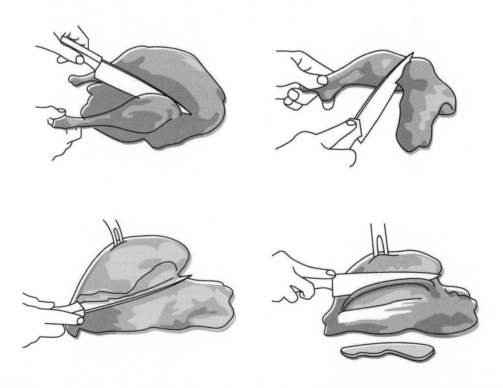

5. Carve down the breast on an angle in thin, even slices. Arrange the white meat together on the serving platter.

6. Repeat on the other side.

Smoked Cornish Game Hen with Polenta Stuffing & Mushroom Gravy

Serves 4

COOKING METHOD: Indirect-Medium

Perfect for a smaller holiday gathering or special occasion, Cornish game hen smokes up deliciously.

INGREDIENTS
4 Cornish game hens

RUB
1 tablespoon olive oil
1 teaspoon kosher salt
¼ teaspoon fresh ground pepper
1 tablespoon chopped fresh savory

POLENTA STUFFING
1 cup milk
1 cup chicken stock or broth
1 cup polenta
1 teaspoon salt
1 tablespoon chopped fresh savory (may also substitute sage or rosemary)

MUSHROOM GRAVY
2 cups chicken stock, heated
16 medium mushrooms, sliced
6 tablespoons butter, divided
4 tablespoons all-purpose flour

BEST EQUIPMENT: Any charcoal, electric, or gas grill or smoker
PREFERRED WOOD: Maple or pecan

STEP BY STEP

1. *Make the polenta stuffing*: Bring milk and chicken stock to a low boil and slowly add polenta while stirring. Stir and cook for 20 minutes. Add salt and savory. Take off heat and put aside.

2. Rinse hens thoroughly and pat dry. Rub olive oil, salt, pepper, and savory on outside and inside cavity. Spoon in approximately 1 cup of polenta per bird. Set aside while you make your fire.

3. Make fire for indirect medium heat and "get your smoke on." Place hens breast side down directly on grill and close lid. Leave them for 40 minutes.

4. *Make mushroom gravy:* While hens are cooking, heat 2 cups of chicken stock on low heat in separate pan. On medium-high heat, sauté mushrooms in 4 tablespoons butter until brown. Add flour and stir. Cook for 5 minutes, stirring constantly so as not to burn. Stir in 2 tablespoons additional butter. Slowly pour heated chicken stock while stirring. Reduce while stirring until it thickens.

5. Remove hens and rest meat for 15 minutes before serving. I like to cut hens in half before plating so guests don't have to, though it lessens the presentation.

Smoked Prime Rib

Prime rib is something people often fear cooking because of its size and expense and the pressure of cooking it to a proper rare/medium rare. Smoked Prime Rib couldn't be easier. The low cooking temperatures make it difficult to overcook, and guests will oooh and ahhh at this special treat.

INGREDIENTS
1 whole or half prime rib (factor 1 pound per person)
3 cups red wine

PRIME RIB RUB

I vary the Basic BBQ Rub as follows:

1 cup kosher salt
½ cup cumin
1 cup chili powder
½ cup paprika
2 cups packed brown sugar

BEST EQUIPMENT: Any charcoal or electric smoker
PREFERRED WOOD: Hickory or maple, blended with a little mesquite
TOOLS: Remote thermometer or instant read thermometer

STEP BY STEP

1. Rub prime rib generously. If smoking a whole rib in a bullet-style smoker, cut in half and smoke one half on each rack.

2. Make fire for slow and low and "get your smoke on." Fill water/drip pan and place under meat.

3. Smoke for 2 hours; then flip and baste with ½ to 1 cup of red wine. Add wood as necessary, about every hour. Baste with wine every 30 minutes.

4. After 3 hours, check internal temperature. I like to insert a remote thermometer in the meat at this time so that I may monitor the internal temperature without opening the lid. Total time will be about 4 hours.

5. For rare, pull at 130°F; medium rare, 135°F–140°F; medium 150°F. Let rest for at least 15 minutes before slicing.

Serve *au jus* (with sauce) or a thin gravy.

Smoked Lamb Shanks with Fig Chutney

Serves 4–6

COOKING METHOD: Slow and Low
These simple, straightforward lamb shanks are a special meaty treat. Save the bones for
Mr. Jones . . . and also for soup the next day.

INGREDIENTS
Mustard Mummy Slather (pg. 54)
4 lamb shanks
Fresh mint
Olive oil
Kosher salt and fresh ground pepper
Fig & Mint Chutney (pg. 68)

BEST EQUIPMENT: Any charcoal or electric water smoker, any offset smoker
PREFERRED WOOD: Grapevines, pecan, or oak
STEP BY STEP
   1. Make your fire for slow and low heat. Use a water pan and "get your
   smoke on."

   2. Make 2 cuts where the meat and bone meet and stuff fresh mint into
   meat.

   3. Rub generously with olive oil, kosher salt, and fresh ground pepper.

   4. Smoke for about 4 hours. Serve with chutney.

Christmas Morning Smoked Scrapple
By The Princess of Pork, Kathy Brown
Independence, Missouri

My grandmother cooked scrapple religiously every Christmas Day. I loved it, and since my mother *didn't*, we ate it only once a year. Brown's recipe adds a smoky twist to this classic.

INGREDIENTS
3 tubes of Corn Meal Mush (or make from scratch)
1 pound plus of Hot J.C. Potter's Country Sausage (from Durant, Oklahoma) or any other good-quality country sausage
1 small Bermuda onion, finely chopped
Honey or maple syrup

TOOLS: Fry pan, 1 washed brick
PREFERRED WOOD: Hickory or apple

STEP BY STEP
1. Mix corn-meal mush with about 1 cup hot water and chop it up to the consistency of corn meal ready to set (thick). Set aside in bowl.

2. Fry sausage and add chopped onion once sausage has just lost its pink color. Do not drain grease.

3. Once onion is soft and sausage is a bit crisped, add to corn meal mush in pot. Mix well.

4. Spoon mixture into a bread loaf pan. Cover with wax paper. Put a brick on top to make it hold shape and set up firm. If you don't have a brick handy, press well into loaf pan. Refrigerate 2 hours to overnight, or freeze until ready to cook. Remove loaf from pan just before placing in your smoker.

5. Make your fire for slow and low and "get your smoke on." Put in smoker directly on the grill rack for 2 hours. Let cool 15 minutes. Slice and serve with honey or maple syrup.

Chapter Thirteen

Accompaniments & Sweet Endings

The matriarch of our family, my Aunt Sandra, could hold three conversations at once and talk each of her conversers under the table. Like her social life, her refrigerator overflowed, almost visibly bulging like a cartoon fridge waiting to explode. Not only did she cram the entire pantry inside (pests are a problem in the Alabama heat), but she saved every scrap for later revival and enjoyment. Lost souls lived, died, and mutated in there. What her refrigerator symbolized to me was her ability to include and feed everyone. She also knew the family history, she was the go-to gal for any genealogy and lore, and she gladly shared her knowledge.

Perhaps surprisingly, Aunt Sandra did not dwell on the past. Family for her was the fabric of life. She planned reunions, picnics, menus, church socials, and all with a sense of creative frugality no one could match. (Her thrift was renowned: At my grandparent's fiftieth wedding anniversary, guests needed only attend a short 15-minute presentation about the property. She of course booked the facility for free.) Those no longer with us were still a part of the living. We even held our annual family picnic in the cemetery so that everyone could be there together, the living and those who had already passed on. We walked to their graves and talked about them, not in sadness of their parting but in the joy of their lives. Then we headed to the picnic to chow down.

When she was first diagnosed with breast cancer, we all knew she could beat it, and she did, at first. Her faith and her ability to laugh at life stood as her greatest armor to cancer. After twenty years of battling myriad cancers, her doctor finally gave her less than a year to live.

"Oh, now that just won't work for me," she told the doctor. "You see, I have my first grandson's graduation from college in the spring, my granddaughter will be born in June, the cruise planned in July, my seventieth birthday in August, and my fiftieth wedding anniversary in September. You're going to have to do better than that."

She did everything on her list, but there came a time when she was ready for the next life, without pain. In true Aunt Sandra fashion, she planned her own funeral. She left behind pages of notes outlining her service, from the speaking line-up to the flower arrangements. But *before* that day, most of the Seattle clan flew out to spend Thanksgiving with the family at a dude ranch in Tennessee. As we drove to the ranch with my Uncle Steve and Aunt Debbie, Aunt Debbie filled me in a bit about Aunt Sandra's latest cancer fight. "She's baffled the medical community. She's one tough lady," she said.

Aunt Sandra had undergone intense chemo the week before, and she spent more time than usual resting in bed. She was a trooper, however, and participated despite what were obviously incredible pain and sickness. She still commanded the feast preparations, though with considerable less air in her sails. As we were departing I made sure to corner her for some face time and a big hug. I knew it was going to be the last time I'd see her, and it was all I could do to hold back the tears. Aunt Sandra, on the other hand, began giving me her slaw recipe, verbatim, for me to try at the restaurant.

Back in the car, I let the tears flow like a spring river. I turned to my Aunt Debbie: "Aunt Debbie, I'm standing there, trying to say goodbye, because I'm pretty sure I'm not going to see her again, and she started giving me her slaw recipe!"

"Mmm," said Aunt Debbie, stroking my hair, "Well, it *is* good slaw."

Family recipes with loads of back story should accompany barbecue. I've shared just a few of my family favorites with some restaurant recipes thrown in as well.

Aunt Sandra's Three-Week Slaw

Serves 10–12

INGREDIENTS
SLAW
1 head green cabbage, about 3 pounds
2 white onions, chopped
1 or 2 carrots, grated
1 green pepper, chopped
1 cup sugar

DRESSING
1 cup apple cider vinegar
1 cup vegetable oil
1 tablespoon celery seed
1 tablespoon salt
1 tablespoon sugar
1 teaspoon dry mustard

STEP BY STEP

1. Shred head of cabbage. Put chopped onion, carrot, and green pepper on top of cabbage. Pour sugar on top and set aside.

2. In a pan, mix the vinegar, vegetable oil, celery seed, salt, sugar, and dry mustard, and bring to a boil. Stir; then bring to a boil again.

3. Pour hot dressing over the dry mixture. Stir and refrigerate overnight.

4. Let stand 3 days; then serve. This will keep up to 3 weeks in your refrigerator.

This recipe is a mix of two versions from Aunt Sandra's daughter Shelli, and Aunt Debbie. Aunt Debbie notes that the original came from the *St. John's United Methodist Church Mission Cookbook,* Birmingham 1989.

Island Slaw

Serves 6–8

My husband and I bump heads about my flair for the inventive when I'm talking to catering clients. I have a bad habit of creating enticing titles to dishes that we've never made. Just as often, we put our heads together and something good comes out of it. A German-theme barbecue? How about a three-cheese streudel for the vegetarians? A Jamaican menu? Thus the Island Slaw was born.

INGREDIENTS
SLAW
½ grilled pineapple (see pg. 90 for grilling fruit)

½ grilled jicama (see pg. 90 for grilling fruit)
½ head green cabbage
¼ chopped red onion
¼ cup chopped fresh cilantro

DRESSING
¾ cup mayonnaise
¼ cup apple cider vinegar
1 teaspoon sugar
1–2 tablespoons barbecue sauce

STEP BY STEP

1. Grill the pineapple and jicama ahead. Dice and combine with shredded cabbage, chopped onion, and cilantro.

2. Mix dressing and pour over slaw. May be dressed 1–2 hours before serving.

Oyi Namul (Cucumber Salad)

Serves 4

My mother-in-law studied Korean at the Army Language School in Monterey, California, while her husband served in the Korean War. In addition to teaching the spoken and written Korean language, the program exposed students to a full cultural program of history, geography, music, art, and food. She wasn't allowed to finish the course because his tour ended, but she still took the exams and graduated, with honors, the second in her class among a high caliber of college kids and officers. Korean food has been a staple in her home ever since. Serve this salad with the Kalbi Beef Short Ribs on page 103, steamed white rice, and some kimchi, if you can handle the heat.

INGREDIENTS
2 medium cucumbers, peeled and sliced
¼ cup green onions, finely chopped
¼ cup soy sauce
¼ cup water
2 tablespoons sesame oil

1 tablespoon rice vinegar

1 tablespoon sugar

3 garlic cloves, minced

1 teaspoon minced fresh ginger

¼ teaspoon cayenne pepper

2 tablespoons sesame seeds, toasted

STEP BY STEP

    1. Mix marinade ingredients together, and pour over cucumber slices. Refrigerate 4 hours.

A delicious alternative to this recipe is *Hobak Namul* (Zucchini Salad). Substitute the cucumbers with 2 small to medium zucchini squashes that have been blanched in boiling water for 1–2 minutes. Put into ice water and slice thinly.

Summer Heirloom Tomato Caprese Salad

I spent a privileged semester studying Italian in Florence. For spring break my friends and I pooled our limited funds together and headed to the Isle of Capri. Even on our student budget, we basked in the Mediterranean spring and swam into shimmering blue or green *grotti*, caves carved out of the island's edge. When we weren't exploring these otherworldly caves, or checking out the *ragazzi* (boys), we dined on the dish of the island: the Caprese salad or sandwich. This salad is no stranger to our shores—many a grocery store deli has made a poor attempt at the thing.

TIP: To chop basil, stack the leaves and then roll them up like a cigar. Chop the "cigar" in thin, angled slices.

The key to a perfect Caprese salad is fresh quality ingredients. It's a summer salad, one that requires ripe-picked tomatoes from the garden or the heirloom tomatoes sold during that short window from July to August at farmer's markets and co-op grocers. Cut up the tomatoes and mix with an equal amount of sliced large Italian fresh mozzarella balls that are stored in water. Drizzle a good extra virgin olive oil, and about half the amount of balsamic vinegar. Toss in a few pinches of kosher salt. Chop up and sprinkle in a few leaves of fresh basil upon serving.

Mom's Biscuits

Makes about 18–24 biscuits

I've made a few digs at my mom's cooking in this book, but her baking is another story. Maybe it's the potter and artist inside her, because my mom knows dough, especially biscuits. What was once a staple growing up we now have to beg her to make ("They're full of all the *bad* stuff," she says). It had been awhile since I made them with her, so I made sure to watch her every move. So much of making biscuits is all in "the feel," as she says, so I've tried to put words to her biscuit feelings. Eat these hot out of the oven, with even more butter if you like, for best results.

INGREDIENTS
2 cups flour
1 teaspoon salt
2 teaspoons double-acting baking powder
2 sticks unsalted butter
⅔ cup ice water

STEP BY STEP
1. Preheat oven to 425°F and grease a cookie sheet.

2. Mix dry ingredients together thoroughly. Cut in cold butter until it looks like corn meal. Incorporate ice water a little at a time with a fork. **NOTE:** Mom said "stir," but stirring is too big a motion for what she does. She pats in the water with the fork.

3. You want to mix gently so as not to overdevelop the gluten in the flour, making the biscuits tough or chewy.

4. Form dough into a ball and pat it down on a floured surface to about ½ inch thick. Cut into a biscuit shape with a flour-dipped drinking glass.

5. Put on a greased cookie sheet. Bake for 10–12 minutes.

Johnnycakes

This recipe came from an afternoon spent in Rangeley Lakes, Maine, carefully writing down Eric's Grandma Helen's recipes while she wove in stories of her life. Johnnycakes are a New England favorite, but their resemblance to hushpuppies makes them an excellent accompaniment to barbecue or smoked fish. This recipe is one that Grandma Helen learned as a bride from her new husband, whom we called Grandy, to appease his "Swamp Yankee" palate. She cooked these on a cast-iron skillet, on a cast-iron Franklin woodstove. The stove is still there in the Maine hunting cabin, though both Helen and Grandy have passed on. Most johnnycake recipes use milk, and some have eggs, but these johnnycakes were from harder times, when fresh eggs and milk were hard to come by. Now we can say they are "wheat and dairy free." The fresh thyme was not in the original recipe, though Grandma Helen loved using fresh herbs from her garden. The beauty of johnnycakes is their simplicity. From this base, you may add cheddar, onions, fresh herbs, or even honey for a sweet cake to complement your menu.

INGREDIENTS
1 cup white cornmeal
1 cup boiling water
2 teaspoons salt
2 teaspoons fresh chopped thyme
Butter, vegetable oil, or lard for pan cooking

TOOLS: Heavy-duty skillet

STEP BY STEP
1. Heat skillet on low to low-medium heat.

2. Mix corn meal and salt; then pour boiling water over it. Mix well and add in fresh thyme.

3. Lightly coat pan with butter or oil. Pour enough batter for a 2- to 3-inch cake.

4. Cook on low heat, turning when one side begins to get golden brown.

5. Serve warm with dinner, or top with maple syrup for breakfast.

Jamaican Festival
....

Makes 12 "Fingers"
A sweet hushpuppy, a Jamaican Festival cuts and complements the jerk seasoning heat. Adding sweet potatoes, while not traditional, makes these good enough to eat alone.

INGREDIENTS
½ cup hot milk
¾ cup cornmeal
Vegetable oil for frying
1 cup all-purpose flour
1 tablespoon baking soda
1 teaspoon baking powder
¼ teaspooon cinnamon
3 tablespoons brown sugar
½ teaspoon salt
1 teaspoon vanilla
½ can sweet potatoes, drained

STEP BY STEP
1. Heat milk and mix in cornmeal. Set aside to cool as you get the other ingredients together.

2. Preheat oil to medium target of 350°F–375°F.

3. Mix dry ingredients.

4. Add vanilla and sweet potatoes to corn meal mixture. Be sure to drain sweet potatoes before adding and squish up into smaller chunks. Mix in with fork.

5. Add dry ingredients to wet until just combined. Overmixing will cause dough to get chewy. Make a long 1-inch-thick roll and cut off 2-inch pieces.

6. Fry up to 6 pieces at a time, for about 5 minutes, turning as necessary until golden brown.

 TIP: Use a candy thermometer to take your oil's temperature. If you don't have one, test one festival "finger" to be sure your oil is at the right temperature. If it is too hot, the outside will burn before the inside is cooked. If it is too tepid, the festival will be oily.

Hushpuppies

Makes about 18 Hushpuppies
A staple side dish along the Eastern Seaboard, hushpuppies go well with pork barbecue or fried fish.

INGREDIENTS
Vegetable oil for frying
1¼ cups white cornmeal
¼ cup flour
¼ teaspoon baking soda
1 teaspoon baking powder
¾ teaspoon sugar
½ teaspoon salt
¼ teaspoon cayenne pepper
¾ cup buttermilk
½ cup grated white onion
1 egg

STEP BY STEP
1. Pour 2 inches of cold vegetable oil in heavy-duty sauce pan and heat to medium. Mix dry ingredients well. Mix buttermilk, egg, and onion in separate bowl.

2. Make a well in the dry ingredients and pour in wet mix. Mix with a rubber spatula until all dry ingredients are incorporated.

3. With a tablespoon or soup spoon, scoop a dollop of batter into oil. Make up to 5 hushpuppies at a time. (Too many will lower the temperature of the oil, making the hushpuppies greasy inside.) Turn over after about 2 minutes. They will take about 4 minutes to cook to a golden brown.

4. With a slotted spoon, transfer to a paper-towel-lined dish, kept warm in the oven. Serve hushpuppies warm.

The Only Potato Salad Recipe You'll Ever Need

The potato gets too much flack for being "white." Those "anti-white-stuff" diets forbidding white sugar and flour write off this incredibly diverse, chock full 'o vitamins, and *forgiving* vegetable that takes on flavors like a champ. With potato salad, your possibilities for variation are endless. Rather than downloading or looking up a new potato salad recipe every time, just use my basic recipe and vary it from there, much like a children's three-part flip book where you can change the head, body, and legs of a character. So here it is . . . drum roll, please . . . the Only Potato Salad Recipe You'll Ever Need:

INGREDIENTS
3 pounds Potatoes (the body)
1½ cups Goo (the legs)
Plus Stuff (the face)

For those of you who just went, "Huh?", I'll explain.

THE POTATO—Changing the variety of potato will give your salad a subtle difference in texture and taste. My "stock" potato is the Yukon Gold; yours may be the faithful russet, or choose one of the hundreds of varieties at farmer's markets across the county.

THE GOO—This constitutes the "wet" dressing of your salad and may include mayonnaise, mustard, sour cream, buttermilk, vinegar, olive oil . . . you get the picture.

THE STUFF—This is everything else that really puts texture, personality, and expression in your salad. Whether you go classic with celery and onions or pickles and hard-boiled egg, go new with fresh dill and red potatoes, or go fancy with caramelized onions, bacon, and blue cheese will change the *face* of your salad. By changing each category, you place a new spin on your salad.

Here is a classic-base potato salad with a list of variations to apply the same formula above.

Classic Picnic Potato Salad

Serves 8–10

INGREDIENTS

THE POTATO
3 pounds Yukon Gold potatoes
3 tablespoons salt in potato water

THE GOO
1/8 cup mustard
1 1/4 cups mayonnaise
1/8 cup dill pickle juice
1 teaspoon salt
1 teaspoon fresh ground pepper

THE STUFF
1 cup chopped celery
1 cup chopped yellow onion
1/2 cup finely chopped dill pickle (or use 1/2 cup dill relish)

STEP BY STEP

NOTE: The most important thing about making a good potato salad lies in the cooking of the potatoes. Undercooked potatoes make all your yummy STUFF irrelevant because the salad is ruined. Overcooking makes the salad a cold mashed potato salad. Here are some tips to making the perfect salad potato:

1. As best you can, use uniformly sized potatoes so they cook in relatively the same time. If you are using a variety of potatoes like the red, white, and blue potatoes for the July 4th salad below, cook the potatoes separately. Not only is there a difference in size, potatoes vary in consistency and starch content, which affects the cooking time.

2. Start your POTATOES in cold water and bring to a boil. This is so the potatoes will cook evenly.

3. Salt the water. This way the salt will soak into the potatoes, not sit on top after they are cooked.

4. Cook POTATOES whole, for approximately 45 minutes. For very small potatoes, back this off to 30 minutes or less depending. Cut very large potatoes such as russets in half or quarters. *How to tell if they are done*: You want to be able to push a skewer smoothly in the potato, without any gritty resistance, yet not have it swoosh through so easily that the potato might fall apart in the skewering.

5. Rinse POTATOES under cold water; then cool completely in refrigerator in a single layer.

6. Once POTATOES are completely cold, remove skin, if desired, and dice in bite-sized chunks.

7. Mix GOO ingredients and pour over potatoes.

8. Mix STUFF together and add in.

9. Let potato salad chill for a few hours to let the dressing fully settle in. Sample it before serving to be sure it has enough salt for your taste. I always go on the slight side of salt for recipes because you may always add more.

Here are just a few variations.

#1 CLASSIC ADDITIONS—Add this STUFF to the above recipe: sweet pickles instead of dill and 6 chopped hardboiled eggs. Swap sweet pickle juice for the dill in the GOO.

#2 NEW POTATO SALAD—POTATO: Use red or new potatoes. Do not peel the red potatoes. GOO: Substitute ¼ cup sour cream for the mustard and pickle juice. STUFF: Swap red onion for the yellow and add fresh chopped dill. Follow the rest of the Classic Picnic Potato Salad recipe.

#3 FANCY—POTATO: Use a more exotic farmer's market potato if desired. GOO: 1 cup mayonnaise, ⅓ cup sour cream, ¼ cup buttermilk, plus salt and pepper. STUFF: 4 cups caramelized onions, ½ cup cooked chopped bacon, 4 ounces crumbled blue cheese, and ½ cup candied pecans (below). Reserve some of the pecans for garnish on top.

TIP: To caramelize onions, heat up pan and add ⅓ cup olive or canola oil on medium heat. Once oil is hot, add onions and sauté for 2 minutes while stirring. Turn down to low and slowly cook for 20–25 minutes until onions are nicely brown and sweet because they have released their sugars.

#4: PATRIOTIC—This is a fun one for the Fourth of July. POTATO: Use 1 pound each red, white, and blue potatoes. If red and white potatoes are different sizes, cook separately. Cook blue potatoes separately and add 2 tablespoons of vinegar to water to retain color. Do not peel the red potatoes, as these give the red color to the salad. STUFF: Use a mix of red and white onion. Follow the rest of the Classic Picnic Potato Salad recipe. Garnish with blue corn chips around edge of bowl.

#5: SICILIAN—This is based on a recipe in *One Potato, Two Potato*, by Roy Finamore & Molly Stevens[1], which brings up a point on variations. Scroll through websites like Epicurius.com for STUFF and GOO ideas; then apply them to your base recipe. GOO: Instead of a mayo-based GOO, use ½ cup extra virgin olive oil, 1 tin of canned sardines in oil, or the equivalent of sun-dried tomatoes in oil if you don't like sardines. The tomato, olives, and capers in the STUFF will add moisture as well to get our base recipe ratios on par. STUFF: Substitute red onion for the yellow. Add 1 cup chopped tomatoes, ⅔ cup chopped olives, 4 tablespoons drained capers, plus 2 teaspoons fresh oregano, ⅓ cup chopped Italian parsley, and ¼ teaspoon red pepper flakes. Nix the pickle.

The Get-Sloshed-While-You-Make-It Warm German Potato Salad

My sister-in-law is Czech, and my oldest brother now lives in Prague with his family. She and I immediately hit it off, as we both have a fondness for cooking when accompanied with plenty of wine and gab time for the cooks. At one of our parties, this German salad took on a life of its own, and in the end we had enough to feed fifty hungry men in lederhosen. We were of course operating without a recipe and started with way too many potatoes. The potatoes soaked up batch after batch of the vinegar, bacon drippings, and mustard GOO like an ever-thirsty sponge. Open a bottle of gewürztraminer before you start and make this salad with a good friend.

INGREDIENTS
3 pounds potatoes (any white or yellow variety)

GOO
1 cup sweet pickle juice
½ cup white distilled vinegar
4 tablespoons spicy brown mustard
Bacon drippings (save them from bacon below)
1 teaspoon salt
1 teaspoon fresh ground pepper

STUFF
1 cup fried bacon, chopped (about 10 pieces)
1½ large sweet onions, caramelized
½ cup finely cut peeled apple
½ cup sweet pickle, finely chopped

STEP BY STEP

1. Cook POTATOES and chill for 20 minutes (see instructions in previous recipe).

2. Fry 5 pieces of bacon on medium low heat to make it crispy and to render the fat. Pour off bacon grease. Fry 4–5 more pieces. (Leave the bacon drippings in the pan.) Put bacon on paper-towel-lined plate and set aside. Chop onions, and caramelize in the bacon oil left in pan on medium low.

3. Chop the apple and sweet pickle. *Prepare the dressing*: Mix sweet pickle juice, vinegar, mustard, salt, and pepper.

4. Dice the slightly chilled potatoes and put in large bowl. Mix in the onions, leaving the drippings in the pan. Add the apple, sweet pickle, and chopped bacon. Pour the GOO mixture into the pan where you just caramelized the onions. Warm up to medium and then pour over the potato salad. Add more salt to taste once all ingredients have been mixed in. Serve warm.

Bar Basics

For any party with a bar, feature a few specialty drinks, and have *some* standards on hand. Keep your guest list in mind, and if there are any stodgy Scotch drinkers or an old friend who insists that her wine be "sweet and pink," keep a small stash away from the crowd. Choosing a theme for cocktails like "Pink Drinks" or "Drinks with Dirty Names" is fun and does not require you to stock the whole bar. If it's a straight beer crowd, be sure to have a light choice and a microbrew and/or import choice. I know at my wedding I stocked Bud Light specifically for a few family members who drink the stuff like Kool-Aid, and I had a nice German beer for my husband's family. They all got along quite well, since they held their favorite beer in hand. Finally, please buy ice: Nobody buys enough ice. It takes a minimum of three bags of ice to fill one medium cooler full of drinks initially, with more needed for re-stock. If you are using bus tubs or non-insulated containers, and it's a hot day, you will need an initial two bags per bus tub plus one bag per hour for restocking. It's just a fact in catering that at some point, there is an ice run.

Jamaican Black Beans with Sweet Potato

Enough for a crowd

These beans draw you in with sweet innocence, then give you a back kick of spice. It's not a burn or a front-of-the-mouth heat, and the dish pairs nicely with the Jerk Pork on page 139 or Donna Moodie's Jamaican Jerk Chicken on page 110. This will mellow with time. Add leftover jerk pork or chicken and you have chili for the next day.

INGREDIENTS
1 pound dried black beans, soaked overnight
7–9 cups water
⅓ cup olive or canola oil
1 large red onion, diced
1 tablespoon cumin
1½ teaspoons allspice (Jamaican allspice if available)
½ teaspoon ground cinnamon
2 teaspoons salt, divided
2 smoked or dried reconstituted habanero (more if you like it hot)
2 smoked or dried reconstituted poblano peppers (see pg. 54 for smoked pepper recipe)

1 15-ounce can sweet potatoes in syrup (don't drain)

3 tablespoons brown sugar

Optional garnish: Top with diced grilled mango and/or chopped cilantro before serving

STEP BY STEP

1. Soak beans overnight by doubling the water level to the beans.

2. Drain and rinse the next day.

3. Sauté red onion in oil until just soft; add cumin, allspice, cinnamon, and 1 teaspoon salt. Add 1 chopped smoked habanero pepper (remove seeds before chopping), and reconstituted dried poblanos.

4. Add black beans and coat with spice mixture. Add can of sweet potatoes with syrup, brown sugar, and 1 whole smoked or dried habanero and stir. Add 5 cups of water and bring to a low boil for 15 minutes.

5. Turn down to medium-low and simmer for approximately 8 hours. Add water as needed. Speed it up by turning up heat slightly, but keep a close eye on the water and stir. In the last half hour of cooking, add another teaspoon of salt.

Cowboy Beans

This is pretty close to the Cowboy Beans we serve in our restaurant. We wanted a bean that was tasty enough to serve with barbecue yet vegetarian to make it an easy catering side. You may of course add smoked ham hocks for additional flavor.

INGREDIENTS

1 pound dried pinto beans

⅓ cup canola oil

1 cup chopped onion

4 garlic cloves, finely chopped

2 fresh jalapeños, finely chopped

1½ teaspoons cumin

1½ teaspoons chili powder

2 teaspoons salt, divided

1 15-ounce can stewed tomatoes, chopped

3 tablespoons prepared mustard

3 tablespoons brown sugar

3 tablespoons molasses

1½ tablespoons apple cider vinegar

4–6 cups water

STEP BY STEP

1. Soak beans overnight by doubling the water level to the beans. Drain and rinse the next day.

2. In a large pot, sauté onions in oil for 2–3 minutes; add garlic and jalapeños. Stir for a few minutes and add in cumin, chili powder, and 1 teaspoon salt. Add beans and coat thoroughly.

3. Add can of tomatoes, mustard, brown sugar, molasses, apple cider vinegar, and 4 cups of water.

4. Bring to a low boil for 15 minutes; then turn down to medium low for approximately 8 hours. Add water as needed. In the last ½ hour of cooking, add another teaspoon of salt.

THE SWEET STUFF
Candied Cayenne Pecans

These addictive little nutters will please your palate with the sweet of the sugar and the kick of cayenne. Put them in salads, like the Fancy potato salad (pg. 244) or a wild greens salad, or just munch on them solo.

INGREDIENTS

4 cups water

1 pound whole pecans, shelled

4 cups sugar, divided

¼ teaspoon cayenne pepper

Canola oil for deep frying

TOOLS: Deep fryer or deep skillet, parchment paper

STEP BY STEP

1. Boil 4 cups of water. (While waiting for water to boil, heat oil in deep fryer or deep skillet on medium heat.) Once water boils, toss in pecans and continue to cook on high for 2 minutes; then remove and drain.

2. Toss immediately in 2 cups of sugar. Pour pecans in hot oil and fry for 2 minutes.

3. Remove with slotted spoon or slotted spatula spoon, shaking off excess oil, and toss in bowl with the remaining sugar and ¼ teaspoon cayenne pepper.

4. Let cool on parchment-paper-lined cookie sheet.

Sweet Tea

In the South, if you order tea, it comes cold and syrupy sweet. Simple to make, this tea gives you a refreshing afternoon pick-me-up, far better than a latte on a hot day.

Step by Step: Pour a pot of boiling water over 3 tea bags, preferably Lipton. Pour in 1 cup of sugar and stir. Let steep for 15 minutes, remove tea bags, then chill in refrigerator.

Grilled Apple Tart Tatin

COOKING METHOD: Combination Direct-Heat Grilling and Indirect Medium

One summer in Alaska, I made this dessert often. Eric and I quit our city jobs and headed to the Redoubt Bay wilderness area to work in an eco-lodge. Guests flew in via float plane to eat at the lodge—the only structure in 180,000 square miles—and to go bear viewing or fishing with the guides. The food we cooked came in with the planes, and our garbage flew out in the floats to keep our camp free of hungry brown and black bears. During the height of the season we served two back-to-back lunches of twenty to thirty guests each, in a small one-room log-cabin lodge with barely a two-butt home-sized kitchen. One-pot meals were the norm. In the evening, however, we served a smaller group of overnight guests and could cook more elaborate fare. This one-pan, one-burner dessert was simple and perfect for cooking in tight quarters. I'm sure I started with *The Joy of Cooking*'s recipe, one of the only cookbooks at the lodge, but I tweaked it over time. Now I like to make it right on the grill. *(Incidentally, you can't grill or barbecue in the bush. Nothing is a louder dinner bell to the abundant wildlife in Alaska. The minute your food hit the grill, you'd have a beary big problem on your hands.)*

INGREDIENTS
PASTRY
1 stick chilled unsalted butter
1 cup all-purpose flour, sifted after measured
¼ cup plus 2 tablespoons pastry flour, sifted after measured
1½ tablespoons sugar
¼ teaspoon salt
3 tablespoons shortening
3 ounces ice water (¼ cup plus 2 tablespoons)

FRUIT FILLING
5–6 apples, a firm slightly tart variety like Macintosh or Braeburn
1 cup sugar
1 stick butter
Optional: Powdered sugar garnish

TOOLS: Food processor, cast iron pan

STEP BY STEP
1. *The pastry dough*: Measure flours by leveling off exact quantities, then sifting in bowl. Slice cold butter and put in food processor with flour, sugar, and salt. Pulse 5–6 times. Add shortening, turn on low, and add ice water. Once water is in, pulse a few more times until dough is just mixed in and starting to clump. If it is crumbly, add a few more drops of water. Turn dough onto floured work surface and gently form into a ball. Wrap in plastic and chill for 1–2 hours. (For more detail on how to make pastry dough, read Julia Childs' *The Way to Cook*, the *Joy of Cooking* section on pastry dough, or your favorite baking book. [2, 3])

2. After dough has chilled at least an hour, roll out on floured surface into a circle about 2 inches larger than your cast-iron pan. Sprinkle with flour;

then fold in half and half again. Set aside on plate in refrigerator while you prep your fire and apples.

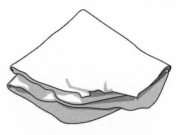

3. Prepare fire for direct heat or preheat gas grill for medium-high heat. If you are using charcoal, lump charcoal is preferred because it burns hotter, with less ash. While coals are starting, quarter and core apples; then cut each apple into 8–10 slices.

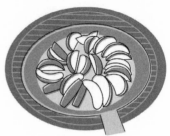

4. Bring out apples, sugar, butter, pan, hot pads/oven mitts, and tongs to grill area. Place pan directly on grill grate and melt butter. Add sugar and stir. Arrange ¾ of the apples in a ring and in the middle.

5. Let mixture boil for 5 minutes; then turn the apples over, maintaining the ring shape. Fill in remaining apples in any spaces. Cook down until butter and sugar mixture caramelizes to an amber color. This can take 20–25 minutes. *Be patient.* Pulling it too early will result in a loose tart that won't hold its shape. Stay with the tart, using your tongs to spoon the juices over the top apples and gently pushing the apples down in place. Take care that the mixture does not boil over, causing sugar to burn on the fire. Pull off the fire before the amber color turns dark. The difference between perfect and scorched is a matter of minutes.

6. Remove tart from fire. *For charcoal*: Lift top grill grate, wearing hot pads, and rake coals to one corner of your grill. Add 10–15 fresh coals to the fire and return grate. *For gas*: Turn off one or two burners so you have enough room to fit pan on indirect cooking side.

7. Get dough out of refrigerator. Place point of dough in center of pan and unfold over apples. Tuck dough into inside of pan. Remember: The pan is still hot! Put tart back on grill, on the indirect side, and close the lid tightly. If you have a remote thermometer, place it next to tart to see if you are close to the target temperature of 375°F. Bake on grill for 30 minutes or until crust is golden brown. Rotate once during cooking to be sure both sides are cooked evenly.

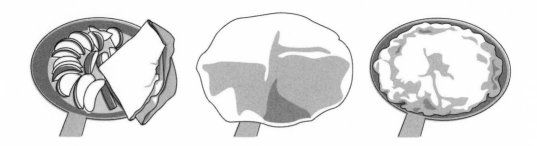

8. Let cool for 20–30 minutes. Place serving plate over pan and turn upside down. Give it a gentle thump and lift off pan. Replace any apples that may have stuck to the pan. Sprinkle with powdered sugar before serving.

Blackberry Cobbler

After salmon, the food that most exemplifies the Northwest is blackberries. While our true native species produce quite small amounts in comparison, the introduced European variety grows so abundantly that it is being considered for the Washington State Noxious Weed list.

I'll never forget when my granddaddy in Birmingham proudly took me to his garden and showed me his blackberries. I was about ten and looked at his puny berries, about half the size of the scrubby bush fruit that grew in every vacant lot and back alley at home. At the time, I didn't know why he would show me some blackberries. It was only later that I realized I'd never seen blackberries cultivated in a garden and that it probably represented a great feat of gardening to grow them in the Alabama heat. Granddaddy liked to make his cobbler and pie syrupy sweet. Even with a kid's sweet tooth, I had to cut it with vanilla ice cream to eat it. But he made it with such care and love, and he watched with a smile while I ate it. My recipe is not nearly as sweet as Granddaddy's cobbler, but I've always thought of it as equally a Northwest and Southern dessert.

INGREDIENTS

FRUIT FILLING

1½ cups sugar

2 tablespoons cornstarch

1¼ cups boiling water

6 cups blackberries, fresh or frozen

TOPPING

2 cups all-purpose flour, sifted

2 tablespoons sugar

3 teaspoons baking powder

1 teaspoon salt

1 stick cold unsalted butter

1 cup buttermilk

STEP BY STEP

1. Grease a 9 x 13 dish and preheat oven to 400°F.

2. *Fruit filling*: Combine 1½ cups sugar and cornstarch, and stir in boiling water. Stir over medium heat and boil for 1 minute. Add berries and bring back to a boil for 1 minute. Pour into buttered pan.

3. *Topping*: Sift together flour, sugar, baking powder, and salt. Cut in the butter, working it with your hands until butter chunks are no larger than a pea. Stir in the buttermilk until a soft dough forms.

4. Drop by spoonfuls over the berry mixture and bake for 30 minutes. Serve with vanilla ice cream, whipped cream, or milk. *Mmmm.*

Mom's Pie Crust
....

Enough for one pie, top and bottom

My mom's pie crust is the kind you can snitch raw. It's the little bit of sugar, and no skimping on the butter, that makes hers stand out. She always put cinnamon and sugar on the leftover pie dough scraps and baked them as a treat for her little helpers.

INGREDIENTS

2 cups all-purpose flour

1 teaspoon salt

½ teaspoon baking powder

1 tablespoon sugar

⅔ cup chilled unsalted butter

2 tablespoons shortening

¼ cup ice water

STEP BY STEP

1. Mix dry ingredients together. Cut in ⅔ cup cold butter and shortening with a fork until it looks like cornmeal. Incorporate ice water a little bit at a time until you can gently form into a ball with floured hands. Divide into 2 balls.

2. Place in middle of a floured board. Using a floured rolling pin, start at the center and roll out to edges in a sun pattern, until dough is ¼ inch thick. Roll your dough a little larger than your pie tin.

3. Reflour rolling pin and roll dough up onto the pin to transfer to the pie tin. Roll the dough back out over the tin. Pat in the dough and prick it in a few places.

4. Add any pie filling, then repeat the steps for making a pie top. Crimp bottom and top crusts together.

5. For a no-bake pie like the Chocolate Cream Pie below, just make a bottom shell and crimp, prick bottom, and bake at 425°F for 10–12 minutes until golden brown.

Chocolate Cream Pie

Makes one pie

My dad's a pie guy, and my mom, as you may have gathered, makes some serious pie. I'm not sure if one made the other so, or whether it was always a symbiotic pie relationship. He loves banana cream pie, but if my middle would allow it, I'd take Chocolate Cream Pie any day of the week.

INGREDIENTS
FILLING
½ cup sugar
3 tablespoons cornstarch
5 egg yolks
2½ cups whole milk
¼ teaspoon salt
3 tablespoons unsalted butter
½ teaspoon vanilla
3 tablespoons cocoa
2 cups chocolate chips

TOPPING
1 cup heavy whipping cream
¼ cup sugar
Dark chocolate bar

STEP BY STEP

1. *Pre-bake pie shell*: Make *half* of the Mom's Pie Crust recipe above. Crimp along edge, prick bottom, then bake at 425°F for 10–12 minutes until golden brown.

2. *Make filling:* Whisk together the sugar, cocoa, cornstarch, and egg yolks until pale in color. Set aside.

3. Heat milk and salt over medium heat until just below boiling. Take off heat and temper the yolk mixture (add a little at a time) into milk. Return to heat and bring mixture to a boil for one minute to fully thicken.

4. Remove from heat and whisk in butter, vanilla, and chocolate chips. Pour custard into a bowl and cover with plastic wrap, allowing it to cool slightly before you add it to the prepared pie shell.

5. Add custard to the prepared pie shell and cool completely in fridge.

6. *Top pie:* Whip cream until almost stiff; then add sugar in gently. Spread evenly over pie in swirls. Top with shaved chocolate as a garnish.

Peach Pie

Makes one pie

One of my favorite memories of visiting our Alabama relatives was their large peach tree in the back yard. It seemed so exotic. We picked those enormous sweet peaches right off the tree, peeled the skin off with our teeth, and bit down. You knew you'd picked a peach at the peak of perfection by the amount of juice dribbling down your arm. You can't get a peach in the grocery store that requires you to eat it outside, slightly hunched over to avoid a river of juice on your shirt. In Seattle for a short window in the summer we get Wenatchee peaches like the Alabama variety at roadside fruit stands and farmer's markets. The rest of the year, we must buy IQF (individually quick frozen) peach slices. Take note of the slight differences in this recipe for using fresh vs. frozen peaches.

INGREDIENTS

2 pounds sliced peaches, fresh or frozen
½ cup sugar
1 tablespoon cornstarch
½ tablespoon lemon juice
Pinch of salt
1 egg, for pie-crust wash
Optional: Pinch of nutmeg or cinnamon

STEP BY STEP

1. Follow the directions for Mom's Pie Crust, above.

2. In a large bowl mix peaches, sugar, cornstarch, lemon juice, and salt. If using fresh peaches, drain off excess juice (into a cup and drink it!) if, after cutting, the peaches are swimming. If using frozen peaches, let them thaw just a little before mixing ingredients.

3. Spoon filling into pie crust; then top with dough and crimp edges together. Egg-wash top and make 6–8 small slits in crust. Bake at 375°F until juices are thick and bubbling. *Note*: To make an egg wash, whisk one egg with a tablespoon of water. Once combined, use a pastry brush to lightly brush pie crust.

She's Smokin': On Turning Forty

Almost a year ago I experienced an almost clichéd "Oh, my god, I'm turning forty soon" crisis. Years previously, I had set the goal of publishing a book by the time I reached the Big 4-0, and with only a few months to go, it didn't look like it was going to happen. Between a restaurant and a toddler, my writing time got sandwiched, and it wasn't a very meaty sandwich.

I don't soul-search quietly. I recall hollering at my husband at 2:00 AM with a spreadsheet in hand, "I've figured it out! We'll sell everything and move out to the woods. I'm serious. I can make soap until the first few book contracts start earning. You can forage for chanterelles, honey!" My husband calmly nodded, knowing this was not the time to bring up practical points with me: "Whatever it takes, babe."

The second part of my turning-forty crisis had to do with a second child. In theory I wanted another baby, but we'd had difficulty conceiving our son, and I didn't see how we could fit a second child in our chaos. Forty loomed as a final line in my mind. I come from a large family, though, and the thought that my son would not have a sibling made me a little sad. I let the dream go, so I said. The maternity clothes and baby clothes, however, never made it to Goodwill.

I got myself out of this pre-forty funk in two ways. The first was that I said my daily mantra, "A writer writes," and reinforced my writing time with steel girders. No more wimpy sandwich time. I began submitting to publishing houses and saw an interesting call for submissions from Seal Press: *Looking for women with expertise in the following areas: Auto Repair, Camping, and Barbecue.* As a writing exercise, I submitted materials to them. I thought

Psssssst! Remember when I said there are no real secrets in barbecue? Well, I fibbed. There is a secret to making great barbecue. Ready? Okay, here it is:

KNOWLEDGE + PRACTICE + A LITTLE LUCK

Don't tell anyone I told you. I hope you've enjoyed the journey, sister. Let me know about it, ask me questions, or tune into my blog: shesmoke.blogspot.com

Website: www.shesmoke.com
email: julierbq@q.com

they were planning a humorous anthology and that perhaps I had a slim chance of writing an essay for them.

The second thing I did was dye my hair pink, purple, and red. It was on my list of Things I Haven't Done, and an easy one to check off. If I wasn't going to have another baby, then it was time I lost the mommy ponytail and spruced things up a bit.

My fortieth birthday came and went. We had a lovely party. A few weeks later, however, I got the email from Seal Press. It said they were interested in my writing a book on barbecue for women. Wow! My dream book and, *hello*, only a few weeks past my fortieth birthday.

In the excitement and initial stages of writing the book, I didn't notice something else was happening too. The week the book contract arrived, so did the results of my pregnancy test.

"Oh, my god," I thought. "Oprah is right. You *can* just manifest it. I should read that *Secret* book."

As I wrap up this book, a new chapter begins. Miss Eloise kindly waited until I finished the book to be born. It is fitting that I've had a girl while writing a book for women. As the only girl in a sea of brothers, I was so excited for a daughter. I can pass on girl stuff to her.

I can't help but think back to my mother, my grandmothers, and great-grandmothers, all the way back to that early woman, using sticks, rocks, and what little else she has to cook a meal of roots, grubs, and a hunk of meat brought back from the hunt. She cooks the meat slowly over a low fire because, well, those wild beasts are pretty tough. Maybe she throws in some aromatic herbs to the fire. And then she smiles, with smoky tendrils dancing in her hair, and utters the words "*Bah bah coo,*" meaning "It is good."

Theme Menus

I'm a theme dork. A party theme, even it if it is just in the menu, makes it all come together. Here are a few menus using the recipes in this book to help you plan your event.

Menu #1 Classic Carolina Pork Pickin' Party

Let your guests participate in pulling the pork and voting on their favorite sauce. Divide the pork into three parts and add a different sauce to each.

Smoked Pork Butt. Factor 10 ounces per person from raw weight (pg. 118).
3 Carolina Sauces: North Carolina Eastern, Lexington, and South Carolina Sauce (pg. 71–73)
Buns, served with Pickle and Onion Tray
Aunt Sandra's Three-Week Slaw (pg. 234)
Hushpuppies (pg. 241)
Cowboy Beans (pg. 248)
Smoked Corn on the Cob (pg. 176)
Peach Pie (pg. 257)
Beverage: Sweet Tea (pg. 250) and Beer
Other Party Ideas: North and South Carolina trivia; blues, bluegrass, and
    country music

Menu #2: Texas Two-Step Party

Texas Two-Step Brisket (pg. 151)

Texas All-Nighter Sauce (pg. 75)

Classic Picnic Potato Salad (pg. 242)

Cowboy Beans (pg. 248)

Fire-Roasted Corn Salad (pg. 93)

Fresh Fruit Salad or Cut Fruit Plate

Beverages: Sweet Tea (pg. 250), whiskey drinks, and Shiner Bock beer

Other Party Ideas: Cowboy hats and Western wear, country music, Texas hold 'em tournament, swing dancing

Menu #3: Jamaican Island Party

Choose one or two meats:

Buried Jerk Pork (pg. 139)

Donna Moodie's Jamaican Jerk Chicken (pg. 110)

Jamaican Jerk Dino Bones (pg. 157)

Island Slaw (pg. 235)

Jamaican Black Beans (pg. 247)

Jamaican Festival (pg. 240)

Grilled Pineapple (pg. 90)

Beverages: Red Stripe beer, mango iced tea, other fruity concoctions

Other Party Ideas: Island-theme decor, reggae music

Menu #4: Pacific Northwest Salmon Bake

Choose a salmon cooking technique from the Salmon Bake chapter: Coast Salish–style racks or pit-cooked salmon, chapter 10

Smoked Mussels & Clams Appetizer (pg. 216)

Roasted or Smoked Corn

Pit-Baked Potatoes

Green Salad

Fresh Rolls and Butter

Beverages: Northwest wines and microbrews

Other Party Ideas: Summer party with volleyball, baseball, or beach activities

Menu #5: Pacific Rim Menu

Thai Chicken Satay appetizer (pg. 96)

Kalbi Beef Short Ribs (pg. 103)

Smoked Duck with Orange-Currant Glaze (pg. 178)

Oyi Namul salad (pg. 236)

Jasmine White Rice

Dessert: Ginger ice cream

Beverages: Jasmine tea, Soporo beer, sake

Other Party Ideas: Volcano centerpiece, Pacific Rim volcano trivia

Fall Dinner Party

Smoked Pork Loin with Grilled Apples (pg. 135)

German Potato Salad (pg. 245)

Johnnycakes (pg. 239)

Grilled Balsamic Greens (pg. 91)

Dessert: Grilled Apple Tart Tatin (pg. 250)

Winter Dinner Party

Smoked Pork Tenderloin with Drunken Port Sauce (pg. 133)

Mom's Biscuits (pg. 238)

Grilled Vegetables (pg. 89)

Dessert: Smoked Cheese Tray (pg. 204) with figs and fresh fruit

Spring Dinner Party

Appetizer: Smoked Romesco and/or Smoked Eggplant Baba Ganoush served with fresh
  bread (pg. 210)

Smoked Lamb Shanks (pg. 230)

Greek Salad (not in book, but you know how to do this)

Grill-Roasted Fingerling Potato Skewers (pg. 97)

Dessert: Chocolate Cream Pie using Mom's Pie Crust (pg. 254–255)

Summer Dinner Party

Appetizer: Smoky Onion Dip with Chips (pg. 209)

Ego-Stroking Baby Back Ribs with Apricot-Zing Glaze (pg. 129)

Smoked Gouda Burgers (pg. 163)

Condiments Tray with Lettuce, Onion, Pickles, and All the Fixin's

Summer Heirloom Tomato Caprese Salad (pg. 237)

Fire-Roasted Corn Salad (pg. 93)

Dessert: Blackberry Cobbler (pg. 253)

Glossary of Terms

BARK—The crust that forms on the outside of barbecue meats like pork butt and brisket from the combination of spice rub and slow and low cooking.

BASTE—To moisten meat with liquid, often with the drippings of the meat. Basting and mopping are basically the same action.

BRINE—A combination of water or other liquids, with salt and usually sugar. Originally used to preserve meats by pickling them, brines add moisture to meats before cooking.

BRISKET—The chest meat of the cow. A tough piece of meat that requires low temperatures and long cooking times to make it tender.

BRISKET DECKLE—Another name for "the point," but also refers to the fattier meat in this part of the brisket.

BRISKET FLAT—Also called the "plate," this is the thin, flat section of a brisket. Often you can just buy a flat vs. the whole packer (see "whole packer").

BRISKET POINT—The thicker section of the whole brisket. Sometimes called the "deckle," it sits on top of the "flat."

BULLET—Name given to some smokers because of their bullet shape. Some examples are the WSM (Weber Smokey Mountain) and the Brinkmann line of water smokers.

BURNT ENDS—The yummy ends of a brisket that get essentially overcooked. Because the ends are thinner, there is a greater concentration of spice rub, making them very flavorful. Some restaurants will "create" burnt ends by re-smoking parts of the brisket to satisfy their customers' hunger for the burnt wonders.

CHARCOAL CHIMNEY STARTER—A cylindrical metal unit with an open grate at the bottom and a heat-resistant handle made for lighting charcoal with ease.

DEDICATED SMOKER—Any rig, grill, or oven designed specifically for cooking slow and low barbecue.

DIRECT HEAT—Cooking over the flames, be they charcoal fire, gas, or wood.

DRIP PAN—A pan placed under the food being cooked to catch drippings. The drip pan can also serve the dual purpose of a water pan.

FACHO—The feminine of macho.

FAT CAP—Layer of fat covering a whole brisket.

GET YOUR SMOKE ON—To add wood chunks or chips to your ready/preheated charcoal, gas, or electric fire. Close lid for 10 minutes to smoke it up before placing food on grill.

INDIRECT HEAT—Cooking foods away from the direct flames. Usually food is placed on one side of a grill, with the fire on the other side, or in a separate "firebox."

MARINADE—A combination of acid (such as vinegar or wine), oil, and seasoning used to soak flavor into foods and soften them with time.

MOP—A thin sauce to baste your meat throughout the cooking process, usually done with a small cotton mop. Though the actual mop gives this application its namesake, a common tool used for mops is a spray bottle.

OFFSET FIREBOX—A separate chamber for the fire from the main grill. Typically the offset firebox will set slightly lower than the main compartment so that smoke travels up into the cooking chamber. Having a separate firebox allows you to manage your fire without opening the grill lid, thereby minimizing heat and smoke loss.

OFFSET SMOKER—A smoker designed with an offset firebox.

PELLETS—Compressed wood sawdust that may be burned as fuel for cooking barbecue.

PIG PICKIN'—Any gathering where pork is pulled directly off a whole cooked hog. Typically the pitmaster will do the pickin' for his or her guests.

PIT—Any grill, oven, rig, dug trench, or smokehouse that cooks with wood as the primary fuel.

PLANK CUT—As in "plank-cut vegetables." A cut along the length of the vegetable in thick slices, about ¼". This gives you a sturdy slice to grill.

PLATEAU—See "Stall."

PULLED PORK—Shredding smoked pork by hand vs. chopping it or slicing it.

REMOTE THERMOMETER—A thermometer with a long cord from the probe to the readout, allowing you to monitor the temperature inside the grill or meat without lifting the lid.

REST—Letting meat sit for typically 10–30 minutes before cutting. This allows the juices, which when hot were pushed to the surface of the meat, to drain back into the meat so that it is juicier upon serving.

RIB RACK—A metal rack for stacking multiple racks of ribs on their side, allowing one to increase the number of racks smoked at once. While there are many for sale, a common rib rack is just a roasting V-rack turned upside down.

RIG—A large mobile smoker unit, typically used for large caterings, competition barbecue, or parked outside of restaurants.

RUB—A spice mixture applied to meat before cooking.

SEAR—To brown meat quickly on direct high heat at the beginning of the cooking time to seal in flavor.

SLATHER—A wet paste, usually done with mustard, used to help the rub "stick" to the meat.

SLOW AND LOW—Cooking at low temperatures, between 185˚ and 250˚, for a long period of time.

SMOKE CHIMNEY—Many dedicated smokers have a chimney placed above the food that draws the smoke across the food, creating a smokier environment and allowing the smoke to escape more slowly than vents. There are those that brag chimney size overzealously.

SMOKE RING—A pink or red ring inside slow-cooked meat (just past the bark) caused by a chemical reaction between the smoke and the meat. Smoke rings make us happy.

SMOKER—Any grill, pit, or oven designed specifically for smoking meats at low temperatures. These come in a variety of of designs and for fuel may use wood, charcoal, wood pellets, gas, or electricity.

STALL—The period of time in which a large, tough piece of meat, like a pork shoulder or brisket, breaks down the connective tissue and becomes tender. The internal temperature "stalls" during this time, not reaching readiness temperature. Time for the stall can be anywhere from one hour to many.

TRIM—The act of removing fat, tendons, or parts of the main cut of meat. For example, some may remove all or part of the fat cap of a brisket before smoking.

WATER PAN—A pan filled with water or a mix of liquids, placed next to the coals and/or under the meat. Water pans combat the drying effect of smoking by replacing humidity into the smoker. Water is also a great temperature regulator and can help maintain even temperatures within the smoker.

WATER SMOKER—A smoker with a built-in water pan, for the purpose of regulating temperature and adding moisture to the cooking chamber.

WOOD CHIPS OR CHUNKS—Pieces of wood used to burn and create smoke on a grill or smoker.

WSM—Weber Smokey Mountain, a popular bullet water smoker.

Resources

My Favorite Barbecue Books by Women

The BBQ Queens, Big Book of Barbecue, by Karen Adler and Judith Fertig. Boston, MA: The Harvard Common Press, 2005. As sassy as their Love Potion for the Swine sauce, the Queens are well known on "the circuit" and feature recipes from barbecue babes from all over the country as well as their own. They'll grill and smoke just about everything, and this (truly) big book tells you how, with humor and wit to boot. The Barbecue Queens together and separately have written over twenty books covering grilling and barbecue topics.

Championship BBQ Secrets for Real Smoked Food, by Karen Putnam. Toronto, Ontario: Robert Rose, Inc., 2006. "The Flower of the Flames" of BBQ, Karen Putnam is barbecue royalty. Read her book. Hands down my favorite barbecue book. It is so well organized, has truly great tips, and satisfies the full range of barbecue levels, from beginner to champion.

Smoke & Spice: Cooking with Smoke, the Real Way to Barbecue, by Cheryl Alters Jamison and Bill Jamison. Boston, MA: The Harvard Common Press, 2003 (revised edition). This well-known duo won the 1995 James Beard Award for this book, and the follow-up, *Sublime Smoke,* is excellent, too.

Taming the Flame, by Elizabeth Karmel. Hoboken, NJ: John Wiley and Sons, Inc., 2005. I like Karmel's focus on the fire and smoke. Each chapter features slow-smoking recipes and grilling recipes to give a full range of cooking options. She has a great website too: www.tamingtheflame.com.

The Way to Cook, by Julia Child. New York, NY: Alfred A. Knopf, 1989. Okay, not a barbecue book, but Julia rocked. She wasn't afraid to sling some meat around either. Hers is such a comprehensive book on cooking technique, it's a treasure trove of information and funny to boot.

More Great Barbecue & Grilling Cookbooks or Related Cookbooks

The Barbecue! Bible, by Steven Raichlen. New York, NY: Workman Publishing Company, 1998. Raichlen has created an entire barbecue universe. This is just one of his many barbecue books; also be sure to catch his PBS show, *Barbecue University,* or check out his website for great tips: www.barbecuebible.com.

The Barbecue Bible, by Linda Tubby. London: Hermes House, 2006. A barbecue book done by a Brit, this cookbook may not be as hard core in its distinction between "barbecue" and "grilling," but Tubby knows the difference. Wonderful recipes with photos and detailed instructions.

How To Grill, by Steven Raichlen. New York, NY: Workman Publishing Company, 2001. One of the most clear, concise, and complete how-to books on grilling. Large, up-close color photos of steps make this a must-have for beginners and veterans alike.

Jerk from Jamaica: Barbecue Caribbean Style, by Helen Willinsky. Berkeley, CA: Ten Speed Press, 2007 edition. Experience the Jamaican contribution and influence on barbecue first hand in this book.

Legends of Texas Barbecue Cookbook, by Robb Walsh. San Francisco, CA: Chronicle Books, 2002. Full of history, lore, and great recipes from one of the great bastions of barbecue—the state of Texas.

The Meat Club Cookbook (Girls only), by Vanessa Dina, Kristina Fuller, and Gemma DePalma. San Francisco, CA: Chronicle Books, 2006. Not a barbecue cookbook, but a cookbook for women who love meat. These gals know their meat and aren't afraid to quilt about it. You'll want to join the meat club, too!

North Carolina Barbecue: Flavored by Time, by Bob Garner. Winston-Salem, NC: John F. Blair Publisher, 1996. Almost mandatory in any barbecue library.

Paul Kirk's Championship Barbecue, by Paul Kirk and Bob Lyon. Boston, MA: The Harvard Common Press, 2004. Though Kirk gives explicit instructions for those who want to compete, you can enjoy the 575 recipes by the "Baron of Barbecue" without leaving your backyard. His extensive slathers, rubs, and marinades alone can keep you busy at the barbie year-round. Try any of Kirk's many books.

Peace, Love, and Barbecue, by Mike and Amy Mills Tunnicliffe. New York, NY: Rodale Books, 2005. I'm a sucker for a story, and Mike Mills weaves his family story and love throughout this also fantastic barbecue cookbook.

On-the-Road 'Cue Books
Barbecue America, by Rick Browne and Jack Bettridge. Alexandria, VA: Time Life Medical, 1999.

Real Barbecue: The Classic Barbecue Guide to the Best Joints Across the USA, by Vince Staten and Greg Johnson. Guilford, CT: Globe Pequot Press, 2007.

Smokestack Lightning: Adventures in the Heart of Barbecue Country, by Lolis Eric Elie. Berkeley, CA: Ten Speed Press, 2005. I love the writing in this book. Elie takes us on a journey from one 'cue joint to the next, each a dark and smoky den of sauce with tales of its owner.

History of Cooking, Barbecue & Eating; Historical Cookbooks; Contemporary Food Writers Who Draw Upon the Past
African American Foodways: Explorations of History & Culture, edited by Anne L. Bower. Chicago, IL: University of Illinois Press, 2007. Essays and commentaries chronicling the influence of African slave cooking and how it serves as a base for our modern American cuisine.

The Carolina Housewife, by Sarah Rutledge. Columbia, SC: University of South Carolina Press, 1979. A facsimile of the original, *The Carolina Housewife by a Lady of Charleston,* 1847, with an introduction by Anna Wells Rutledge, 1979.

Cornbread Nation series, books 1–4, by The Southern Foodways Alliance and Contributors, edited by John Egerton. Chapel Hill, NC: University of North Carolina Press: Center for the Study of Southern Culture, University of Mississippi, 2002–2008. I love this series. Essays and articles by some of the best food writers on the planet.

How To Cook a Wolf, by M.F.K. Fisher. New York, NY: North Point Press (Farrar, Strauss and Giroux), 1942. The heavyweight champion of food writers, Fisher enjoyed a renowned friendship with James Beard.

Larissa's Breadbook, Baking Bread and Telling Tales with Women of the American South, by Lorraine Johnson-Coleman. Nashville, TN: Rutledge Hill Press, 2001. Barbecue and bread making seem kindred spirits to me, and bread making remains even today largely in the female domain. Male bread makers fight the same stigmas women have at the grill. The stories and recipes in this book just make you want to bake bread with your girlfriends.

A Love Affair with Southern Cooking, by Jean Anderson. New York, NY: Harper Collins, 2007. Food writer, historian, and champion Jean Anderson writes the story behind each recipe in this collection. History timelines of food and agriculture fill the side bars, from the cotton gin to the Gin Fizz, from Colonel Sanders to Coca-Cola. If you love cookbooks and food history, trawling *her* bibliography for titles is like finding a gold mine.

Mrs. Hill's Southern Practical Cookery and Recipe Book, by Annabella P. Hill. Columbia, SC: University of South Carolina Press, 1995. A facsimile of the original, *Mrs. Hill's New Cook Book,* 1872 edition, with historical commentary by Damon L. Fowler.

Savage Barbecue: Race, Culture, and the Invention of America's First Food, by Andrew Warnes. Athens, GA: University of Georgia Press, 2008. A fascinating discussion on the origins of barbecue.

Serve It Forth, by M.F.K Fisher. New York, NY: North Point Press (Farrar, Straus and Giroux), 1937. Feisty Ms. Fisher knew about food.

Smokehouse Ham, Spoon Bread, & Scuppernong Wine: The Folklore and Art of Appalachian Cooking, by Joseph E. Dabney. Nashville, TN: Cumberland House Publishing, Inc., 1998.

A Thousand Years over a Hot Stove, by Laura Schenone. New York, NY: W.W. Norton and Co., 2003. A beautiful book telling the story of women through cooking.

What Mrs. Fisher Knows about Old Southern Cooking, by Abby Fisher. Bedford, MA: Applewood Books, 1995. With historical notes by Karen Hess. First published in 1881 by the Women's Cooperative Printing office in San Francisco. Noted as the first African

American cookbook, Fisher's story is one of incredible success out of dire beginnings. She overcame slavery, made the arduous trip out west (during which she birthed one of her eleven children), became known for her award-winning recipes at fairs and society in San Francisco, and then published a cookbook without the ability to read or write.

About Buying Natural Meats, Shopping Locally & Sustainable Farming

The Farmer and the Grill: A Guide to Grilling, Barbecuing and Spit-Roasting Grassfed Meat, by Shannon Hayes. Richmondville, NY: Left to Write Press, 2007.

Holy Cows and Hog Heaven: The Food Buyer's Guide to Farm Friendly Food, by Joel Salatin. Swoope, VA: Polyface, Inc., 2004.

The Omnivore's Dilemma: A Natural History of Four Meals, by Michael Pollan. New York, NY: Penguin, 2007.

Pasture Perfect: The Far-Reaching Benefits of Choosing Meat, Eggs, and Dairy Products from Grass-Fed Animals, by Jo Robinson. Vashon Island, WA: Vashon Island Press, 2004.

Some Favorite Websites, Blogs & Forums

www.amazingribs.com—Craig "Meathead" Goldwyn's website and blog. Full of right-on, straight-from-the-smoker information. I especially like his use of the word "porknography."

www.barbecuebible.com—Steven Raichlen's huge website of barbecue and grilling tips and information.

www.bbq-4-u.com—BBQ Central's forum, complete with podcasts of BBQ Central radio show archives.

www.chilefire.com—an obsession with spice.

www.eatwild.com—Jo Robinson's extensive website about grass-fed and pastured meats. See above for information about her book, *Pasture Perfect.*

www.sustainabletable.org—a website that clarifies sustainability and takes it from idea to actual resources.

www.weberbbq.com—Plenty of great barbecue and grilling information on this site. I particularly like the site's Annual Grillwatch Survey, which tracks trends and topics of everything grill.

Barbecue Association Links

California Barbecue Association—www.cbbqa.org
Florida Barbecue Association—www.flbbq.org
International Barbeque Cookers Association—www.ibcabbq.org
Iowa Barbeque Society—www.iabbq.org
Kansas City Barbeque Society—www.kcbs.us
Lone Star Barbecue Society—www.lonestarbarbecue.com
Mid-Atlantic Barbecue Association—www.mabbqa.com
National Barbecue Association—www.nbbqa.org
New England Barbecue Society—www.nebs.org
North Carolina Barbecue Society—www.ncbbqsociety.com
Pacific Northwest Barbecue Association—www.pnwba.com
South Carolina Barbeque Association—www.scbarbeque.com
Texas Gulf Coast BBQ Cooker's Association—www.tgcbca.org
World Barbecue Association—www.wbqa.com

Equipment Companies & Related Equipment

The Big Green Egg, www.biggreenegg.com, 3417 Lawrenceville Hwy., Tucker, GA 30084-5802, 770/934-5300.

Brinkmann, www.brinkmann.net, The Brinkmann Corporation, 4215 McEwen Rd., Dallas, TX 75244, 800/468-5252.

Char-griller, www.chargriller.com, PO Box 30864, Sea Island, GA 31561, 912/638-4724.

Cookshack, www.cookshack.com, 2304 N. Ash St., Ponca City, OK 74601-1100, 800/423-0698.

Hasty-Bake Ovens, www.hastybake.com, 1313 S. Lewis, Tulsa, OK 74104, 800/4AN-OVEN.

Pitt's & Spitt's of Austin, www.pittsandspitts.com, 10016 Eastex Fwy., Houston, TX 77093, 800/521-2947. Higher-end Texas smokers with an excellent reputation.

Traeger Pellet Grills, www.traegergrills.com, 800/872-3437.

Weber-Stephen Products, www.weber.com, 200 E. Daniels Rd., Palatine, IL 60067-6266, 800/474-5568 (for grilling questions), 800/446-1071 (for customer service).

Cedar wraps or papers, www.barbecuewood.com. A full line of grilling papers. Also available in alder, cherry, maple, pecan, and white oak. Set of 10 for $14.95 and up depending on size. See below for full contact information.

Remote external thermometers, A few that I like or that others have recommended to me:

> **Comark:** www.comarkltd.com. I use this standard remote thermometer. I can set the alarm to sound when my temperature gets too low or high.

> **Tel-Tru:** www.teltru.com. Tel-Tru offers a full line of barbecue remote thermometers, plus replacement thermometers made for specific brands like Weber and the Big Green Egg.

Grill baskets, These are available in most home improvement stores for less than you will find at kitchen stores.

Fiskars Roll-Sharp, www.fiskars.com, enter "house wares." This is the manufacturer's site, and getting to the housewares section is not very direct. To find where to buy the Roll-Sharp, try your local culinary or craft stores for distribution, or try E-bay.

Charcoal & Wood Suppliers

Barbecue Wood, www.barbecuewood.com, PO Box 8163, Yakima, WA 98908, 800-DRYWOOD (800/379-9663). Your one-stop online barbecue store for wood, grills, and barbecue accessories.

Maine Grilling Woods, www.mainegrillingwoods.com, 33 Lakeview St., Lincoln, ME 04457, 207/794-8232. A full range of sustainably harvested woods. They have bulk boxes and smoker dust for stovetop and electric smokers, and they offer free shipping.

Nature's Grilling Products, www.naturesgrilling.com, 706 Front St., Suite 2, Louisville, CO 80027, 720/890-8797. See interview in Chapter 1. They have briquettes, chunk wood charcoal, wood chunks, and chips.

Pimentowood.com, www.pimentowood.com, 9303 Plymouth Ave. N, Suite 101, Golden Valley, MN 55427, 612/868-JERK. Pimento wood from Jamaica for your jerk barbecue. Practices sustainable harvesting.

Western Cookin' Chunks & Smokin' Chips, www.woodinc.com. 1799 Corgey Rd., Pleasanton, TX 78064, 830/569-2501. Ron Lawson of Western Cookin' Chunks gave me some guidelines for picking good charcoal. There shouldn't be sparking—this means the charcoal contains moisture. Too much smoke means too much wood is left in the mix.

Though they no longer carry their lump charcoal made in Kentucky from renewable resources, they harvest their mesquite, pecan, and hickory locally and carry a few green products. What I liked about them is they admitted that harvesting sustainably was not their original focus but that "as a business with a long-term business plan, it happened naturally." Alder comes from Pacific Northwest mills and fruit trees from Illinois farms that are already clearing orchards for new species.

The Rainforest Alliance's Smartwood program recognizes companies that have Forest Stewardship Council certification or use products with certification to create something new. Search their database at www.smartwood.org, email them at info@ra.org, or call 212/677-1900.

International

Basques Hardwood Charcoal, www.basquescharcoal.com, 121, rue Saint-Alphonse, Sainte-Luce, Québec, Canada, G0K 1P0, 418/739-4894 ext. 151, or 800/463-0909. Canadian charcoal, mostly sugar maple. No trees are expressly cut for charcoal. They use cuttings and trees not fit for the lumber specifications, and mill scraps. No treated wood from cabinetry or furniture is used in their charcoal. They also sponsor a few barbecue competition teams, one of which is the female-led team Diva Q, who are winning big on the circuit. See chapter 6 for an interview with the Diva herself, Danielle Dimovsky.

The United Kingdom has a long tradition of making charcoal that is making a comeback. They stress "bioregional charcoal" to keep U.K. 'cuers in the smoke without cutting down rainforests halfway around the globe. Two companies on the forefront of the movement:

> **The Bioregional Charcoal Company,** www.bioregionalhomegrown. co.uk, BedZED Centre, 24 Helios Rd., Wallington, Surrey, U.K. SM6 7BZ, 020/8404-2300, email: brcc@bioregional.com. Certified by the Forest Stewardship Council.

The Dorset Charcoal Company, www.dorsetcharcoal.co.uk, Tudor Cottage, Pidney, Hazelbury Bryan, Dorset DT10 ZEB, 012/5881-8176. Find great articles about the dangers of imported charcoal from the South American rain forests.

Kamado Lump Charcoal, www.kamado.com, 877/257-6871 or 619/819-5120. Sustainably harvested tamarind and "coconut charcoal" made from coconut meat. Follows strict guidelines from Indonesia. While it is not local in terms of shipping it to the United States, it *is* an international source that is meeting certain standards.

Bulk Spices, Salts & Barbecue Sauces Online

Atlantic Spice Company, www.atlanticspice.com, 2 Shore Rd., North Truro, MA 02652, 800/316-7965.

Monterrey Spice Company, www.herbco.com, 719 Swift St., Suite 62, Santa Cruz, CA 95060, 800/500-6148.

Mountain Rose Herbs, www.mountainroseherbs.com, PO Box 50220, Eugene, OR 97405, 800/879-3337. Bulk certified organic herbs and spices.

Simply Cajun, www.simplycajun.com, 221 Belle Maison Dr., Lafayette, LA 70506, 337/989-1758. Online store for authentic Cajun and Louisiana products, or for a giggle at the pickled pig lips for sale.

www.bbqsauceofthemonth.com—Great site that showcases small-run barbecue sauces and rubs from around the country, many from competitive barbecue teams.

Salt Works, www.saltworks.us, 15000 Wood-Red Rd., Suite B-900, Woodinville, WA 98072, 425/885-7258. Great prices and selection. Most quantities are in 55-pound bags, so get a few friends to split.

Bibliography & Notes

Introduction
1. Ragir, Dr. Sonia. "Diet and Food Preparation: Rethinking Early Hominid Behavior." *Evolutionary Anthropolgy: Issues, News, and Reviews,* Vol. 9, Issue 4, 2000, pp. 153-155.
2. ibid.
3. ibid.

Chapter 1: Tools of the Trade
1. Weber 19th Annual Grill Watch Study (2008).
2. Consumer Affairs Directorate, "An Investigation into Barbecue Accidents," 2000. U.K. Dept. of Trade and Industry, p. 12.

Chapter 3: Barbecue Smoke & Mirrors
1. Clayton, Lawrence, ed. *The De Soto Chronicles. The Expedition of Hernando de Soto to North America in 1539-1543.* Tuscaloosa, AL: University of Alabama Press, 1993.
2. Warnes, Andrew. *Savage Barbecue: Race, Culture, and the Invention of America's First Food.* Athens, GA: University of Georgia Press, 2008, p. 48.
3. Hill, Anabelle P. *Mrs. Hill's Southern Practical Cookery and Recipe Book,* Columbia, SC: University of South Carolina, 1995. A facsimile of *Mrs. Hill's New Cook Book,* 1872 edition.

Chapter 4: Meat Mixology

1. Putnam, Karen. *Championship BBQ Secrets for Real Smoked Food*. Toronto, Ontario: Robert Rose, Inc., 2006.
2. Garner, Bob. *North Carolina Barbecue: Flavored by Time*. Winston-Salem, NC: John F. Blair Publisher, 1996.

Chapter 7: Big & Beefy

1. Beef labeling sourced by National Cattlemen's Beef Association on behalf of The Beef Checkoff, and USDA website guidelines.
2. Robinson, Jo. *Pasture Perfect: The Far-Reaching Benefits of Choosing Meat, Eggs, and Dairy Products from Grass-Fed Animals*. Vashon, WA: Vashon Island Press, 2004.

Chapter 8: Birds for Birds

1. National Chicken Council website, 2007, taken from USDA statistics with permission.
2. Child, Julia. *The Way to Cook*. New York: Alfred A. Knopf, 1989, p. 164.
3. USDA Economic Bulletin, number 38, June 2008, and National Chicken Council website, 2007, taken from USDA statistics.
4. USDA website and National Chicken Council website, 2007, taken from USDA statistics.

Chapter 9: Julie's Soapbox

1. Loerch, S.C. "Efficacy of Plastic Pot Scrubbers as a Replacement for Roughage in High-Concentrate Cattle Diets." *Journal of Animal Science* 69, No. 6, 1991: pgs. 2,321-28.
2. Wolf, B.W., L.L. Berger, and G.C. Fahey, Jr. "Effects of Feeding a Return Chewing Gum/Packaging Material Mixture on Performance and Carcass Characteristics of Feedlot Cattle." *Journal of Animal Science,* No. 11, 1996: pgs. 2,559-65.
3. See Jo Robinson's website (www.eatwild.com) for an exhaustive list. I originally began reading studies one by one through scientific journals, but I found her list to be so complete that I could not do better. Both the studies above were found through *her* bibliography.
4. An example is this study by W.A. Gebreyes, P.B. Bahnson, J.A. Funk, J. McKean, P. Patchanee. *Seroprevalence of Trichinella, Toxoplasma, and Salmonella in Antimicrobial-free and Conventional Swine Production Systems*. Research paper, College of Veterinary Medicine, Department of Veterinary Preventive Medicine, The Ohio State University, Columbus: Research Communications, The Ohio State University, April 5, 2005.
5. Transcript, USDA, Food Safety and Inspection Service public meeting on "Product Labeling: Definition of the Term 'Natural,'" December 2006, Washington, DC.

6. Bahnson, Peter. "Risk Factors for the Occurrence of Drug Resistant Salmonella spp. in Commerical Swine Production." Research paper, University of Wisconsin-Madison, 2004.

7. Salatin, Joel. "The Polyface Farm Model," featured in the Weston A. Price Foundation quarterly journal, *Wise Traditions in Food, Farming and the Healing Arts,* Summer, 2002.

8. Robinson, Jo. *Pasture Perfect: The Far-Reaching Benefits of Choosing Meat, Eggs, and Dairy Products from Grass-Fed Animals.* Vashon, WA: Vashon Island Press, 2004.

9. Long, Cheryl, and Tabitha Alterman. "Meet Real Free-Range Eggs." *Mother Earth News,* October/November 2007 issue. See their website for updates to these studies. They've now added a study with Vitamin D, finding that pastured eggs (or, "true free-range") contain four to six times the amount of vitamin D as standard eggs.

Chapter 10: The Pacific Northwest Salmon Bake

1. Porter, Frank W. III. *The Coast Salish Peoples.* New York: Chelsea House Publications, 1989.

2. A wonderful photo in the University of Washington Special Collections Division is captioned "Indian women cooking salmon on a wooden rack on the Swinomish Reservation in the 1940's" (photo by Bertelson, negative #1741). Photos of earlier times in *The Coast Salish Peoples* noted above, and other publications, suggest that more often than not, smoke roasting the salmon fell on the shoulders of the tribes' women.

3. Lilliwaup Community Club, *Hood Canal Kukbuk,* 1970, by permission.

Chapter 13: Accompaniments & Sweet Endings

1. Finamore, Roy, and Molly Stevens. *One Potato, Two Potato.* Boston: Houghton Mifflin, 2001.

2. Child, Julia. *The Way To Cook.* New York: Alfred A. Knopf, 1989.

3. Rombauer, Irma S., Marion Rombauer Becker, and Ethan Becker. *The Joy of Cooking.* New York: Scribner. I use the 1996 edition. "The Pies and Tarts" chapter, pp. 856–865, discusses pie dough in detail.

Index

regional differences, 44–48

bar tips, 247

Basic Barbecue Rub, 51

Basic Brine, 63

bean dishes, 247–249

beef: Bistecca Fiorentina, 105; Gas-Powered Brisket, 153–154; grades, 144; Grass-Fed Beef Brisket, 160–161, 163; grilling times and temperatures, 82, 83, 160, 161; Jamaican Jerk Dino Bones, 157, 159; Kalbi Beef Short Ribs, 103; labeling guidelines, 144–145; Not Your Mama's Smoked Meatloaf, 164–166; per-person serving calculations, 106; Simple Pleasures Grilled Steak, 102; Skirt for Skirts, 104; Smoked Gouda Burgers, 163–164; Smoked Prime Rib, 228–229; steak cuts, 100–101; Texas Two-Step Brisket, 151–153; *See also* brisket; burgers; short ribs

Beer Brine for Beef, 64

Beer-Can Chicken & Smoked Corn, Smoked, 176–178

beer-can chicken stand, 18

Big Green Egg, 7, 34

Bird Quarterly slicing method, 170–171

Biscuits, Mom's, 238–239

Bistecca Fiorentina, 105, 107

Black Beans with Sweet Potato, Jamaican, 247–248

Blackberry Cobbler, 253–254

Bone Sauce, 65

box-style electric smokers, 7

Brined Smoked Turkey, 222–227

brines, 49, 62–64, 223

brisket: barbecue tips, 148–150; burnt ends, 157; buying tips, 145, 146; carving tips, 154–156; characteristics, 146; doneness tests, 150; Gas-Powered Brisket, 153–154; Grass-Fed Beef Brisket, 160–161, 163; grilling times and temperatures, 160, 161; resting period, 150–151; smoking tips, 146–147; Texas barbecue, 143; Texas crutch, 147; Texas Two-Step Brisket, 151–153

Brown, Kathy, 230

Browns Point, Washington, 192–193

Brunswick stew, 45

BTUs (British thermal units), 10–11

bullet smokers, 6, 34

burgers: patty makeovers, 98–100; salmon, 201; Smoked Gouda Burgers, 163–164; Turkey-Zucchini Burgers, 100

burgoo, 47

Buried Jerk Pork, 139–142

C

calibration, thermometer, 17

California barbecue, 48

campfires, 37; *See also* pit barbecues

Candied Cayenne Pecans, 249–250

caramelized onions, 245

Carolina Pulled Pork, 118–126

Cave Woman slicing method, 169

cedar, 15

cedar stakes, 197–199

cedar wraps, 18, 113–114

Certified Angus beef, 144

charcoal briquettes: definition, 12; fabrication methods, 14; fire-starting guidelines, 27–29, 80–81; heat readiness test, 81; quantity guidelines, 35

charcoal grills: briquette quantity guidelines, 35; direct-heat grilling, 30; fire-starting guidelines, 27–29, 80–81; heat readiness test, 35, 81, 86; indirect-heat grilling, 31; slow and low cooking, 33; smoking tips, 32; wood quantity guidelines, 35–36

cheese, smoked, 204–208

chef tongs, 16

cherry wood, 15

chicken: carving tips, 169–172; Donna Moodie's Jamaican Jerk Chicken, 110–111; food sources, 167–168; Grilled South Carolina Mustard Thighs, 109–110; grilling times and temperatures, 82, 83, 174–175; labeling guidelines, 182–183; love handles, 171; per-person serving calculations, 106; safety guidelines, 174, 175; Simple Barbecue Half Chickens, 172–173; Smoked Beer-Can Chicken & Smoked Corn, 176–178; Smokin' Hot Wings, 181–182; Thai Chicken Satay with Peanut Sauce, 96–97

chimney fire starters, 13, 28–29

Chocolate Cream Pie, 255–256

Christine's Nirvana Smoked Tomato Bruschetta, 212–214

Christmas Morning Smoked Scrapple, 231–232

Citrus & Clove Brine, 63–64

Clams & Mussels, Smoked, 216–217

Classic Picnic Potato Salad, 243–245

Cobbler, Blackberry, 253–254

cocktails, 247

Cocoa Bliss Rub, 53

cold-smoked cheese, 204, 205–206

coleslaw, 234–236

Collins, Dick, 193

combination grilling, definition of, 86

commercial meat industry, 185–187

competition barbecue, 131–132, 137–138, 158, 230

cooking times and temperatures, 82–85, 124, 125, 160, 161, 225

copper wire brushes, 17–18

Cornish game hens: grilling times and temperatures, 174–175; Smoked Cornish Game Hen with Polenta Stuffing and Mushroom Gravy, 227–228

Corn Salad with Lime-Cumin-Honey Dressing, Fire-Roasted, 93–94

Corn, Smoked Beer-Can Chicken & Smoked, 176–178

cost concerns, 189

country style ribs, 126

Cowboy Beans, 248–249

Crock-Pot method, 126

cross-contamination, 175

Cryovac-packaged meat, 51

Cucumber Salad (Oyi Namul), 236–237

cutting boards, 17

D

danger zone, 39

dedicated smokers, 4

desserts: Blackberry Cobbler, 253–254; Chocolate Cream Pie, 255–256; Grilled Apple Tart Tatin, 250–253; Grilled Fruit, 90–91; Mom's Pie Crust, 254–255; Peach Pie, 257

digital thermometers, 16

Dimovski, Danielle, 137–138

dips, 208, 209–210

direct-heat grilling, 30–31

disposable foil pans, 17

disposable latex gloves, 17, 38

distance from fire, 5

Diva Q East Meets West Pork Loin, 138–139

Donna Moodie's Jamaican Jerk Chicken, 110–111

Drunken Port Sauce with Dried Fruit & Stilton, 69–70

dry rubs, 49, 56

duck: grilling times and temperatures,

Acknowledgments

A big sloppy kiss and thanks to my husband for his support doing what needed to be done, whether it was working through a recipe, taking our son to the park so Mom could write, or putting up with my moment-to-moment emotional rollercoaster. This book would not have happened without you. Hugs to my best little guy, Xander, who let me know he missed me by saying, "How about Daddy write the book and you stay home and play?", and to my little Eloise, thank you for waiting until your due date so that I could finish the book.

I thank my family for their support, especially Mom and Dad for extra babysitting, Melissa too. And thanks Mom for attacking my ever-teetering pile of laundry. Thank you to my brothers for their words of encouragement and for taste-testing my recipes (I know that was a huge sacrifice, guys).

To the B-girls, my smokin' posse of women who helped me along the way: Molly Blaisdell, Holly Cupala, Carrie Duncan, Christine Gaffney, Annie Gage, Amy Gregory, Lene Hansen, Nora Nelson, Mary Nolan, Kathryn Olsen, Laurie Olsen, and Katy Viswat, thanks for your recipe testing, reading through chapters, cheerleading, and, in Amy's case, even traveling to Kansas City with me. You surrounded me with community, offered up comments with such kindness, and helped make the process fun. Each of you brought something unique to the table and I thank you for sharing at my table.

To my editor and publisher, Krista Lyons, and all the amazing people at Seal Press who brought this book to publication, thank you for giving me the amazing opportunity to write this book and for your expertise in making it happen. Thanks to my publicist, Eva Zimmerman, for spending most of a day tracking down five pounds of Fed Ex'd pulled pork. Thanks to Tabitha (designer) and Tim (illustrator) for making this a beautiful book.

A special thanks to Tom Wallin, president of the Pacific Northwest Barbecue Association, for his expert comments on my drafts. To Drew and Charlyn Wingard, for their sharing of the family salmon bake secrets. To Brian Fransen, Kelly Kerrone, and Dick Collins for their time talking about Browns Point. To Tracy Rector, executive director of Native Lens, for her expertise on Pacific Northwest Coastal Native Americans. To Joel Salatin, for talking with me about pastured meats and sustainable farming. You are such a rock star in my mind, and I was thrilled you answered your phone! To the FSIS for answering my questions on natural labeling and to all the small farms and producers mentioned in this book for sharing their stories and expert opinions.

A shout-out and thanks to all the amazing folks who shared their morsels of meat, passion, stories, and tips, including Squeal of Approval for their open arms at the Kansas City American Royal (and their beer); Kathy Swift, of the Wild Bunch Butt Burners; Lynnae Oxley, of Sugar's BBQ & Catering; Kathy Brown, the Princess of Pork; Donna Moodie of Marjorie; Christine Gaffney; Sten Skaar and his Big Green Egg; Lake High, of the South Carolina Barbeque Association; Ricky Ginsburg, of the Florida Barbecue Association; Danielle Dimovsky, of Diva Q; and Chris Wirken, who organized a great tour at the 2008 American Royal Barbecue Competition.

A hearty thanks to the staff at Smokin' Pete's BBQ, who put up with my frantic calls saying, "I just can't come in today—I have five things going in the smokers and a chapter due by Friday!"

And last but not least, thank you to all the women who said, "I need a book like that!" and for encouraging me to write the book in the first place.

About the Author

Writer, mother, and owner of Smokin' Pete's BBQ in Seattle, Julie Reinhardt thinks smoking pork butt might just help women find balance in their hectic lives. Even if they don't find inner peace, they will find a tasty piece of tender meat at the end of the day. Julie has worked with food most of her life, from dishwasher to catering director and restaurateur. She's cooked under the stars, for rock stars, and for a five-star general.

© Julie Reinhardt

Notes

Notes

Notes

Notes

Notes

Notes

Notes

Notes

Notes

Notes

Selected Titles from Seal Press

For more than thirty years, Seal Press has published groundbreaking books. By women. For women. Visit our website at www.sealpress.com. Check out the Seal Press blog at www.sealpress.com/blog.

Women Who Eat, edited by Leslie Miller. $15.95, 1-58005-092-1. Women both in and out of the culinary profession share their stories about the many ways food shapes and enhances their lives.

The List: 100 Ways to Shake Up Your Life, by Gail Belsky. $15.95, 1-58005-256-8. Get a tattoo, ride in a fire truck, or use food as foreplay—this collection of 100 ideas will inspire women to shake things up and do something they never dared to consider.

The Boss of You: Everything A Woman Needs to Know to Start, Run, and Maintain Her Own Business, by Emira Mears & Lauren Bacon. $15.95, 1-58005-236-3. Provides women entrepreneurs the advice, guidance, and straightforward how-to's they need to start, run, and maintain a business.

The Bigger, The Better, The Tighter the Sweater: 21 Funny Women on Beauty, Body Image, and Other Hazards of Being Female, edited by Samantha Schoech and Lisa Taggart. $14.95, 1-58005-210-X. A refreshingly honest and funny collection of essays on how women view their bodies.

DIRT: The Quirks, Habits, and Passions of Keeping House, edited by Mindy Lewis. $15.95, 1-58005-261-4. From grime, to clutter, to spit-clean—writers share their amusing relationships with dirt.

How to Cook a Dragon: Living, Loving, and Eating in China, by Linda Furiya. $16.95, 1-58005-255-X. Part insightful memoir, part authentic cookbook, How to Cook a Dragon is a revealing look at race, love, and food in China from Bento Box in the Heartland author Linda Furiya.